S0-ARO-052

ISSUES IN POLITICAL ECONOMY

A Critical Approach

By the same editors

ECONOMICS: AN ANTI-TEXT
Edited by Francis Green and Petter Nore

Issues in
Political Economy

A Critical Approach

Edited by

Francis Green

and

Petter Nore

© John Grahl, Francis Green, Mike Ball, Petter Nore, Laurence Harris,
Sue Himmelweit, Ben Fine, Stephen J. Lord, Simon Mohun 1979

All rights reserved. No part of this publication
may be reproduced or transmitted, in any form
or by any means, without permission.

First published 1979 by
THE MACMILLAN PRESS LTD
London and Basingstoke
Associated companies in Delhi Dublin
Hong Kong Johannesburg Lagos Melbourne
New York Singapore and Tokyo

Typesetting by Reproduction Drawings Limited
Sutton, Surrey

Printed in Great Britain by
LOWE AND BRYDONE PRINTERS LIMITED
Thetford, Norfolk.

British Library Cataloguing in Publication Data

Issues in political economy.
  1. Economics
  I. Green, Francis II. Nore, Petter
  330 HB171

  ISBN 0–333–25376–0
  ISBN 0–333–25377–9 Pbk

This book is sold subject to the standard conditions of the Net Book Agreement.

The paperback edition of this book is sold subject to the condition that it shall
not, by way of trade or otherwise, be lent, re-sold, hired out, or otherwise
circulated without the publisher's prior consent in any form of binding or cover
other than that in which it is published and without a similar condition including
this condition being imposed on the subsequent purchaser.

Contents

List of Contributors

All contributors to this volume are teachers of Economics: LAURENCE
HARRIS, SUE HIMMELWEIT, BEN FINE and MIKE BALL at Birkbeck
College, University of London; JOHN GRAHL and SIMON MOHUN
at Queen Mary College, University of London; STEPHEN J. LORD
at Keele University, PETTER NORE at Thames Polytechnic, and
FRANCIS GREEN at Kingston Polytechnic.

Editors' Introduction

There is a tendency among some modern Marxists to disregard ortho-dox economics altogether, to cast it aside and to brand it as mere apologetics, as the voice of vested interest. According to this view one can only expect the orthodox economist to come up with theories and policies that justify capitalist relations, and one should be con-cerned only with the political propaganda value of these theories, not with their intellectual merits. This book is conceived in opposition to this tendency. As socialists and Marxists we none the less consider that it is important to take orthodox economics seriously, to examine what it has to say, to untangle and to understand the origins of its basic conceptions.

Why is this necessary? First, there are elements of value in the writings of orthodox economists. It would be foolish to suppose that bourgeois economics is a completely unified body of thought and practice, and it remains true that much work that is centred at very concrete levels of analysis is indispensable to understanding the world. How, after all, can we claim to know the workings of capitalism if we do not know, for example, how a banking system works? The point is not to abjure this kind of concrete knowledge, but to try to locate it within a materialist understanding of capitalism. Moreover it is clearly part of such a materialist analysis to understand the character of the ideologies that are produced by it, and so from this point of view it is vital to examine the essence of bourgeois economics.

Second, there is the most important reason for our approach: simply that every year thousands of students of economics, the world over, are confronted by issues of great importance and are urged to theorise them from the framework of bourgeois economics. This book is written for those people who are dissatisfied with that framework or who want to have a broader perspective than they are able to gain from the point of view of the orthodoxy. It is therefore conceived in the same spirit as our earlier book, *Economics: An Anti-Text* (Macmillan, 1977). In our introduction to that book we pointed to the developing crisis of economics theory in the face of the world crisis of capitalism. There is no sign of any solution to the problems and inadequacies of orthodox economics. Nor is there the slightest prospect at the moment of a return to the conditions of the post-war boom. There seems therefore to be a continuing need for analyses of orthodox economics, for attempts to investigate closely its failures. The difference between the *Anti-Text* and the current offering is mainly that here we have treated each issue in greater depth, and have therefore been able to direct attention to the policy and the political implications of economic theory. But also the subjects treated here on the whole require a more advanced knowledge of economics than was required for the *Anti-Text*, and so are meant for undergraduate students who have reached the intermediate level or above.

The issues discussed in this book are ones which the student is bound to confront at one time or another in studying orthodox economics and its application to the capitalist economy. They fall into three broad categories. Part A tackles the important questions of economic methodology and provides an assessment of the extent to which the post-war development of econometrics, and of empiricist methodology in general, has fulfilled its claim to provide economics with the tools wherewith to validate its theories in confrontation with empirical observations. The assessment is that this endeavour has failed. In the second part come two fundamental issues concerning the policies of the state: the theory and practice of costbenefit analysis, and the analysis of oil and of the origins of state oil policies. In each case it is shown how orthodox economics prescribes and explains these policies; the explanation is subjected to a critique, and an alternative Marxist analysis is proposed. The same approach is used again in the final category, which is a discussion of issues in economic theory. These issues are chosen both for their fundamental importance within the method of orthodox economics and for their close relevance for the theorising of contemporary capitalism. Part C ends with a chapter on the nature of ideology in neoclassical economics, using the analysis that springs directly from Marx's *Capital*; this discussion is supplemented by an introduction to the difficult and somewhat controversial contemporary problems within the Marxist theory of ideology.

We should mention finally that while all the contributors naturally adhere to the philosophy with which our book is conceived, there are certainly points of disagreement on some areas of debate which overlap two or more chapters. All the issues have, in the course of their production, been discussed by all of the contributors and have therefore benefited in their final form from this group criticism. But each chapter remains naturally the final responsibility of its author.

F. G.
P. N.

PART A

Issues in Economic Methodology

CHAPTER 1

Econometric Methods in Macroeconomics: a critical appraisal

John Grahl

INTRODUCTION[1]

The Marxist critique of contemporary bourgeois economics is often
weakened by a failure to recognise the *scientific* content of bourgeois
analyses and constructions, by a tendency to dismiss all that is produced in the orthodox camp as mystificatory and apologetic. Such
attitudes reveal a misunderstanding of the capitalist economy itself,
for it is by no means true that capitalist social relations are reproduced
quite spontaneously – which would leave bourgeois social science no
other role than to disguise the real nature of an automatic mechanism.
Conscious co-ordination and regulation, requiring an accurate understanding of economic processes, play an important part in capitalist
economy at the level both of the enterprise and of the state (including
in the latter the supra-national state apparatuses such as IMF or OECD
which are a major feature of contemporary imperialism). Further,
this necessity for an adequate grasp of real economic relations, for a
scientific economics, develops with the capitalist mode of production
itself, with the complexity of its internal structure, as production
increasingly becomes a socially unified process. Thus the critique
of political economy, today more than ever, must be able to explain
the 'rational core' of bourgeois theories: it is this rational content,
however mystified in its formulation, however limited by the unvoiced
assumption of the permanance of capitalist social relations or overlaid
with vulgar apologetics, that gives orthodox economics its real strength
as an ideology.

From this point of view, one can try to sketch out what is rational in the development of econometric methods, as a necessary step to understanding the ideological function which these methods came to perform. That rationality resides in the objective necessity of using highly developed statistical procedures, in particular quantitative *models,* in a wide variety of economic applications concerned with the production, analysis and regulation of economic processes. And this necessity grows with the degree of organisation of the economy itself, that is to say with the development of the productive forces under capitalism. Very schematically, we can associate the key problems which have stimulated the elaboration of econometric techniques with the major historical periods of industrial capitalism. First, then, ·comes the problem of *demand* – of the estimation of demand curves in particular markets – which is clearly posed by the transition to monopoly capitalism. Giant enterprises, engaged in the struggle to control whole sectors of production and distribution, need precisely this kind of information (Wold, 1952, is the classic exposition of the sub-discipline in this stage of its development).

The next important stimulus is associated of course with the accelerated development of State Monopoly Capitalism (SMC) in the years following the Great Depression and the Second World War. The massive advance of state economic intervention required the systematic provision of quantitative information in a form suited to guide the determination of economic policy (above all of fiscal policy). It is with these exigencies that econometrics may be said to have come of age, with the first production of economy-wide models, and it is this stage of development which is examined below.

The following critique of econometrics thus starts from these considerations – that is, it takes both the scientific and ideological sides of the subject as closely integrated with the historical formation of SMC, in particular with the reflection of this phase in Keynesian thought. (Although it is noted that Keynes as an individual was highly cynical about econometric procedures.) Thus the ideological abuse of econometrics and its scientific failures are tightly bound up with the fortunes of Keynesianism as an economic philosophy.

The weaknesses of Keynesianism are revealed today with ever greater brutality in the crisis of capitalism itself; they are, besides, discussed elsewhere in this volume. For our purposes it is necessary to emphasise only two aspects.

The first of these is the violence done by Keynesian thought to the reality of capitalist economy in its very constitution of 'macro-economics' as an autonomous object of inquiry. The project of successful state regulation by fiscal means requires that the macro system exhibit general properties of coherence and consistency to admit of its manipulation, and, further, that the fiscal and financial apparatuses of the state possess sufficient particularisation from the laws of capitalist development to form an adequate regulatory agency. Since in reality these conditions were only fulfilled to a limited extent in a particular stage of development of capitalism's productive forces, and through a specific historical balance in the class-struggle, Keynesianism is today threatened with the most final condemnation of any science – the disintegration of this object of inquiry as an ordered and relatively autonomous totality. Here we see the consequences of viewing both the state and the economy in abstraction from the antagonistic social relations which they both embody. In econometric macro models the consequence is that there is usually implicit con-fusion of the distinction between economy and policy-maker with that between object and subject of control. This perspective eliminates any possibility of a dialectical grasp of relations between state and economy (consider the fate of the Phillips curve as a 'menu of policy choice').

The second, closely related, weakness of Keynesian theory is, quite simply, its lack of any genuine historical dimension. This is already suggested in the *General Theory's* treatment of the Malthus–Ricardo dispute as immediately relevant to the modern era: Malthus, it seems, was right all along (contrast this with the classic Marxist account of the same dispute in section 2 of Luxemburg (1971)). This historical myopia of econometricians is at times almost unbelievable. The most elementary recognition of the historical nature of its object would, in the author's opinion, go far towards stripping econometrics of at least its most silly pretensions and towards defining its true (by no means negligible) practical scope.

A cautionary word is in order here on Keynesianism and SMC. There is no intention to identify the two: it is only assumed that within one phase of SMC and within certain countries, above all Britain and the United States, Keynesianism was a key element of the dominant ideology; and that fiscal interventions at the macro-economic level constituted during this phase the paradigm of state economic intervention, though by no means its most important manifestation either historically or quantitatively. Throughout this phase econometrics played a significant, even indispensable, role as an instrument of policy-formation – which specifies its actual scientific value and the limitation of its real achievements.

On the other hand, the tendency to regard this battery of techniques as a comprehensive solution to the problem of empirical verification in economic science, as, in Malinvaud's (1970) definition, 'the empirical determination of economic laws', is simply an illustration of the limits of Keynesianism itself, of the point at which it oversteps its real historical basis and becomes a mythology. (This extension is very comparable to one of the most elementary abuses of statistics, namely an illegitimate extrapolation from insufficient experience.)

The above remarks indicate the framework in which the following critique was attempted. The critique itself, however, is of an 'immanent' nature; it tries to exhibit the limitations of econometric methods and the contradictions of econometric methodology by contrasting its actual practices with its own criteria of validity. This procedure means that what follows lacks the sharpness of a direct Marxist anatomy, relating ideological developments to the movement of the class struggle in material and intellectual production. It may, however, have a compensating advantage in supplying arguments and analyses easily fitted to polemical purposes.

The plan of the chapter is this: some comments on the philosophical climate in which macro-econometric models were first designed; an examination of their central core, the Keynesian income – expenditure model as an object for quantitative statistical determination; the failures of econometric procedures at three levels, those of statistical procedure, applied economics and economic theory; finally, there is an examination of right-wing objections to econometrics since it seemed to be the case, in this field at least, that the contradictions within bourgeois thought are an illuminating guide to its critique.

1   METHODOLOGY OF ECONOMETRICS

It is difficult today, when so much of economic theory and method is looked on as highly problematic, to appreciate the impact made on the science by the emergence of econometric techniques. After three decades which have failed to fulfil the promise of the new approach, it is now defended in less extravagant terms;[2] but we can present as by no means untypical of its earlier period Koopmans's claim to be developing procedures of simultaneous estimation which were to permit the reduction of 'observed economic regularities' to 'underlying behaviour patterns, institutional rules and laws of production' (Koopmans, 1947). In those days it was not a question of defence but of attack – Koopmans's declaration, for instance, being part of a highly polemical assault on traditional approaches to the measurement of business cycles. In retrospect it would seem to be such claims, rather than any achievements, which established the subdiscipline. (Vining, 1949, in his reply to Koopmans, already felt the 'tyranny of a new orthodoxy'.)

Econometric modelling, of course, was only the spearhead of a general neopositivist assault which pretended to a complete re-structuring of the discipline. Henceforth there were to be neither speculative theoretical constructions nor descriptive empirical inquiries; theory and evidence were to be reunited on a new, and more satisfactorily scientific, basis. Today the conjunction of serious economic instability with widespread doubt as to the status of economic theory has reawakened the interest of many economists in methodological problems of both social science and science in general; and it is precisely the post-war neopositivist position which has become in its turn the target of widespread criticism.

However, it is not necessary here to pursue the theory of econometric modelling into the misty realms of epistemology. For, with hindsight, it is clear that, as the research method proper to economic science, econometrics never had any substantive methodological underpinnings and that all its claims to logical rigour rest on a positivism so shallow that it would now probably be rejected as an illegitimate offspring by the positivists themselves. Coddington (1972) has enumerated some of the most obvious weaknesses of the position – in particular the colossal assumption required of a completely unproblematic conceptual context in which the variables, relations, and data used by the model-builder retain, throughout the inquiry, an unchanging and unambiguous meaning.

What is more interesting, is the tendency which Coddington identifies for positivism, when it is pushed to a thorough-going defence of model-building *as scientific method,* to degenerate into an extreme pragmatism of 'instrumentalism'.[3] For, from any less simplistic methodological position, it is clear that econometric models are just that – instruments of investigation within some wider context.[4] Thus to treat models as themselves expressing and validating theoretical positions merely blinds us to this wider framework, which on examination usually turns out to be, if anything, not economic theory, but economic policy.[5]

Thus, while, as will be argued below, in many of the purely theoretical applications of econometric macro models no clear context can be found to give the investigation a determinable *scientific* meaning, work conducted with a policy orientation – to guide and correct macro-economic policy decisions – does have a coherent *practical* context, which would appear to be the only appropriate one for the practice as it was developed. Certainly the aspiration to guide policy measures is explicit in much of the pioneering work in the field – Tinbergen (1951, 1954), for example, whose interests in econometrics and economic planning are obviously complementary, or Phillips, whose work on distributed lags is clearly related to his investigation of economic regulators (Phillips, 1954, 1956). From this point of view, it is no accident that it was just at the time when a new degree of state intervention in economy had achieved its first successes, and promised more, that the claims of the econometricians were advanced most rigorously: the two optimisms, for method and policy application, are in fact the same.

But if this is the real 'home ground' of econometrics, then its continuous representation as the proper instrument of theoretical inquiry calls into question the neutrality of theory itself, and we are then no longer dealing with a matter of purely academic concern. For such a situation amounts to the assertion, as a methodological proposition, that the techniques, *and hence their true, policy-guiding context,* are basically sound. And if the fundamental failures of the method are treated as purely technical matters we will be strongly impelled to treat the present failures of macro-economic policy as a technical problem also. Many today would agree that such are among the dangers to which a naïvely positivist methodological position has exposed the discipline.

2   THE SOURCES OF ECONOMETRICS

In his much-discussed book, Axel Leijonhufvud (1968) argued that post-Keynesian macro-economics, through a premature formalisation, had failed to embody in its models some of the most important of Keynes's theoretical insights. In particular, the 'income–expenditure' model, however fruitful in short-run policy applications, simplified the economics of the *General Theory* to the point where its revolutionary implications for the theory of value could be first minimised and subsequently altogether neglected. Following Clower (1965), Leijonhufvud sees Keynes as locating a major malfunction in the capitalist system, in the way a market economy disseminates information and co-ordinates the action of its elements. The result is completely subversive – of Marshallian micro-analysis, of orthodox monetary economics and of General Equilibrium theory. The 'income-expenditure' model, on the other hand, has come to co-exist quite amicably with the whole corpus of traditional economic analysis.

The discussion has important implications for the status of econometric methods. For it is the equations of the income – expenditure model (or its derivatives) which provide econometrics with its principal field of application. It is not immediately relevant here whether or not Leijonhufvud's work is accurate exegesis; what is material is the content of 'Keynesian' models. Conventional interpretations of empirical macro economics see in it a *confrontation* between theory and evidence. If Leijonhufvud's critique is valid then this view can no longer be maintained, because the equations involved do not represent any coherent theoretical position. What econometrics amounts to in such a context is exactly what Koopmans condemned in his unsophisticated predecessors, 'measurement without theory'.

It is difficult not to see in the later work of the 'Keynesians' themselves an implicit recognition of the justice of these remarks. Klein, who occupied a central place in the early spread of Keynesian theory and pioneered the construction of econometric macro-models now writes:

> I look upon the Keynesian theory as essentially a system of equations. While I may once have been satisfied with the explanatory value of a small version of that system expressed in just two or three equations, I now feel that intelligent discussion cannot be carried on unless this system is expanded to include fifteen to twenty or even more equations. (Klein, 1968, p. 223)

Klein no longer represents a theory in a model; he identifies the theory with the model. He asserts that his 'Keynesian' approach is universal – underdeveloped economies, socialist economies, fast-growing capitalist economies like Japan in the 1960s – all are suitable objects for the same battery of techniques (Klein, 1968, 1964). However, in his survey of macro models in different countries he accepts the most varied formulations of the same function, for instance the investment equation. At the same time he adopts an agnostic position on the *theoretical* validity of the *General Theory:*

> On the question of labour supply, however, Keynes was definitely confused and in error. He suggested that labour supply is a function of the money wage and not the real wage. Of course, we can show the possibility of an under-employment equilibrium if there is an assumed 'money illusion' or inhomogeneity in the supply behaviour of workers. Schumpeter stressed repeatedly that the challenging theoretical problem was to make all the classical assumptions about behaviour under perfect competition and then show the possibility of an under-employment equilibrium. This is the problem that must be faced by Keynesian economists. (Klein, 1968, p. 210)

That is to say, on 'revisiting' the Keynesian revolution in 1968 Klein avoids reaching a conclusion on the central theoretical (and empirical) proposition of the *General Theory*. What we have is a complete acceptance of Leijonhufvud's terms for peace between the Keynesians and the neoclassical school. 'The theoretically important is the practically trivial and the practically important is the theoretically trivial.'

What, then, is there of Keynesian theory in Klein's 'system of equations'? The element that remains, both as an implication of Keynes's theory and as a property common to empirical macro models is that output and income are determined *in the first instance* by the level of aggregate demand. The rest of the structure, in so far as it is not dictated by this consideration, is arbitrary. Now this implies that it is the estimation of the parameters of the consumption function that provides econometrics with its proper field of inquiry. On the other hand, the formal income–expenditure model seemed at first to offer far more scope for statistical analysis.

The classical statement of this model by Hicks (1937) uses three equations: the consumption function relates savings to income and the rate of interest; the investment function relates investment to the same two variables; the liquidity preference function does the same for the demand for money. The system is closed by a policy equation specifying the terms on which money is supplied to the economy. In equilibrium, savings equals investment and the demand for money equals its supply: thus income and the rate of interest are determined. All empirical macro models descend from this original.

Two points are important for the present argument. First, the *IS–LM* system has no equation for the supply of labour. Implicit in it is the proposition that employment passively follows the demand for final output. If this is not the case then the analysis holds only for money, not real income and the model ceases to be purely demand determined. On the other hand, the reason the level of income is demand-determined depends critically on what happens in the labour market. (If, for instance, there is simply a fixed money wage, then there is little theoretical novelty in the system.) Thus the *IS–LM* model suppresses an important part of Keynes's theoretical discussion. In this it is followed by its 'empirical' successors: even when they include labour market equations these are so closely linked to subsidiary specifications of the output – employment and price – wage relations that they cannot be construed as embodying Keynesian (or any other) theory.

Second, the Hicksian system, being formal, treats all the equations *symmetrically*. This is an elegant procedure but whether or not the equations of 'Mr. Keynes and the Classics' capture the essence of the *General Theory,* it is clear that Keynes could never have given them equal standing as empirical *regularities*. Only the consumption function is stable it is the source of Keynes's policy conclusions where fiscal intervention, relying on the stable multiplier, is chosen to compensate for shortfalls in investment expenditure as opposed to unreliable monetary measures. Subsequent empirical work simply ignored the distinction. Taking the early investigation of the consumption function as a pattern the other two relations were attacked with the same weapons – though with notably less success. This agenda is already explicit in Tinbergen's 'The Significance of Keynes' Theories from the Econometric Point of View', where just these three relations are considered. What is important to Tinbergen is Keynes's 'way of thinking, i.e. thinking in rather simple relations between the macro-economic variables', which provides the statistician with a 'transparent' object for investigation (Tinbergen, 1948).[6]

The argument is that the automatic extension of econometric analysis, from the multiplier problem to macro economics as a whole, involves extensive theoretical distortions. This can be brought out more strongly if we examine the question from the points of view of pre-

Keynesian theory. In an early statement of his anti-empiricist position Hayek defined the challenge presented to neoclassical economics by the business cycle. Disequilibrium states as such naturally gave no problem to the theorist. The difficulty lay in sustained, systematic and cumulative departures from the equilibrium in all markets. The place of statistics here is secondary to that of economic analysis:

> Just as no statistical investigation can prove that a given change in demand must necessarily be followed by a certain change in price, so no statistical method can explain why all economic phenomena present that regular wave-like appearance which we observe in cyclical fluctuations. This can be explained only by widening the assumptions on which our deductions are based, so that cyclical fluctuations would follow from these as a necessary consequence, just as the propositions of the theory of price followed from the narrower assumptions of equilibrium theory. (Hayek, 1933, p. 30)

The multiplier is a key element in the Keynesian resolution of this dilemma. Aggregate income becomes a strategic variable in the system and the mechanism which sustains cumulative movements away from equilibrium becomes clear. But the multiplier alone is not a complete solution because it merely describes expansionary and deflationary processes. It remains to answer the questions: what initiates these movements? and why do not market responses rapidly bring them to an end? Thus the multiplier process is complemented by an explanation of the volatility of investment expenditures and by an analysis of the capital and labour markets. From this point of view Keynes's theory operates at a variety of levels, with a complex relationship to the institutions and agents of the capitalist economy. For econometric purposes, however, there is only one level – the correlations between statistical aggregates. The consequence is a double violence – to theory and reality at the same time.

3 MULTICOLLINEARITY AND THE PROBLEM OF STRUCTURAL CHANGE

We have already described the rigid methodological position held by the mainstream of post-Keynesian macro economists. It is now necessary to go into some details of the way in which this methodology, with its almost complete faith in econometrics, came to grief.

The standard textbooks on econometric procedure consist of, first, an account of the (by now) classical method of multiple regression, and, second, a discussion of the problems of that method – serially correlated disturbances, simultaneous equation bias, errors of observation and so on. For each of these there is then developed a solution (of greater or lesser generality, more or less practical efficiency) in the form of more complex techniques; 'progress' in this development is reported as rapid in some areas, slow in others.[7] What such expositions uniformly fail to do is to confront the two most critical problems in the use of the classical method: multicollinear regressors and parametric or 'structural' change. As the technical papers accumulate, and applied studies (each containing an acid critique of its predecessors' methodological naiveté) are piled on top of them one's suspicion grows that the neglect of these two fundamental problems is not in spite of, but because of the fact that these alone are not problems within, but problems of econometrics. Between them they squeeze the range of applicability of its procedures down to a field of very narrow compass indeed.

High levels of collinearity pervade virtually the entire range of macro-economic time series. Price and output indices, employment data, money and interest-rate series, all exhibit roughly the same kind of short-run movements. Over longer periods many also have strong trend components which can often be modelled by the same functional form – linear or exponential. The source of this situation is not difficult to identify: it is simply the generality, the all-pervasiveness of the processes under study, of the rhythm of cumulative expansions and contractions within capitalist economies.

The consequences of high degrees of collinearity are also well known. Within a given model it makes for imprecise results – a set of estimated parameters with high variances and high covariances so that it is not clear to which of the included independent variables should be attributed the main determining roles in the model. More importantly, in the explanation of any particular aggregate magnitude there will in many cases be a large number of models which provide adequate fits to the data; a large number of subsets of variables drawn from the available published series will provide us, to use the standard jargon, with hypotheses that are not refuted at the x per cent level of significance.

Now since the choice of a model is necessarily prior to the assessment of its correspondence to the data, one has not fully stated the problem when one talks of high variances and standard errors of estimated parameters. In fact, a competent practitioner of the art will usually be able to overcome this and obtain reasonably well-defined results, at the cost of a certain amount of *ad hoc* juggling with the various elements of the study. But all that happens when this is done is that the problem of multicollinearity is transformed into the less embarrassingly obvious problem of omitted variables. The question of choice of model reappears as soon as one asks whether there are not other possible explanatory variables, collinear with those actually used, which deserve inclusion in the equation system – as soon as one asks, in effect, whether the results presented are not hopelessly biased.

It is very important to grasp here that multicollinearity is not a problem of econometric *procedure*. In so far as any technique can, classical methods already constitute an optimal procedure. Multiple regression itself is the statistically efficient way of treating collinear independent variables and its use has no justification except to do just this. Such uncertainty as remains after multiple regression has been applied to the model is a problem of the *data*: the figures simply do not contain enough information to answer the question posed of them.[8] In the context of applied macro-economics, that is to say, the movements of the economic system exemplify in an acute manner a central dilemma in all social sciences (as in all historiography): how do we disentangle the determinants of a social process from its concomitants, cause from concurrence?

In practically every area of macro-economic research (investment, inflation, growth, money, and the rest) this fundamental lack of information permits the survival of the most diverse and contradictory theoretical positions, quite unmarked by two decades of 'rigorous' application of the appropriate econometric techniques. Only if a much richer and more varied source of information than the existing short-data series were to be found, could these techniques begin to help us discriminate between genuinely different prior hypotheses.

But it is just when we seek these fuller sources of information that the other jaw of the trap springs shut on econometric practice: the problem of structural change. For, on immediate reflection, there are only two ways in which supplementary information can be found. First, one can simply assume it – a clear solution in some practical problems no doubt but hardly so if our concern is with the validation of theory. Alternatively, one can collect more observations. But by their nature we can only obtain more observations of macro aggregates by lengthening the time period under consideration and then the question arises: are we observing the same process? As is well known to those involved in the field, all too frequently the answer is no.

Once again the problem appears both within particular models and, more critically, as affecting choice of model. In the former case the econometrician usually considers the question as one of time-variation in the parameters of an equation. In this technical sense, something can be done about structural change: one can cite both the work on statistical tests of the stability of parameters by Brown, Durbin and Evans (1975) for instance; and the various techniques for 'tracing' time-varying structures discussed in Wall (1937) – although the simplest of these, the inclusion of a linear time trend, is by no means the least useful. Such a reaction to the problem has at any rate the merit of recognising that the growing mass of available time-series data is not proportional to our information about a given structure – as fast as new data appear the old become obsolete, putting an upper bound to the precision of our estimates and returning the resource of public records to its traditional exploiter, the economic historian.[9]

In two ways, however, structural change is much more than a parametric problem. First, there is simply the rapidity and suddenness of the discontinuities. The past few years, of course, have given the most dramatic examples of this: output–employment, G.D.P.–imports, wages–unemployment and other central relationships of macroeconomics are once again largely uncharted. One can express this in terms of the apparently technical problem of choice of functional form, i.e. whether a relationship is best modelled as linear, logarithmic or whatever. In practice this is usually a matter of very little consequence, until it is too late, when new observations start to show very large negative or positive errors of prediction. That is to say, the practical problem of non-linearities in fitted equations is simply that of failed extrapolations from linear models. The kind of mechanisms involved – ceilings and floors, thresholds and triggers, sudden accelerations and slowdowns – are already notoriously difficult to model and estimate. When it is realised that it is just the most essential observations for such modelling that have yet to be made, it becomes impossible.

Second, partly as a corollary of those discontinuities but also as a simple consequence of the evolution of the economy in general, structural change has the most severe implications for the choice of models and their use in the evaluation of conflicting theoretical positions. For the changes in question cannot be expressed usefully as combinations of alterations in paremeter values and in the values of exogenous variables. Experience has repeatedly shown that entire models become redundant over quite short periods of time. As striking instances one could refer to Walters (1969), who finds radically different behaviour of the money–output relation in three eras, or again to the very high degree of obsolescence in the formulation of inflation and investment models; but the problem is increasingly admitted to be quite general. The only exception is perhaps that most people spend what they get very shortly after they get it. Hence most of this relation is roughly stable.

The evidence is, then, that current econometric procedure is vitiated by the actual poverty of its data sources for theoretical purposes. What is perhaps needed as one part of the solution is an explicit *economic* theory of parameters. Some indication of what such a theory might involve can be found in the work of Kalecki (1954). In his *Economic Dynamics* this writer makes clear exactly what kind of event is likely to affect the validity of his short-run aggregate relations. (This is done by presenting these equations in the form of identities with certain ratios among the variables fixed over the cycle, though the particular technique used by Kalecki is not of primary importance.) Such an approach is, of course, inspired by a Marxist conception of the forces behind structural change properly so called – here, for instance, the degree of monopolisation. Apart from Kalecki's work nothing of the kind exists apart from theoretical disaggregations which refer us back simplistically to the individual firm or household. Meanwhile the lack of scope for genuine advance in the field is concealed only by the fact that the real barrier – lack of information in a set of short multi-collinear time series with high noise levels – at the same time permits the endless production of spurious reformulations.

More speculatively, one could perhaps relate the problem of parametric change to a key concept of Marxist economics, that of *proportionality*. While the necessary ratios between different sectors of capitalist economy are established only by continuous departure from these proportions themselves, and 'disproportionality' is a central element in the crises by which economic structure is modified; in socialist economy agreements between the realised proportions and those of the plan is, according to Lenin, an important index of social control over economic development. Further, the democracy of the planning progress, which tends to align the goals of the agents of implementation with those of the agents of control, would condition the extent to which planned proportions could be optimally determined and then achieved. One sees here a possibly important role for econometrics, in a modified form, in the economy of the future.

In the present socialist society econometrics may be marked by weaknesses similar to those described in this chapter. At least this was the view of Varga (1968): 'there is no open revisionism among us [Soviet economists: JG]. Repercussions of revisionist ideas are sometimes encountered in a concealed form only among the champions of econometrics. (p. 12.)

4 THE TYPICAL MACRO MODEL

Having seen how the limitations of econometric methodology appear as *statistical* obstacles to its application, we pursue the theme by examining the way in which these limitations have conditioned the development of applied macro-economic research. Here – although of course they constitute only a fraction of the work done – economy-wide models give us a good framework in which to examine general trends in the field.

If, then, we trace the line of evolution of such models from their beginnings in the work of Tinbergen (1939) and Klein and Goldberger (1955), we see it increasingly accepted that these are short-run models centred on the immediate determinants of aggregate demand and its immediate consequences for output, prices and employment. This is a necessary restriction if what has been said about structural change is correct, but one that undercuts a whole range of the theoretical functions originally envisaged for such models. The K–G model was initially estimated with data spanning the U.S. economy from the twenties to the fifties – who would now be so bold?

The failure to tackle questions of long-run development by these means is common knowledge, but it is less widely realised that it extends also to the whole complex of problems associated with investment and the cycle: that is to all but the very short-run.

It is, however, clear that, from the point of view of prediction and control, the entire econometric investigation of aggregate investment expenditures has been simply a waste of time. This conclusion emerges from Jorgensen's survey articles (predating the current disturbances in capitalist economies which can hardly have helped matters); but it is already ironically implicit in the Brookings model, which relegates the investment theorist to the humble task of predicting investment anticipations data, while the econometrician proper is given the bread-and-butter job of transforming anticipations into actual expenditures (Jorgensen, Hunter and Nadiri, 1970a,b; Jorgensen, 1965; Eisner, 1965). Theoretically things are just as bad, for the two main positions – 'accelerator' and 'neo-classical' – result in such similar equations (investment as a function of a series of lagged output variables) that it is far-fetched to claim that empirical studies of macro data could discriminate between them. Further, it is doubtful whether the propositions under test retain, in any meaningful sense, the status of theory. In general the concept of investment as *any* stable function of a few arguments is quite inconsistent with the critical work of Shackle (see, for instance, his *Time in Economics*, 1958); while the manner in which Jorgensen formulates his 'neoclassical' position, in particular, has been sabotaged by the prolonged theoretical debate on growth and distribution.[10] To deny this would be to admit to a fundamental confusion about what economic theory is, let alone how it might be validated.

Given these structural weaknesses in the econometric analysis of capital formation, one could hardly anticipate a satisfactory treatment of economic fluctuations. In fact, such cyclical properties as macro models possess arise from their use of the Slutsky effect: oscillations as a consequence of random disturbances whose impact is distributed over time by lags in the model. It has proved impossible to find any but highly damped cyclical tendencies within the deterministic part of the specified structures.

Now the immediate theoretical implication of such findings is that the economic structure is in reality intrinsically stable, and that its actual performance will be more or less free from fluctuations as the environment in which it functions is more or less smooth and un-troubled. If acceptable, this would be a conclusion of some importance – one could attribute the present economic upheavals, for instance, to the delayed working of extrinsic factors.

For several reasons, however, this kind of inference is highly problematic, since all that has been achieved is this: equations fitted over a given time period, when 'shocked' in a simulation exercise with random disturbances of the same order of magnitude as the residuals in the sample, exhibit fluctuations of the same character as those observed in that sampling period. In such an exercise this result is not particularly sensitive to the specification of the model employed, always providing that it contains sufficient dynamics in the form of distributed lags. A 'naïve' equation, simply relating an aggregate such as G.D.P. to its own past values and a disturbance will show the same sort of cyclical behaviour; and one can make a set of variables oscillate with the same frequency by imposing 'indecomposability', i.e. allowing each to be related directly or indirectly to all the others in any way, regardless of whether the interconnections have any sensible explanation. After all, Slutsky's classic paper (1937) can be interpreted in two ways: a set of random disturbances when smoothed will give rise to a sinusoidal wave; but, equally, any sinusoidal wave, of whatever origin, can be modelled as a moving average of random disturbances.

Examined in greater depth, the standard result of 'exogenous' cycles is really a necessary consequence of the method of econometricians, forced by the lack of information in their 'observations' to approach the problem of fluctuations in isolation from that of capitalist economic development in general. Very strong reasons can be adduced to show the actual inseparability of growth and fluctuations. This is so whether we consider the economic history of industrial capitalism or the traditional corpus of trade-cycle theory (Schumpeter, 1961, Hayek, 1933, for example);[11] but it becomes brutally explicit in post-war thought on the subject since the latter is formulated in mathematical terms. In the equation systems of Hicks (1950) or Goodwin (1969) 'inseparability' may be translated as 'non-linearity'.

Malinvaud is clear in rejecting non-linear theory on practical, not theoretical, grounds:

> Some do in fact think that general fluctuations in economic activity only reflect the fluctuation of certain exogenous quantities which dies away naturally. But others think that the economic system is essentially unstable, that every initial disturbance tends to propagate and amplify over time. In this case a good model should be unstable near its equilibrium position, and describe the obstacles which put an end to explosive evolutions. It would be necessarily non-linear. (Malinvaud, 1970, p. 539.)

We can add that given the limitations on data described above, Malinvaud's 'good model' would also be 'necessarily' inestimable. (Desai, 1973, has put one of Goodwin's models into a form where quantification is conceivable but this is hardly the same as convincing results.)

In practice, then, the econometrician is forced to investigate dynamic phenomena with stable linear difference equations. This predetermines his results which contradict historical knowledge and distort modern and traditional dynamic theory. Pasinetti spells out what happens:

> Can the differential equation representing the multiplier-accelerator interaction, *in general* (and independently of the number of time lags), explain a movement of fluctuating growth? The answer is no. The solution of such a differential equation will contain as many roots as the order of its characteristic equation. No matter how many such roots may be, only one of them (or only one pair of conjugate complex roots) will eventually dominate all the others. And the shape of the dominating path will indeed crucially depend on the values of the parameters. In any case, it will be *either* a path of exponential growth or a path of cyclical fluctuations. (Pasinetti, 1974, p. 70.)

We have discussed only the central structural flaw in macro models. Others could be listed – in particular the difficulty of establishing any satisfactory link between the money and commodity markets. It is more convenient, however, to pass now to the current state of research. Here a recent survey of models of the U.S. economy is illuminating (Fromm and Klein, 1973). A lengthy comparative study of these projects is made and the work pronounced in moderate language a success; but Fromm and Klein's criterion of success or failure is no longer any light thrown on the nature of economic processes, but what is termed 'convergence'. By this, it turns out, Klein does not mean convergence *with reality* but *convergence of the various models with one another*. The rationale for an entire sphere of academic work has thus been internalised: henceforth any external criticism is irrelevant and the activities of the model-builders are only to be assessed by their own majority vote. But economic history menaces even this most modest of achievements: a sharp dissenting note asserts the *divergence* (and superior predictions) of an odd model out constructed on monetarist rather than 'Keynesian' principles (Bodkin, 1973). As we move from an era of relative stability to one of rapid inflation this claim is plausible, but we can believe that even the econometricians of the Federal Reserve Bank of St Louis will prove, in the event, to have possessed but a temporary truth.[12]

5 THE THEORY AND PRACTICE OF MACRO-ECONOMICS

It is hardly an exaggeration to say that the result of adopting econometrics as the main investigative technique of economic science has been the divorce of theoretical work from the whole field of measurement and application. We now give some details of this break.

On the side of application, then, the rationale for econometric macro models has gradually shifted. There is less interest in the estimation of simultaneous equation systems and the associated problems of statistical inference; the model-builders are more likely to be preoccupied with the mathematics of dynamic systems and the prediction of stochastic processes. The orientation is practical, more concerned with forecasting than explanation – economy-wide models in particular no longer tend to be single projects for academic purposes but part of the routine functioning of official or semi-official agencies such as the Treasury or NIESR in the United Kingdom. But the same applies to macro-economic research in general: it is the policy-oriented economist rather than the theorist who is likely to have recourse to econometric techniques.

The change in rationale may be summarised as the substitution of an 'engineering' approach for an analogy with the experimental procedures of natural science. Further correlates can be traced, for example the attempt to ground empirical macro relationships in individual behaviour functions which used to enliven the literature with such entertaining contortions has been largely abandoned. The administrator is more concerned with the stability of a relation than its micro-economic pedigree and there never was any reason why one should guarantee the other since the household or the firm is precisely as subject to historical change as the society of which it is a part.

Thus the models which are presently constructed are explicitly designed for short-term policy problems: in every way they are less ambitious than the first essays in the field. Further, no governmental or private economic action is ever likely to be based immediately on econometric results; predictions as given by the model are always critically adjusted before they are used to inform policy.[13]

Now to some extent this separation of prediction from parameter estimation, hypothesis testing, and so on is compatible with econometric theory: efficiency and unbiasedness often turn out to be separable attributes in that one may pursue the first in abstraction from the second. It has been appreciated since the 1950s that if with the model

$$y = a + bx + u$$

one is concerned with the prediction of y rather than the determination of b, then a non-zero covariance between x and u such as arises from omitted variables is no problem provided it is stable, i.e. provided the nature of the bias does not change between the sampling period and the predicition period. In such a case one wishes to know not b but $E(y/x)$, and there is scope for some technical debate as to how this may be done efficiently. For two reasons, however, this transformation of science into art is highly unsatisfactory.

First, if our sole concern is efficient prediction we have no use for simultaneous equation theory which is concerned centrally with consistent parameter estimation. But this is to discard econometrics, since this theory is all that distinguishes econometrics from mathematical statistics in general, and it is impossible to justify the academic weight of the subdiscipline within economic science by referring to its application in these terms.

Second, there is the more substantial point that nothing that has been said should be taken as suggesting that econometrics is more capable of performing its new, limited role than its old and grandiose one. There is no evidence (Fromm and Klein's survey conspicuously fails to offer any) that the use of expensive and time consuming econometric procedures improves economic predictions even in the short run. Chancellor Healey recently had some sharp words for his short-term Treasury forecasters when he discovered this. And the importance accorded to these techniques contains this danger, that since policy decisions cannot be informed by economic theory via the established investigative procedures, they will not be informed by it all. For the problem of bias cannot be ignored for ever – sooner rather than later the covariance of x and u will turn out to be a non-linear function of time. The separation of prediction and policy from the formulation of theory is always temporary and relative: in changing environment one cannot for long control what one does not understand.

Turning now to economic analysis, we see that, in developments over the last two decades, theory has gradually been emancipated from the techniques which pretended to subject it for the first time to the rigours of the scientific method. After the early days of the 'Keynesian revolution' when the elucidation and measurement of expenditure multipliers was the order of the day, the focus of theoretical attention naturally shifted to other areas such as economic growth or monetary theory. For the reasons outlined above these proved far less tractable in terms of measurement.

In these areas there was no real possibility that theoretical developments could be constrained and ordered by a series of 'refutations'. In the field of economic growth, for example, the distance between theory and experience is so great, and so many subsidiary transitions have to be made before econometric estimation becomes possible, that any discrepancies between model and data can always be explained away. Could results from work such as Denison's (1967) settle any of the issues between 'Cambridge' and a 'neoclassical' growth theorist? The real danger has proved the contrary one, that with a well-defined but practically useless method of investigation, thoughts on growth would become too free, involving the production of numerous models so specialised and elaborate as to be remote from all experience. In other words the realities, both historical and contemporary, which should always influence analytical thought to some extent, have frequently been neglected.

In such a context, applied work loses its importance, always following theory, rarely preceding and informing it. The new methodology prescribed a rigid sequence – hypothesis, test, refutation, new hypothesis. But with its failure all interaction between analysis and the examination of economic phenomena is jeopardised. Instead what happens is a series of unrelated adventures – theoretical contribution, unconstrained analytical discussion using over-specialised mathematical models, and finally a host of unreal 'econometric studies' which everybody, quite correctly, ignores.

This is the general situation in the discipline: what we possess is a methodology which prevents the theorist from examining the object of his inquiry.

6 CRITICS OF ORTHODOX METHODOLOGY

It is argued above that the rise of econometric methodology was conditioned by the very specific problems associated with the first implementation of demand management policies. This thesis is supported by the fact that the most penetrating criticism of orthodox positions has come from the opponents of fiscal intervention.

On the practical level an outstanding critical contribution is that of Streissler (1970). In his *Pitfalls in Econometric Forecasting* this writer presents econometric procedure as a series of 'transitions', pointing out the concrete difficulties of each stage: the conception of a theory; its representation in a mathematical model; linearisation of the model and the introduction of stochastic components; and estimation with actual data. From the other side there are also the numerous transitions through which primary economic observations themselves must go before their emergence as macro time series in official publications. Each stage is marked by its own difficulties, its own necessary approximations and probable distortions, and their cumulative result is the extreme dubiety of the method as a whole.

Streissler's general arguments are reinforced by George Polanyi's detailed study of the forecasting record of the National Institute for Economic and Social Research, a (semi-official) body which has consistently taken an optimistic view of the value of econometric technique. It is interesting here that the failures of the method are intimately associated by Polanyi with policy failures:

> Inaccuracy on a substantial scale, therefore, seems to be a hazard that is unlikely to be avoided by using more refined techniques. One way out would be to abandon forecasting altogether. But this may be impracticable. . . . A much more promising approach would recognise the inevitable inaccuracy of forecasts and the limitations of demand management in attempting to regulate short-term fluctuations in activity and the balance of payments. (Polanyi, 1973.)

These examinations are valuable, indeed essential. But, in itself, the work of Streissler and Polanyi is limited in its methodological implications: these may be summed up as the absolute need for caution both in econometric estimation, and even more in any government action based on its results. This is a conclusion which will clearly be more welcome to economic liberals than to interventionists.

For a deeper critique of quantitative work in economics, though cognate with Streissler's in its economic philosophy, we can turn to the work of Hayek. In his 'The Theory of Complex Phenomena' we find a useful summary account of his epistemological objections to the kind of ambition exemplified by econometrics, as, in Malinvaud's definition, 'the empirical determination of economic laws':

We may well have achieved a very elaborate and quite useful theory about some kind of a complex phenomenon and yet have to admit that we do not know of a single law, in the ordinary sense of the word, which this kind of phenomenon obeys. I believe this to be in a great measure true of social phenomena: though we possess theories of social structures, I rather doubt whether we know of any 'laws' which social phenomena obey. (Hayek, 1967, p. 42.)

This conclusion is the more devastating for econometrics in that it attacks the *aspirations* of the discipline, not its necessarily limited achievements for which particular apologies are always available. Hayek reaches it by considering the complexity of the phenomena of 'life, mind and society' as opposed to those investigated by physics. Whereas the latter may be able to predict particular events, the biologist, psychologist or economist may be constrained to the prediction of certain kinds of pattern formed by very large numbers of elements – their particular constellation being, for practical purposes, unknowable.

Ironically, Hayek is concerned when making this argument to reconcile his view of the social sciences with Popper's theory of scientific discovery. It is difficult not to feel that he does this with subtlety and realism, exposing in the process the crudity of the 'neo-positivist' position which underlies much of contemporary economic research. Social theories must often be 'algebraic' since we are in fact unable to substitute particular values for the variables and obtain numerical results. This will be the case with general equilibrium theory, for instance. But to make this admission is not to deprive such theory of scientific status.

Such a theory will, of course, in Popper's terms, be one of small empirical content, because it enables us to predict or explain only certain general features of a situation which may be compatible with a great many particular circumstances. It will perhaps enable us to make only what M. Sriven has called 'hypothetical predictions', dependent on yet unknown future events; in any case the range of phenomena compatible with it will be wide and the possibility of falsifying it correspondingly small. But as in many fields this will be for the present, or perhaps for ever, all the theoretical knowledge we can achieve, it will nevertheless extend the range of the possible advance of scientific knowledge. (Hayek, 1967, pp. 28–9.)

Thus the criticism of econometrics advanced by the economic liberals is very cogent on a variety of levels, and its political orientation, while it may explain, cannot justify the general neglect of these views by professional economists. This neglect, indeed, carries the disturbing suggestion that the dominance of orthodox methodology may itself be unconsciously political, buttressed more by the patronage of departments of state than by any scientific validity.

But in associating economic liberalism with a resistance to contemporary methods of economic investigation, one should not ignore the exception which proves the rule. It is one thing to argue that the government does not possess the knowledge required to intervene usefully in the economy. The Monetarists go farther, asserting that in the absence of such action the economy would come into balance with reasonable speed and fluency. An easy corollary, however, of rapid equilibration in other markets is a similarly rapid adjustment of the demand for money to its supply; and in the attempt to establish this most implausible of contentions, anti-interventionists have been ready to employ every suspect technique, every ambiguous device, of their 'Keynesian' opponents. They would appear, in many cases, to have bettered the instruction.[14]

8 CONCLUSION

None of the discussion above should be interpreted as a Luddite assault on the alliance of economic theory with mathematics and statistical theory; nor, in particular, is it meant to suggest that economics can do without quantitative models any more than other branches of contemporary science. On the other hand, it is argued, first, that it is no longer realistic to look for solutions to problems of empirical economic research within econometrics itself. These problems are too deep-rooted in the whole structure of contemporary economics, in the way in which it is articulated into its various subdisciplines, for such an approach to be more than an evasion of fundamental difficulties in methodology, economic theory and statistical technique.

Second, in retrospect it becomes increasingly clear that the present organisation of economic science was largely conditioned by the establishment of a post-war economic order where early successes masked the myriad problems implicit in massive state intervention in capitalist economies. In the radical restructuring of that organisation required by contemporary economic developments the validity and status currently accorded to econometric methods of investigation will necessarily be early victims.

NOTES

1. This is a revised version of 'Econometric Methods in Macro-economics: A Critical Assessment', which first appeared in the *British Review of Economic Issues*, vol. 1, no. 1 (Nov 1977). I would like to thank my colleagues at Queen Mary College Economics Department, in particular Ian Drury, for help with this paper.

2. Desai (1976), for instance, admits: 'The gap between theory and application is still wide. . . . with a few exceptions those who excel in econometric theory keep away from the messy contact with data'. (p. viii).

3. Friedman (1953) is the clearest example.

4. This is not to prejudge their fitness for such a function which is considered below.

5. Althusser, from a totally different position, makes a statement quite congruent with Coddington's: 'I only discuss and reject the theory of models as an *ideology of knowledge*. . . The empiricist conception of the model as an ideology of knowledge obtains all the appearances necessary for its imposture from the confusion between the *technical instrument* that a model in fact is, and the concept of knowledge.' (Althusser and Balibar, 1970, p. 39). One is not making a linguistic point. Some writers, Marxist and otherwise, use the term 'model' for any scientific production, whatever its level of abstraction and generality. For instance Marx's theory of capitalist development is sometimes described as a model. The point is rather that these various levels do exist and are necessarily distinct in epistemological status. The higher (more abstract) levels are marked by the complexity and sophistication of their conceptual structure. Lower levels in the first place presuppose this kind of conceptual development and second are limited by instrumental simplifications, omissions, adaptations needed to put the abstract theory in relation with more specific conjunctural situations. This is the sense in which the pair theory model is used here – econometric models being low-level productions indeed.

6. That Keynes himself would not have agreed with this assessment is shown by his reaction to Tinbergen's early work which is, incidentally, an amazing anticipation of the problems of economic methods. (Keynes, 1939).

7. Thus it is not unfair to define econometric theory as a series of footnotes to the Gauss–Markov Theorem.

8. 'Information' is to be understood here both in its usual sense and with the technical meaning it has in statistical theory.

9. Although one notes (with despondency rather than surprise)

the continued good health of the 'new econometric history', having recently been shown a paper with a massive statistical annexe and the breath-taking title, 'Britain in the Napoleonic Wars: A General Equilibrium Analysis'.

10. The same applies to the use of aggregate production functions in the study of growth processes: no matter how useful the results of such work are as *description,* they can hardly be claimed to test a well-specified theory.

11. Schumpeter (1935) states that his theory excludes the econometric separation of economic development into cycle and trend:

> the trends of our time series are not due to influences distinct from those that create the cyclical fluctuations but simply embody the results of these latter. To these 'result-trends', as the author calls them in his workshop, it is entirely unwarranted to apply formal methods of the type of least squares.

12. The above has considered only the most ambitious part of applied macro-economic research, though criticism of work confined to particular variables, or specific sectors and markets is to some extent implicit. On the other hand, detailed criticism of inflation-models, labour-market models, and so on is as endless as these productions themselves. We can, however, raise the general question of the *autonomy* of the various sectors isolated for econometric investigation – meaning by this the theoretical legitimacy as well as the practical value of examining phenomena such as labour-market participation rates, or the impact of incomes policies, in abstraction from an overall vision of the economic system.

13. To formalise this a *posteriori* doctoring as an exercise in 'Bayesian estimation' is, in all probability, a waste of time.

14. See Kaldor (1970). Brainard and Cooper (1975) give this (generous) assessment of an entire debate:

> there was an effort stimulated by Milton Friedman and David Meiselman, to determine whether Keynesian or monetarist models provide a better explanation of money income. In retrospect, it appears clear that it is not possible to discriminate between competing macro-models simply on the basis of in-sample fit. Given the highly serially and cross-correlated nature of economic time series, the range of choice variables for use in any model, and

the flexibility in the specification of lags, marvellous fits of historic data can be obtained by models with widely different implications for the behaviour of the economy and its response to policy. Out-of-sample forecasts provide a better test, but it appears difficult to discriminate between the simple Keynesian and monetarist models on this basis.

Given the fact that economic data do not distinguish sharply between competing views, the *plausibility of theoretical explanation will continue to bear heavy weight in distinguishing among alternative hypotheses* as well as in guiding our exploration of the data.' [emphasis added] .

REFERENCES

Althusser, L., and Balibar, E. (1970) *Reading Capital* (London: New Left Books).

Bodkin, R. G. (1973) '"Discussion" of Fromm and Klein' (1973) *A.E.R.* vol. 63, p. 410.

Brainard, W. C., and Cooper, R. N. (1975) 'Empirical Monetary Economics: What Have We Learned in the Last 25 years?', *A.E.R. Papers and Proceedings,* p. 167.

Bray, J. (1975) 'Optimal Control of a Noisy Economy with the U.K. as an Example', *J.R.S.S.,* Series A, vol. 138, p. 339 (with discussion).

Brechling, F., and Hahn, F. H. (eds) (1965) *The Theory of Interest Rates* (London: Macmillan).

Brown, R. L., Durbin, J., and Evans, J. M. (1975) 'Techniques for Testing the Constancy of a Regression Relationship over Time', *J.R.S.S.,* Series B, vol. 37, p. 149.

Clower, R. W. (1965) 'The Keynesian Counter-Revolution: a theoretical appraisal', in Brechling and Hahn (1965).

Coddington, A. (1972) 'Positive Economics', *Canadian Journal of Economics,* vol. 5, p. 1.

Denison, E. F. (1967) *Why Growth Rates Differ: Post-war Experience in 9 Western Countries* (Washington: Brookings Institution).

Desai, M. (1973) 'Growth Cycles and Inflation in a Model of the Class Struggle', *Journal of Economic Theory,* vol. 6, p. 527.

Desai, M. (1976) *Applied Econometrics* (London: Allan).

Duesenberry, J. S., Fromm, G., Klein, L. R., and Kuh, E. (eds) (1965) *The Brookings Quarterly Econometric Model of the United States* (Amsterdam: North-Holland).

Eisner, R. (1965) 'Realisation of Investment Anticipations', in Duesenberry *et al.* (1965).

Feinstein, C. H. (ed.) (1969) *Socialism, Capitalism and Economic Growth: Essays presented to Maurice Dobb* (Cambridge: Cambridge University Press).

Friedman, M. (1953) 'The Methodology of Positive Economics', in *Essays in Positive Economics* (Chicago: University of Chicago Press).

Fromm, G., and Klein, L. R. (1973) 'A Comparison of Eleven Econometric Models of the United States', *A.E.R.,* vol. 63, p.335.

Goodwin, R. M. (1969) ' A Growth Cycle', in Feinstein (1969).

Gordon, R. A., and Klein, L. R. (eds) (1966) *Readings in Business Cycles,* A.E.R. Series (London: Allen & Unwin).

Haberler, G. (ed.) (1950) *Readings in Business Cycle Theory,* A.E.R. Series (London: Allen & Unwin).

Harris, S. E. (1948) (ed.) *The New Economics* (London: Dobson).

Hayek, F. A. (1933) *Monetary Theory and the Trade Cycle* (London: Cape).

Hayek, F. A. (1967) 'The Theory of Complex Phenomena', in *Studies in Philosophy, Politics and Economics* (London: Routledge & Kegan Paul).

Hicks, J. R. (1937) 'Mr. Keynes and the Classics: A Suggested Intepretation', *Econometrics,* vol. 5, p. 147.

Hicks, J. R. (1950) *A Contribution to the Theory of the Trade Cycle* (Oxford: Clarendon Press).

Jorgensen, D. W. (1965) 'Anticipations and Investment Behaviour', in Duesenberry *et al.* (1965).

Jorgensen, D. W., Hunter, J., and Nadiri, M. I. (1970a) 'A Comparison of Alternative Econometric Models of Quarterly Investment Behaviour', *Econometrica,* vol. 38, p. 187.

Jorgensen, D. W., Hunter, J., and Nadiri, M. I. (1970b) 'The Predictive Performance of Econometric Models of Quarterly Investment Behaviour', *Econometrica,* vol. 38, p. 213.

Kaldor, N. (1970) 'The New Monetarism', *Lloyds Bank Review,* no. 97, p. 1.

Kalecki, M. (1954) *Theory of Economic Dynamics* (London: Allen & Unwin).

Keynes, J. M. (1939) 'Professor Tinbergen's Method', *Economic Journal,* vol. 49, p. 558.

Klein, L. R. (1964) 'The Role of Econometrics in Socialist Economies', in *Problems of Economic Dynamics and Planning: Essays in Honour of Michael Kalecki* (Warsaw: Polish Scientific Publishers).

Klein, L. R. (1968) *The Keynesian Revolution,* 2nd ed. (London: Macmillan).

Klein, L. R., and Goldberger, A. S. (1955) *An Econometric Model of the United States 1929-1952* (Amsterdam: North-Holland).

Koopmans, T. C. (1947) 'Measurement without Theory', *Review of Economic Statistics,* vol. 29, reprinted in Gordon and Klein (1966).

Leijonhufvud, A. (1968) *On Keynesian Economics and the Economics of Keynes* (New York: Oxford University Press).

Luxemburg, R. (1971) *The Accumulation of Capital* (London: Routledge & Kegan Paul).

Malinvaud, E. (1970) *Statistical Methods of Econometrics* (Amsterdam: North-Holland).

Pasinetti, L. L. (1974) 'Growth and Income Distribution', in *Essays in Economic Theory* (London: Cambridge University Press).

Phillips, A. W. (1954) 'Stabilisation Policy in a Closed Economy', *Economic Journal* vol. 67, p. 265.

Phillips, A. W. (1956) 'Some Notes on the Estimation of Time-Forms of Reactions in Independent Dynamic Systems', *Economica,* vol. 23, p. 90.

Polanyi, G. (1973) *Short-Term Forecasting: A Case Study,* I.E.A. Background Memoranda, no. 4.

Schumpeter, J. A. (1935) 'The Analysis of Economic Statistics', *Review of Economic Statistics,* vol. 17, p. 2, reprinted in Haberler (1950).

Schumpeter, J. A. (1961) *The Theory of Economic Development* (New York: Oxford University Press).

Shackle, G. L. S. (1958) *Time in Economics* (Amsterdam: North-Holland).

Slutsky, E. (1937) 'The Summation of Random Causes as the Source of Cyclic Processes', *Econometrica,* vol. 5, p. 105.

Streissler, E. W. (1970) *Pitfalls in Econometric Forecasting,* I.E.A. Research Monograph, no. 23.

Tinbergen, J. (1939) *A Method and its Application to Investment Activity* (No. 1 of League of Nations series on Statistical Testing of Business Theories) (Geneva).

Tinbergen, J. (1948) 'The Significance of Keynes' Theories from the Econometric Point of View', in Harris (1948).

Tinbergen, J. (1951) *Econometrics* (London: Allen & Unwin).

Tinbergen, J. (1954) *Centralisation and Decentralisation in Economic Policy* (Amsterdam: North-Holland).

Varga (1968) *Politico Economic Problems of Capitalism* (Moscow: Progress).

Vining, R. (1949) 'Koopmans on the Choice of Variables to be Studies and of Methods of Measurement', *Review of Economics and Statistics,* vol. 31, reprinted in Gordon and Klein (1966).

Wall K. D. (1973) 'Solution of the Discrete Time Tracking Problem Using Dynamic Programming', PREM Working Paper KW30 (London: Queen Mary College).

Walters, A. A. (1969) *Money in Boom and Slump:* an empirical enquiry into British experience since the 1880's, Hobart Paper, 12 (London: Institute of Economic Affairs).

Wold, H. (1952) *Demand Analysis – A Study in Econometrics* (Uppsala and New York: Wiley).

CHAPTER 2

The Consumption Function: a study of a failure in positive economics

Francis Green

1 INTRODUCTION

Bourgeois economics would like to present itself in two ways: on the one hand as an integrated body of thought wherein all branches of the subject are related and wherein conclusions follow logically from premises; and on the other hand as a science wherein the theories have been and are being properly and adequately confronted by empirical evidence.

Now it is unlikely that any bourgeois economist would claim that his subject really achieves this in every aspect. Rather, in his eyes it is an ideal to be aimed at, and at the same time some sort of standard against which the current state of economics is to be measured. But there are some areas where this ideal is claimed to be nearly reached and where the only limitations on the extent to which it is achieved are given by the inadequacy of the data (rather than of the theory). One such area is the theory of the consumption function. To see why, let us briefly recall the history of this relationship.

In 1936 Keynes announced to economists the fundamental importance of a simple relation between the aggregate consumption and the aggregate income of individuals. As is well known, this provided the spur to a number of attempts to discover this function, using both cross-section and time-series data, attempts which were at first successful but which after a few years met with a number of anomalies. These were that the cross-section results of simple linear regressions of consumption on income did not properly tally with the time-series results, and that the time-series (aggregate) consumption function did not appear to be stable over a long period: it appeared to be shifting upwards over time.

Apparently in response to these anomalies, Friedman announced in 1957 the importance of his concept 'permanent income', which was designed to alter the nature of the consumption function in such a way as to place it within the framework of utility theory. And more or less at the same time Modigliani and Brumberg (1954) developed their 'Life-Cycle' Hypothesis of saving, which also was based on utility analysis. Thereby arose what is proclaimed to be the finest showpiece of the neoclassical/Keynesian synthesis. Here was a merging of a concept in macro-economics, which helped to explain the determination of macro-economic variables (such as the levels of national income and of employment), with the established methods of microeconomic theory.

Moreover, this marriage of utility theory and macro-economics is held to be confirmed by empirical evidence. There can be few other areas in economics which have been subjected to so much empirical testing. Since the mid-1950s there have been of the order of two hundred studies of consumption functions, most of which have been within the framework of Friedman's Permanent Income Hypothesis (PIH). It would seem, from the sheer quantity of published material, that with so much evidence apparently for the PIH or at least some aspects of it, and with little evidence which unambiguously refutes it, that the theory is now firmly established on an empirical basis. Thus the popular history of the consumption function attempts to convey the impression of a dual success story. It brought together the methods of micro- and macro-economic theory. Thus Modigliani and Brumberg could claim that the Life-Cycle Hypothesis 'has the advantage that the hypotheses on which it rests are explicitly stated as specifications of the consumer's utility function'.[1] But, even more important, it signalled the successful application of positivist methodology within economic science; that is, it purported to exemplify the method whereby the adequacy of a theory is judged by its ability to make predictions about observable data and to survive attempts to refute it. Thus we find, for example, the statement in a widely used textbook that 'the basic idea of the permanent income concept and the broad framework of the theory has, however, passed the empirical tests – if not with flying colours then with enough correspondence to suggest that the theory is the best one we have'.[2,3]

Because this story is well known to the student of economics, and because it is quite frequently pushed to the fore as one of the more successful confrontations of 'theory' and 'fact' in modern economics, it makes an interesting case study in the methodology of positive economics. For this popular history is at the same time unquestionably false. It is my main task in this paper to demonstrate that this is so. I intend to examine the nature of the many tests of the PIH and show to what extent it is true that this theory has been established on an empirical basis. And my conclusion is that the theory has in fact failed to be validated by the 'evidence' *in its own terms*, in the sense that *no* evidence has been adduced that serves to discriminate between it, the PIH, and alternative theories. That does not mean that the PIH has actually been 'disproved' by the evidence and that I am thereby accusing proponents of the theory of ignoring such evidence. Indeed, it is virtually impossible to disprove such a theory as there are always a battery of extra assumptions needed to make the tests operational which can be jettisoned in the face of anomalous results. But it does mean that there are no *empiricist* reasons for preferring the PIH. We find here therefore the continued use of estimated aggregate consumption functions for forecasting and policy purposes, an example of the tendency referred to in Chapter 1 for econometrics to find its only justification in a context that is basically *practical* and ultimately unscientific.

It is as well to be clear from the start that this is not a chapter about what constitutes good scientific methodology. It is, to repeat, a *case study* in methodology (albeit one which by debunking a supposedly successful application of positive economics thereby somewhat discredits the methodology itself). For this reason I must naturally stick to the rules of this methodology if I am to claim that the bourgeois theory does not in this case conform to its own criteria. In particular, this means that I must tacitly accept, for these purposes, the empiricist dichotomy between theory and evidence, and so from now on I shall use uncritically such concepts as 'fact', 'observation', 'refutation', etc. In so doing, the scope of my argument is naturally restricted. But, for the economist, the importance of the conclusions is undiminished, for the consumption function plays a central role within the neoclassical/Keynesian synthesis.

The main argument is developed in the next and longest section of this chapter. Given the conclusion at which I arrive, it becomes necessary to examine the reasons why the PIH and LCH have found such success in the economic literature. These reasons are not hard to find, but it is none the less important to analyse the ideological role that the theories perform. This constitutes the third section. Finally, in the fourth section, I examine briefly the reasons why it is not surprising that the PIH and LCH have failed to be empirically validated; there I conclude that, even apart from questions of methodology, the theories fail because they are based on an individualistic and therefore inadequate view of the economy.

2 THE NEOCLASSICAL THEORY OF SAVING AND THE CONSUMPTION FUNCTION

(a) FISHER'S THEORY

The Permanent Income and Life-Cycle Hypotheses (PIH and LCH) may properly be termed 'neofisherian' theories, as they are based on the work of Irving Fisher. The latter proposed in 1932 a theory of interest, and, in his 'First Approximation' to that theory, he assumed that each individual consumer possesses a utility function which describes his preferences for consumption at different periods of his life. The essence of the theory is that these preferences are 'autonomous'; that is, they are given from outside the field of economics. In particular, the preferences are sharply distinguished from the means whereby they are satisfied, from the income he expects to receive at different periods of his life. Knowing this stream of income the consumer must, however, make sure that his planned consumption at each period can be paid for either from the income in that period or from borrowing or from drawing down savings of previous periods. This constraint is expressed by saying that the present value of his consumption stream must equal the present value of his income steam. He is then assumed to maximise his utility, a function of his consumptions in each period, subject to this constraint.

There are three important aspects of this theory. First and foremost it is a neoclassical theory – it is an application of the much-used optimising framework, in this case to the problem of allocation over time. Second, following on from this, it is an institution-free theory. By this it is not meant to imply that institutions do not affect the level of savings for it may be that the institutions of an economy substantially affect individuals' budget constraints. Rather it is implied that institutions do not affect individuals' preferences directly.

The implications of this view are that the individual's propensity to save is 'natural' – that is, part of his human nature; thus the neoclassical view rules out any idea of class. (see below, Section 3) More concretely, the institution of the joint-stock corporation has no effect on individuals' preferences for saving; the corporation is seen as an extension of, or as representative of, the individual.[4] Third, the theory is in a crucial sense future-oriented. The savings decision is assumed to be made with regard only to the future and present consequences, and in the light of future and present incomes. The past is relevant only in so far as past saving has determined current endowments and incomes. We shall see below how, in the many so-called tests of the theory, this crucial dimension is invariably lost – that is, how not one of the tests succeeds in separating out a statistical regularity that is not much more easily explained as the effect of the past rather than of the future.

The PIH and LCH are both attempts to 'operationalise' Fisher's theory. In almost all respects they are identical even though their approaches are different, the PIH focusing on a flow variable, permanent income, the LCH focusing on a stock, individual wealth. Since by far the greatest number of tests have been in the framework of the PIH, and since all these tests are implicitly tests also of the LCH, I shall restrict my survey largely to the PIH, reserving only a few final comments for the LCH.

(b) THE PIH MODEL[5]

The result that emerges from the assumed maximisation of utility subject to the budget constraint is that consumption in any period depends only on R, the present value of the income stream, and r, the rate of interest. In particular, if we take the current period, the conclusion can be written:

$$C_1 = f(R, r). \tag{1}$$

This result stresses that a change in current income, Y_1, could only affect C_1 in so far as it changes R; and also, that changes in future income, (Y_2, Y_3, etc.), would affect current consumption, since they enter into the determination of R. Friedman then defines 'permanent income', y_p, as the perpetual flow of income that would be derived from a constant stock of wealth R, given the interest rate r. Thus:

$$y_p = rR. \tag{2}$$

Therefore the consumption function is:

$$C_1 = g(y_p, r). \tag{3}$$

It is stressed at this point that the concept of permanent income is intrinsically related therefore to the Fisherian theory.

Friedman then made certain assumptions about the likely form of a consumer's utility function, the implication of which is that consumption is proportional to permanent income:

$$C_1 = k(r) y_p. \tag{4}$$

This assumption has often incorrectly been taken to be the essence of the PIH (though not by Friedman); it is not. If it is found to be false – and most of the evidence suggests this – it is possible to revert to equation (3) which really does contain the essence of the theory. All important tests of the PIH can be seen as attempts to test equation (3). In order to have such a test it is necessary to specify how y_p, a theoretical variable, corresponds to concrete, observable data (remembering that this correspondence between 'theory' and 'fact' is assumed to be unproblematical). This is done in the following model. Observed income and consumption are divided into two parts:

$$Y = y_p + y_T \tag{5}$$

$$C = c_p + c_T, \tag{6}$$

where y_p, permanent income, corresponds to the theoretical concept derived from Fisher's theory; Y_T is transitory income; c_p permanent consumption corresponds to planned consumption as given by equation (3); C_T is transitory consumption. It is implicit in the definitions and in the theory that the permanent and transitory components are independent of each other; most important is the assumption that neither component of consumption is affected by the size of transitory income:

$$^\rho C y_T = 0, \tag{7}$$

where ρ stands for correlation coefficient.

In addition, from equation (4) we have

$$C_p = k y_p \tag{8}$$

or, if we do not take a proportional function, but instead a simple linear function

$$C_p = k_0 + k_1 y_p. \tag{8}$$

In tests of the PIH attempts are made to specify y_p in a number of ways (c_p is, actually, usually specified as simply equal to C, observed consumption). These ways always involve some function of current and past incomes, either directly, or indirectly via relationships with socio-economic characteristics such as occupation. But, to have a test of the PIH, it is not always necessary to specify y_p for every member of a sample of data. Let us now consider two ways in which the model has been tested many times by researchers:

(i)   In possession of cross-section samples of household saving and consumption behaviour, researchers have grouped households according to certain categories. They have argued that with certain groups, e.g. farmers, permanent income is likely to deviate from observed income more on average than with other groups (non-farmers). One way of saying this is that the proportion, P_y, of the variance of observed income within a group of consumers that is accounted for by the variance of permanent income tends to be low for groups like farmers, whose individual incomes tend to vary a lot from year to year. How can this assumption be used? Turn now to the results you would expect from plotting on a graph C against observable income Y, or better from a regression of C on Y. According to the PIH, C is really a function of y_p, not of Y. Therefore the regression coefficient of C on Y (i.e. the estimated marginal propensity to consume) will *understate* the dependence of C on y_p, since Y

is only partially determined by y_p, the rest being contributed by y_T which does not affect C. In fact, in a well-known calculation (see Appendix, p. 55) it can be shown that the expected value of the estimated coefficient will come to $k \operatorname{var} y_p / \operatorname{var} Y$ (which is less than k), assuming equation (8) is the 'true' relationship. If now we calculate the income elasticity of consumption, η_{CY}, at the mean point of the regression, this involves dividing by k (assuming zero transitory income on average), since k is thereby the average propensity to consume. Thus we have the result:

$$\eta_{CY} = \frac{mpc}{apc} = \frac{\operatorname{var} y_p}{\operatorname{var} Y} = P_y \text{ (to use Friedman's notation).}$$

(9)

It follows that for groups where P_y is thought to be relatively low, e.g. farmers, the measured income elasticity of consumption, η_{CY} is predicted also to be low. This prediction of the PIH has figured in many of the tests thought to establish it.

(ii)   A second way in which the model has been tested has been applied either to individuals, or to sample groups, or to aggregate time-series data. This is, simply, that if there are reasons for expecting y_p to be high relative to Y, then it is likely that C will also be relatively high. The commonest case of this prediction is that when the aggregate economy is in recession, aggregate Y is thought to be less than y_p; therefore the aggregate consumption ratio, C/Y, will be relatively high (that is, above its trend value) in times of recession, and vice versa.

I shall describe below in more detail the various types of test that have been performed, but the two ways I have just mentioned in fact cover a large proportion of such tests, and because they illustrate well the main point of my argument, I wish now to consider more closely the nature of these two tests. In particular, it will be noticed that *permanent income is being specified by using the past as a standard against which to compare the present*. Thus the typical argument is that if observed income is high relative to what it was in the past (or if it lies above past trends), then it is said that transitory income, y_T, is positive, that is, y_p is less than Y. Or, similarly, if within a cross-section sample there are many individuals whose incomes deviate a lot from their past incomes then it is argued that the variance of transitory income is high;

that is, that P_y is low. It appears then that although the theory of the PIH is based on the future, in the actual tests the past is being used as the measure of the future. This is especially important in the light of the existence of another, much simpler, explanation of consumer behaviour which stresses the importance of habits on consumption, and therefore of the influence of the past on the present. This other explanation is one aspect of the Relative Income Hypothesis (RIT) as developed by Duesenberry (1949). In this theory it is envisaged that current consumption is determined not only by current income but also by habitual levels of consumption enjoyed in the past. This theory was in existence before the PIH was introduced and, as we shall see, all the facts explained by the PIH can also be explained by the Habit Persistence Hypothesis (HPH). Although this argument is yet to be proved, the essential point can however already be seen: by using the past as a 'proxy' for the future, *none* of the tests of the PIH can serve to discriminate between it and the simpler HPH. The word 'none' is stressed here because although the resemblance between the PIH and HPH has long been recognised, it has usually been claimed that somehow the PIH goes beyond the HPH.

We can pursue this argument first by showing that a simple HPH model produces the same two predictions outlined above as are made by the PIH.

(c)   AN HPH MODEL

The notion of habit persistence is at the same time both simple and superficial: Brown (1952) states that 'the habits' customs, standards and levels associated with real consumption previously enjoyed become "impressed" on the human physiological and psychological systems and this produces an inertia or "hysteresis" in consumer behaviour. Because of this inertia, consumer demand reacts to change in consumer income with a certain slowness. . .' A related but not identical idea is suggested by Marglin (1974), who argues that consumption lags behind income as consumers take time to learn how to spend increases in income. Similar notions to these have been suggested by other writers not committed to the neoclassical approach. They all have in common the view that consumption is affected by the past. If this view is now supplemented by a simple linear specification for the consumption function, we have the following two ways (among others) in which the HPH may be (and has been) simply modelled:

$$C_t = a_1 Y_t + a_2 Y_{t-1} \tag{10}$$

or $\qquad C_t = a_1 Y_t + a_2 C_{t-1} \tag{10'}$

(subscripts $_t$, $_{t-1}$ refer to time periods; the variables refer either to individual or to aggregate measures).

Before proceeding I must emphasise that there is nothing neo-classical about the HPH model of consumption. If consumers are subject to habitual behaviour they cannot also be pursuing a utility maximisation strategy. It is no defence for neoclassical economics to claim that the habits are somehow arrived at rationally and therefore that habit behaviour is rational behaviour. For we cannot sensibly talk of consumers rationally allocating their consumption over time periods if it is during those time periods that their consumption and savings habits are being formed. It follows that the notions lying behind equations (10), and (10)', though simple, must be regarded as essentially non-neoclassical. But from either of specifications equations (10) and (10)' it is possible to derive predictions identical to the two derived above for the PIH.

First, suppose that past income (in the case of equation (10)) or past consumption (in the case of equation (10)'), is relatively low compared to current income. Then the consumption to income ratio will also be low. For example, in the upsurging and boom of the trade cycle Y is increasing fast, so that Y_{t-1} is relatively small compared with Y_t; hence the consumption to income ratio will be on the low side of its long-term value. This is the same prediction as for the PIH, only using different language.

Second, I must consider the implications of specifications such as equations (10) or (10)' for the estimates of income elasticity of consumption, η_{CY}, that would be derived from a regression of C_t or Y_t only. Thus, suppose that equation (10) were the 'true' relationship but that we were to carry out an ordinary least-squares regression of C on Y for a sample cross-section of households. The estimated marginal propensity to consume would be greater than a_1, if current income is positively related to lagged income, but it would be less than $(a_1 + a_2)$ to the extent that the correlation between current and lagged income is less than perfect. To be precise, if we calculate the estimated income elasticity of consumption (See Appendix, p. 60) we obtain:

$$\eta_{CY} = \frac{a_1 + a_2 \, \rho_{01}}{a_1 + a_2} \tag{11}$$

where ρ_{oj} stands for the correlation coefficient between current income and income lagged j periods. From equation (11) it can be seen that, if in our sample cross-section it is thought that ρ_{01} is relatively low (as for example with farmers or any group whose incomes vary a lot from year to year), the estimated value of η_{CY} should be relatively low, compared to other samples which are thought to have more stable incomes. This prediction is exactly the same as that made by the PIH. For the PIH method of testing equation (9), above, is to use ρ_{01} as a proxy for P_y.

Furthermore a similar argument holds if instead of equation (10) we were to specify equation (10)$'$ as our HPH model. In that case the estimated income elasticity is given by (see Appendix):

$$\eta_{CY} = (1 - a_2)(1 + a_2\rho_{01} + a_2^2 \rho_{02} + a_2^3 \rho_{03} + \ldots),$$
$$(11)'$$

and again we have the prediction that the lower are the correlation coefficients between current and past incomes, the lower will be the observed income elasticity of consumption.

Indeed, a similar prediction is bound to hold whenever it is specified that consumption depends on current income and on lagged values of income and consumption. This prediction has been used time and time again in order to 'confirm' the PIH. It is never acknowledged that it is derivable also from the much simpler HPH.

(d)   TESTS OF THE PIH[6]

Let us now see how these ways of testing the PIH are put into practice, by considering some examples. As stated above, there have been a very large number of such tests published in the last twenty years, so a comprehensive survey is impossible without going to book length. In principle it would be necessary to cover every test in an overall assessment, given my argument that there are *no* valid tests that have discriminated between the PIH and the HPH. That would be a tedious exercise if it were really necessary. However, fortunately I can rely on a good secondary source, Mayer (1972), to ensure that there are no valid and relevant tests that I have not considered.[7] For present purposes I have classified the many tests into five types, and I illustrate my argument with examples of each type.

TEST TYPE 1

Tests which use extraneous information about (var y_p/var Y).

The essence of this type of test has already been described. The method is to consider a sample cross-section of households of a particular type and to ask whether P_y (= var y_p/var Y) is likely to be relatively high or low for that sample. In a typical test, Friedman[8] found that η_{CY} was lower for a set of farm families than for non-farm families and concluded this was evidence in favour of his PIH. As we have seen above, however, the HPH would also predict this. All other tests of this type fall into the same pitfall.

In one case, however, Friedman went further: he claimed to have made the prediction numerically precise. He analysed a set of cross-section data that gave information on each household's income and consumption over a number of years. He calculated the income correlation coefficients, ρ_{oj}, assumed that ρ_{oj} = var y_p/var Y and used these calculations to estimate the values of η_{CY}. He found that the estimated values came very close to the actual observed values of η_{CY}. This, he claimed, was strong evidence for his theory. However, this 'evidence' must be discounted completely. Friedman never performed any statistical tests to see just *how* close his estimates of η_{CY} were to the actual values; and Mayer has since shown that the estimates are not much closer than you would have expected on any naïve model.[9] Moreover, Mayer then went on to perform the same test on a new set of data and found that the estimates of η_{CY} were wildly inaccurate. It is, further, significant that *no* other researcher has ever reproduced numerically precise accurate estimates of η_{CY} by this method.

TEST TYPE 2

Tests that use extraneous information on the mean transitory or mean permanent income of a group.

An example of this type of test is the case where the consumption patterns of black families and white families in the United States are contrasted.[10] Comparing samples of each type of family it was found that, despite the fact that the overall average propensity to consume of white families was lower than that of the black families, *at a given income level* the white families spent on average more than black families. The PIH (or LCH) explanation is this: the mean income of a group is an estimate of mean permanent income for members of that group. If we compare black families and white families with the same observed income the former have none the less on average a lower permanent income, y_p, since mean income is lowest for them. Hence the black families spend less than the white families.

But the HPH has the same implication. The mean income and consumption of the group of black families represent a rough estimate of the habitual level of consumption to which they have been accustomed. Thus if again we compare black and white families with equal incomes the white families will consume more than the black families simply because they are likely to have been accustomed to a higher level of consumption in the past.

This test, and others of its type, also fail to discriminate between the PIH and the HPH. The reason is the same as ever: the PIH is implicitly using the past as the standard whereby permanent income is judged.

TEST TYPE 3

Tests which specify y_p or y_T directly or indirectly from socio-economic variables.

In these tests attempts are made to estimate y_p for a household via its various socio-economic characteristics. A good example of this is the 'Group Means' tests. Households may be classified into numerous groupings and sub-groupings based on location, education, occupation, family type and so on, and the basic principle of these tests is that for each member of a sub-group y_p is estimated to be equal to the average measured income of that sub-group. Given this assumption a number of tests have been performed to show the dependence of C on y_p,[11] and on the whole this prediction is confirmed. Yet the PIH does not have a monopoly on this kind of prediction. First, Duesenberry's Relative Income Hypothesis makes the same prediction: individual consumption depends (partly) on the average incomes of the group to which the individual relates, because of the tendency for the individual to try to emulate his neighbour.

Second, the HPH (which is often thought of as part of the Relative Income Hypothesis) also predicts the same thing,[12] for the mean income group is an index that is liable to be positively related to the habitual consumption and income of individuals in the group. Thus, again, the standard by which y_p is measured is implicitly obtained from the past, and the tests fail to distinguish the PIH from the HPH.

TEST TYPE 4

Tests that specify y_T from extraneous information on the nature of an income receipt.

The most famous example of this kind is the 'windfalls' debate. A windfall receipt of income will be classed as almost wholly transitory income and should therefore, according to the PIH, be saved. There have been several studies in the literature of groups of households that contain some households which received windfalls (such as pools wins, war reparations payments). The broad conclusion of these studies is that the marginal propensity to consume windfall income is less than the marginal propensity to consume ordinary income receipts - though in most cases it is greater than zero. Many of the tests are for one reason or another inconclusive. But it is again the case that the HPH predicts the same thing: if a household is subject to habitual consumption behaviour which changes only slowly, it is to be expected that a sudden large rise in income resulting from a windfall receipt would not affect consumption all that much.

TEST TYPE 5

Tests which specify y_p from current and past measured income.

The most important examples of this type of test are those which specify and estimate aggregate consumption functions. Within this category we may consider first of all the standard observation that the cyclical behaviour of the aggregate consumption ratio differs from its long-run behaviour. This was one of the original 'anomalies' of the simple Keynesian consumption function, wherein current consumption was a simple linear function of current income:

$$C_t = a + b \, Y_t. \tag{12}$$

Researchers in the immediate post-war period found that this function equation (12), fitted the data well for the short run, but that in the long run the function shifted upwards over time. Moreover it was found that the average propensity to consume C_t/Y_t was relatively low in boom periods and high in recessions.

The PIH explained this anomaly by saying that in boom periods y_T is positive and hence the savings-ratio is relatively high. We have noted above, however, that this is also explained by the HPH. Indeed the few uses of the HPH in the economist's literature are to be found at that time – before the PIH had been introduced – in precisely this connection.

Since then, there have been a large number of studies which estimate aggregate consumption functions by specifying y_P as a function of current and past incomes. Not one of these is capable of distinguishing the PIH from the HPH. There is no predetermined way in which y_P is to be estimated. Friedman asks us to estimate it in such a way as seems best to fit the data. Given that, we could say the same for the HPH. Therefore the particular consumption function which seems best to fit the data (according to the standard statistical criteria) could equally well be said to be derived from the HPH as from the PIH.

One commonly used example shows the similarity between the two in a particularly obvious way. In this case, y_P is estimated from an 'adaptive expectations' hypothesis:

$$y_{Pt} - y_{Pt-1} = \beta(Y_t - y_{Pt-1}) \tag{13}$$

That is, the extent to which y_P adapts each period is determined by the difference between current observed income and permanent income of the previous period. Rearranging equation (13) we have:

$$y_{Pt} - (1 - \beta) y_{Pt} - y_{Pt-1} = \beta Y_t. \tag{14}$$

Assuming that transitory consumption is negligible:

$$C_t = k y_{Pt}. \tag{15}$$

Take this same equation, lagged one period, and multiply by $(1 - \beta)$:

$$(1 - \beta) C_{t-1} = k (1 - \beta) y_{Pt-1}. \tag{16}$$

Subtracting equation (16) from equation (15), and using (14), we have:

$$C_t - (1 - \beta) C_{t-1} = k [y_{Pt} - (1 - \beta) y_{Pt-1}], = k\beta Y_t,$$

and hence

$$C_t = k \beta Y_t + (1 - \beta) C_{t-1}. \tag{17}$$

This aggregate consumption function, derived from the PIH, can now be estimated, as it only contains observable variables. But a glance at equation (14), which is one specification of the HPH, shows that in this case the two theories are indistinguishable: the aggregate con-sumption functions are the same.[13]

If this is not enough to demonstrate that aggregate consumption functions are of no use for testing the PIH – or the LCH, or almost any of the various competing theories, two more points may be added. The first is that the aggregate data is very unreliable. Data on aggregate savings depend on the particular accounting definition of saving used, and it has been shown for both the United States and the United Kingdom that it makes a lot of difference which savings data series is used – so much so that estimates of the marginal propensity to save transitory income vary between 0.32 and 0.60 in one study;[14] depend-ing on the data series. And yet this data problem is ignored by most researchers. Second, different types of aggregate consumptions are rarely tested against each other on the same set of data in an effort to compare their predictive performances. And in one test where this actually is done, by Mayer (1972), the aggregate consumption derived from the PIH and the LCH do not fare particularly well.

There seems to be no conclusion other than that aggregate con-sumption functions do not throw any light on the differing micro-economic theories of consumption behaviour.

(e)   TESTS OF THE LIFE-CYCLE HYPOTHESIS (LCH)

Most of the tests of the PIH can also be considered as tests of the LCH; they are based in the same theoretical framework. To that extent, since many of the tests of the LCH are based on aggregate con-sumption functions, these must be discounted for the reasons given above.

However, unlike the PIH, the LCH pays particular heed to the effect of age on consumption and saving behaviour. It is observed, for example, that the average individual generally saves for all but the first few years of his or her earning span, and dissaves – that is, draws on past savings – during the retirement period. Moreover, other variables related to consumption vary over the life-cycle – for example, the average number of people in the family. Does the fact that people may be observed saving for retirement and dissaving after retirement, constitute evidence for the LCH? Here we must distinguish between life-cycle factors and the LCH. The importance of life-cycle factors for aspects of behaviour would seem to be obvious. Thus, for example, the behaviour of the retired person is liable to be different from that of a young person. But that is not what the LCH consists of. The LCH assumes that individuals formulate optimal life-time consumption strategies based on autonomous preferences (that is, on preference functions which do not change when economic conditions change). This is to say far more than simply that people save. Clearly people do save, and often for specific purposes. But that fact cannot be used as confirmation of the LCH.

(f)   SUMMARY AND CONCLUSION OF TESTS OF THE PIH AND LCH

The broad conclusion so far is that there is no valid evidence, amongst the many studies of the PIH and the LCH, that is consistent with these theories and yet inconsistent with the HPH.

Two more points may be made conveniently at this stage, although they are not essential to my line of argument. First, I have not troubled so far to summarise the extent to which each aspect of the PIH is consistent with the evidence. I have implicitly conceded the proposition that the marginal propensity to consume transitory income, (mpc_{y_T}), is less than the marginal propensity to consume permanent income, (mpc_{y_p}). The PIH, however, actually proposes more than this: it predicts that the mpc_{y_T} is zero. Upon this the evidence is on the whole inconclusive as it turns out to be very difficult to test, for a number of technical reasons, though it may none the less be stated that there exist many tests which suggest that it is positive and quite large. By comparison, there is conclusive evidence that the proportional relationship between permanent consumption and permanent income, equation (4), is invalid. As Mayer says, at the end of his exhaustive study: 'This [proportionality] hypothesis has been strongly disconfirmed by the tests. . . Some of these tests are the result of studies undertaken by several investigators using different sets of data and different techniques. . . Of all the many tests which have been undertaken by friends of the hypothesis, *not a single one supports it*'.[15] But, as I have stated above, this only rejects one, non-essential, part of the PIH. In the light of this particular conclusion it seems almost amazing that some textbook accounts of the PIH give such prominence to the proportionality hypothesis.

Second, for lack of space I have not devoted much attention to the Relative Income Hypothesis – that is, to that aspect of it which proposes that a household's consumption behaviour depends a lot on other households' consumption levels. A large amount of the quoted evidence for the PIH could also be accounted for by this Relative Income Theory. Thus, to this extent my argument that the evidence fails to distinguish between the PIH and alternative non-neoclassical theories is reinforced.

But, to return to the essential thread of the argument, I must finally reconsider whether there are any other empiricist reasons for preferring the PIH as an explanation of observed behaviour. Friedman himself gives reasons for the alleged superiority of the PIH. He states: 'in so far as we choose [the PIH], it is because we regard it as simpler and more fruitful than others that have come to our notice, or because we can find additional evidence consistent with ours but not with some of these others.'[16] The second part of this sentence cannot be accepted – it has been the object of this paper so far to show that there is *no* 'additional evidence' which is not explicable in terms of other theories, in particular the HPH. But what about the first part of the sentence?

A little consideration will show that this has to be rejected also. The PIH is not a 'simple' theory. If we are to take its theoretical basis in Fisher's theory seriously – and there is little point to it if we do not – we see that even if many simplifying assumptions are made (such as the neglect of uncertainty) the PIH still requires us to assume that the consumer makes what is inevitably a complex calculation as to the optimal consumption plan. As against this, the HPH is really much more simple: consumers are influenced by habits as well as being constrained by income, and we choose to specify this relationship in the simplest way – by a linear function of current income and of past consumption or income. Superficial as this statement is, it is sufficient to explain the relevant statistical evidence. So the criterion of 'simplicity', even if we were to concede that this is an adequate criterion for preferring one theory to another, cannot be used in favour of the PIH.

There is also the criterion of 'fruitfulness'. The fruitfulness of the PIH has generally been vastly exaggerated. What it boils down to in the end is that consumption depends on other things besides current income. Since those 'other things' (such as past consumption habits, or family size and needs) would be expected to affect consumption anyway, for other reasons, the PIH is not really particularly fruitful. Against this, it might be claimed that the PIH (or LCH) is more fruitful than the HPH as it makes predictions about the effect of future income on consumption. But this brings me back to my already stated argument – that whenever the PIH is operationalised the element of the future is always dropped.[17] Its essential basis, the theory of Irving Fisher, is thereby never tested.

Finally, another aspect of fruitfulness might be claimed, namely that the PIH is able to produce numerically precise predictions. But, as I have already reported above (regarding Friedman's precise predictions of income elasticities), additional assumptions are needed to be so precise, and, anyway, when the tests were repeated the predictions were wildly inaccurate. Thus the 'fruitfulness' criterion also cannot be used in favour of the PIH.

The PIH (and LCH) are neither simpler nor more fruitful than the HPH, nor is there any evidence that can be explained by them and not by the HPH. There is nothing for it but to return to my basic conclusion of this section: that the tests of the PIH and LCH that researchers have performed have failed to establish the superiority of these theories over others *on empiricist grounds*. The empiricist economists simply do not live up to their own standards.

3 IDEOLOGICAL FUNCTION OF THE PERMANENT INCOME AND LIFE-CYCLE HYPOTHESES

Why have the PIH and LCH apparently stood the test of time? Why do researchers and theorists continue to use them as a framework for their work? The main reason would seem to be that these hypotheses are grounded within the neoclassical method, and in particular within the theory of utility. This method, is first of all, individualist, for it treats individuals as the basic units of analysis. The preferences of individuals are autonomous – in the sense that they are assumed to be unaffected by economic relationships into which the individuals enter.[18] Thus the method leaves no room for any concept of class or of social relations. To exclude class as a relevant concept at the ground floor of a theory of saving is an extremely important achievement for ideology. For its implications are that property ownership and especially the ownership of capital, derives from savings done in the past. If a capitalist owns an amount of capital, then this ownership is his reward for savings decisions made in the past according to the methods of utility maximisation. If a worker does not possess sufficient means to become a capitalist, then this also is explained by his failure to save enough in the past. It is his own decision. The consequence of the neoclassical method is that everyone must bear the responsibilities for his own position; nothing can be attributed to his class situation.

The second aspect of the neoclassical method, in its guise as basis for the PIH and LCH, is that it is supportive of the ideology that 'consumption is the purpose of economic activity', that is, that the ultimate end of production in capitalist society is the satisfaction of consumer preferences for material consumption to the greatest possible extent. This is the essence of the doctrine of 'consumer sovereignty'[19] In this context, the PIH and LCH, based as they are on Fisher's lifetime savings theory, assume that the purpose for all the wealth accumulation in the economy is that it should be consumed at a later stage in life; people save early in life in order to consume more later on in life. This is in direct contrast to the Marxist analysis of the capitalist economy which sees that most (though not all) 'wealth' accumulation is in fact the *accumulation of capital,* which is not a means towards an end, but is an end in itself.

These are the general points which are necessary to mention since they are the most fundamental. We need in addition to gain some insight into why the PIH and LCH have acted as the 'vehicles' for the expression of the neoclassical method. For this the development of the PIH and LCH must be seen within the context of the development of post-war economics. Broadly speaking, this could be called the history of the neoclassical/neoKeynesian synthesis. The PIH and LCH first enabled a fusion to be enacted between the older neoclassical economics and the recently triumphant Keynesian economics. Later on they could be used to undermine the latter.

The fusion was necessary in order to maintain the methods of neo-classical economics in the face of the Keynesian analysis. Keynes's theory apparently explained all the important things about the work-ings of the economy – in particular why it was prone to cycles and to depressions, and what to do about them. The PIH and LCH – by tacking themselves on to the Keynesian toolbox in giving a micro-economic, neoclassical, explanation of the consumption function, rescued Fisher's theory from oblivion. In so doing they sowed the seeds for an attack on Keynesian analysis which was part of an overall resurgence of neoclassical economics at the expense of Keynesianism. There were two aspects to the attack on Keynes – a policy aspect and a theoretical aspect -- in which the PIH and LCH participated.

First, they imply that the marginal propensity to consume transi-tory income is zero or, at least, very low. Therefore the multiplier, which is the inverse of the marginal propensity to save, is low and not likely to be much different from one. If so, that would mean that government intervention in the economy (for example, by increasing expenditure, or by reducing taxation) would have little effect to stimu-late the economy. The Keynesian policy would appear to be of little use. Thus the PIH and LCH may be, and have been, used as components of an attack on the efficacy of state intervention.

There is no doubt an aspect of truth in this claim that the power of the multiplier is overestimated by the Keynesians. If, for example, we were to consider other theories of the consumption function, such as the HPH, it is apparent that the effect of changes in current income on current consumption may not be as great as was originally imagined in the context of the Absolute Income Hypothesis (AIH). However there is no evidence from the PIH and LCH that the marginal propensity to consume current income is zero. Moreover, the PIH counts the purchase of consumer durables (cars, houses and so on) as savings rather than consumption. While one may debate the relevance of this distinction in the microeconomic context, it is clear that from the macroeconomic point of view the purchase of, say, a car would stimulate the economy, and if a tax cut were to lead people to buy more cars then the multiplier effect of a tax cut still retains its relevance.

Second, there is a theoretical reason why the PIH and LCH could be used in the general attack on Keynesian economics. No space is available here to describe how and why it was criticised. The aspect which concerns us here is this: could below-full employment equilibrium be explained within a Keynesian framework without making the assumption that money wages were downwardly rigid? It turned out to be of some theoretical (though dubious practical) importance whether, when prices fell in a recession while nominal money balances remained constant, people's consumption demands increased as a result of the increase in the real value of their money wealth.[20] Thus, in turn, it mattered as to whether, in the aggregate, consumption is increased by an increase in aggregate wealth. A number of consumption funtions have been estimated which do appear to support the existence of such an effect. The PIH and LCH are considered relevant here because they provide a neoclassical rationale for the importance of wealth in the consumption function.

We see then, in summary, that the neoFisherian theories of the consumption function have played a key role in the attempt to integrate the neoclassical and the Keynesian methods into one, bourgeois, mode of analysis, whose parts are consistent with each other; and that the effect of this has been to aid the reproduction and expansion of the dominance of the neoclassical method in the bourgeois economist's way of analysing the economy, of doing research and of teaching.

Here is an example of a real failure of positive economics that is at the same time an ideological success. Only if we see through the apparent complexities of these theories and discover how shallow is their real empirical basis can we begin to weaken their ideological grip.

4 CONCLUDING REMARKS

The popular conception of the history of the consumption, that sees it as a more or less successful application of the positivist method to neoclassical economics and at the same time a validation of the synthesis of microeconomics and macroeconomics, is a false one. Instead, I have argued, the neoFisherian theories should be regarded as aspects, important ones, of the neoclassical ideology.

In conclusion, it is necessary to point out that the failure to validate the theories is not just a problem of insufficient data in a complex world. (If that were true the recipe for improvement would be clear: spend more funds on research, collect more data.) The real problem lies rather in the individualistic method of neoclassical economics. It is this that prevents an understanding of movement and change in the economy. It is this that gives rise to misconceptions about the role of saving within the economy. A more adequate conception starts instead with the concept of capital accumulation, and out of this it is clear that saving cannot be treated in the undifferentiated way that neoclassical economics sees it. Rather, the 'savings' of capitalists must be distinguished from the savings of workers. The orthodox view rules that out by assuming an aggregate relationship which treats all consumers as alike; the orthodox consumption function fails to take account of the different positions which members of different classes occupy within the capitalist mode of production. Instead, the motives of capitalists and workers should be distinguished conceptually.

The capitalist, as bearer of capital, has no option but to accumulate, and to aim continually for the maximum production of surplus value. This is so because capital accumulation occurs under the coercive force of competition; a capitalist could not decide to stop accumulating, for in that case he would be taken over by larger capitals or go out of business – he would thereby cease to be what he is, a capitalist. The rate of accumulation of capital is determined by a host of factors, primarily governed by the state of class struggle. It is not determined by the individual psychological propensities to consume and save of capitalists. On the other hand, the purpose of workers saving is not the accumulation of capital.[21] The coercive force acting upon workers is the need to sell their labour-power, and thereby to be able to obtain the means of subsistence whereby they may reproduce their labour-power. In the vast majority of cases the whole of the worker's wage is used up in this process; thus we can say that their consumption is sufficient to enable the reproduction of labour-power. However, where possible – that is, where the wage is high enough – the workers may save in order to ensure against the eventuality of a future reduction of income due for example to being thrown out of work. In particular many workers nowadays are forced to save part of their wages in pension schemes, to enable themselves to survive after they have left the work force. These savings payments may also be considered as part of what is necessary for the reproduction of labour-power. For an adequate subsistence level of income must be sustained for workers even after they have retired; it is nowadays necessary for the smooth reproduction of labour-power for the capitalist system, given that the expectations of workers have been so considerably raised by the growth of Western capitalism.

These remarks, which provide no more than the elementary beginnings of a Marxist conception of the economy and of those flows of funds called 'savings' within the economy, must however remain a mere postscript to the main themes of this paper. For it is not my purpose here to develop an alternative theory of saving or of the consumption function.

Appendix

THE ESTIMATED INCOME ELASTICITY OF CONSUMPTION

Consider a linear regression of the form:

$$C_i = a + bY_i + u_i, \tag{A1}$$

where u_i is a normally and independently distributed random-error term. The expected value of the estimate of b, the marginal propensity to consume, obtained from a data sample, will be given by:

$$\hat{b} = \frac{\text{covar}(C, Y)}{\text{var } Y} = \frac{\sum\limits_i (C - \bar{C})(Y - \bar{Y}),}{\sum\limits_i (Y - \bar{Y})^2} \tag{A2}$$

Where 'covar' and 'var' stand for 'covariance' and 'variance'.

(i)   THE PIH MODEL

Assuming for convenience that transitory consumption is zero, we have, from equations (5), (6) and (8):

$$\hat{b} = \frac{\text{covar}(k y_p, y_p + y_T)}{\text{var}(y_p + y_T)} \tag{A3}$$

$$\hat{b} = \frac{k \text{ var } y_p}{\text{var}(y_p + y_T)} + \frac{k \text{ covar}(y_p, y_T)}{\text{var}(y_p + y_T)} \tag{A4}$$

By assumption, y_p and y_T are independent,

hence $$\hat{b} = \frac{k \text{ var } y_p}{\text{var}(y_p + y_T).} \tag{A5}$$

Hence, according to the PIH, the estimated income elasticity, assuming average transitory income is zero is:

$$\eta_{CY} = \frac{\text{var } y_p}{\text{var}(y_p + y_T)} = P_y, \tag{A6}$$

which is equation (9).

(ii)   THE HPH MODEL

Assuming instead that consumption is given by equation (10), equation (A2) becomes:

$$\hat{b} = \frac{\text{covar}(a_1 Y_t + a_2 Y_{t-1}, Y_t)}{\text{var } Y_t} \tag{A7}$$

$$= a_1 + a_2 \frac{\text{covar}(y_{t-1}, Y_t)}{\text{var } Y_t} \tag{A8}$$

Assuming, for convenience, that the standard deviation, σ, of income remains the same in each period, equation (A8) may be rewritten:

$$\hat{b} = a_1 + a_2\ \rho_{01} \tag{A9}$$

Assuming also that mean income remains the same in each period, the estimated income elasticity evaluated at the mean will be:

$$\eta_{CY} = \frac{a_1 + a_2\ \rho_{01}}{a_1 + a_2} \tag{A10}$$

which is equation (11). Altering the assumptions made would make the expression more complex but would not alter the essential argument of the text.

Making the same assumptions, except using equation (10)$'$ as our specification of the HPH model we would obtain:

$$\hat{b} = \frac{\text{covar}\,(a_1\ Y_t + a_2\ C_{t-1}, Y_t)}{\text{var}\ Y_t} \tag{A11}$$

$$\hat{b} = a_1 + \frac{a_2\ \text{covar}\,(C_{t-1}, Y_t)}{\text{var}\ Y_t} \tag{A12}$$

If equation (10)$'$ is now used again to substitute for C_{t-1} in equation (A12), and the process is repeated endlessly we obtain the series:

$$\hat{b} = a_1 + a_1\ a_2\ \rho_{01} + a_1\ a_2{}^2\ \rho_{02} + a_1\ a_2{}^3 \rho_{03} + \ldots \tag{A13}$$

The average propensity to consume at the mean point is obtained from

$$\bar{C} = a_1\ \bar{Y} + a_2\ \bar{C}, \text{ hence}$$

$$\frac{\bar{C}}{\bar{Y}} = \frac{a_1}{1-a_2} \tag{A14}$$

Hence, the estimated income elasticity, evaluated at the mean is:

$$\eta_{CY} = (1 - a_2)\ (1 + a_2\ \rho_{01} + a_2{}^2\ \rho_{02} + a_2{}^3\ \rho_{03} + \ldots), \tag{A15}$$

which is equation (11)$'$ from the text.

NOTES

1. Modigliani and Brumberg (1954) p. 48.
2. Walters (1970) p. 265.
3. It is fair to say here that not all textbook accounts are as categorical as this. There are some that give equal status to alternative theories such as the Relative Income Theory (RIT), e.g. Lindauer (1971); but more generally, in accounts where the RIT is mentioned it is implicitly or explicitly treated as inferior to the PIH and LCH and on the occasions where reasons for this are given they are, as this paper demonstrates, invariably spurious. Outside the textbook the PIH is accepted even less critically. Thus Ferber (1973) argues that 'the concept of permanent income seems to be firmly established as both operational and highly meaningful' (p. 1309). And indeed a flip through the pages of the *Journal of Economic Literature* shows that every year the vast majority of articles on the consumption function use the language of the PIH.
4. Given this view, one might have expected some effort to have been directed to testing this proposition. It is well known that the 'post-Keynesian' school assume a different propensity to save out of personal income than out of the retained income of corporations, contrary to the neoclassical view. Yet very few attempts to test such a proposition have been made; and those few have been inconclusive.
5. In an attempt to maintain the flow of my argument I have considerably restricted the technical part. For a more detailed exposition the reader should consult an appropriate textbook, e.g. Johnson (1971). Some important calculations have been placed in an Appendix to this paper (p. 55).
6. The reader who is less interested in the details of the tests could skip this section without losing the flow of the argument.
7. What follows in the text is perforce only a small sample of the many existing tests. However as far as possible they are representative of all other tests not alluded to. I have noted references in only a few cases where it may be thought to be particularly helpful for the reader. For a full bibliography see either Mayer (1972) or Ferber (1973).
8. Friedman (1957) pp. 58–69.
9. See Mayer (1972) pp. 81–7.
10. See, for example, Fisher and Brown (1958).
11. See, for example, Eisner (1958).
12. The two hypotheses are combined by Duesenberry (1949).
13. Some textbook accounts draw attention to the lack of a con-

stant in equation (17), and, arguing that the HPH model should be specified to contain a constant term, claim that this makes the PIH and HPH consumption functions different. Such an argument is wishful thinking. There is no evidence that the proportionality hypothesis is correct. Besides, the proportionality hypothesis (and hence the lack of a constant term in equation (17)) is not an essential part of the PIH.

14. Taubman (1968); Odling-Smee (1973).

15. Mayer (1972) pp. 347-8.

16. Friedman (1957) p. 157.

17. It is fair to say that there have been three pieces of research that have tried to show the effect of future income on consumption: Watts (1958), Gustman and Stafford (1972) and Mayer (1972) ch. 13. These tests come to no conclusion. Apart from the fact that Mayer concludes differently from the former two, it remains true that the former two, who claim to have found some small effect of future income, never properly confront the problem of separating out the effect of the future from the effect of the past on the households in their data sample.

18. See Himmelweit (1977) in Green and Nore (1977) ch. 2.

19. See Mohun (1977) in Green and Nore (1977) ch. 4.

20. The most sophisticated development of this analysis is by Patinkin (1965).

21. For an elaboration of this argument, see Harris (1976).

REFERENCES

T. M. Brown (1952) 'Habit, Persistence, and Lags in Consumer Behaviour', *Econometrica* (July).

J. Duesenberry (1949) *Income, Saving and the Theory of Consumer Behaviour* (Cambridge, Mass: Harvard University Press).

R. Eisner (1958) 'The Permanent Income Hypothesis: Comment', *American Economic Review* (June).

R. Ferber (1973) 'Consumer Economics: A Survey', *Journal of Economic Literature* (Dec).

F. Fisher and R. Brown (1958) 'Negro-White Savings Differentials and the Modigliani-Brumberg Hypothesis', *Review of Economics and Statistics* (Feb).

I. Fisher (1961) *The Theory of Interest* (New York: Kelly).

M. Friedman (1957) *A Theory of the Consumption Function* (Princeton, N.J.: Princeton University Press).

F. Green and P. Nore (eds) (1977) *Economics: An Anti-Text* (London: Macmillan).

A. L. Gustman and F. P. Stafford (1972) 'Income Expectations and the Consumption of Graduate Students', *Journal of Political Economy* (Nov/Dec).

L. Harris (1976) 'Interest, Credit and Capital', *Income and Society,* vol. 5, no. 2 (May).

M. B. Johnson (1971) *Household Behaviour: Consumption, Income and Wealth* (Harmondsworth: Penguin).

F. Lindauer (1971) *Macro-economics,* 2nd ed. (New York: Wiley).

S. Marglin (1974) 'What Do Bosses Do? Part 2', *Review of Radical Political Economics.*

T. Mayer (1972) *Permanent Income, Wealth and Consumption* (Berkeley: University of California Press).

F. Modigliani and R. Brumberg (1954) 'Utility Analysis and the Consumption Function: An Interpretation of Cross-section Data', in K. Kurihara, *Post-Keynesian Economics* (Brunswick, N.J.: Rutgers University Press).

J. C. Odling-Smee (1973) 'Personal Saving Revisited: More Statistics, Fewer Facts', *Oxford Bulletin of Economics and Statistics.* vol. 35 (Feb).

D. Patinkin (1965) *Money, Interest and Prices* (New York: Harper & Row).

P. Taubman (1968) 'Personal Saving: A Time Series Analysis of Three Measures of the Same Conceptual Series', *Review of Economics and Statistics* (Feb).

A. Walters (1970) *An Introduction to Econometrics,* 2nd ed. (London: Macmillan).

H. Watts (1958) 'Long-Run Income Expectations and Consumer Saving', in Dernburg, Rosett and Watts (1958) *Studies in Household Economic Behaviour* (New Haven, Conn.: Yale University Press).

PART B

Issues in Economic Policy

CHAPTER 3

Cost – benefit Analysis: a critique

Michael Ball

1 INTRODUCTION

Cost–benefit analysis (CBA) is an attempt to provide a set of rules to evaluate whether any element of state expenditure should or should not be undertaken. In par icular, it is concerned with providing criteria for judging the usefulness of projects which will produce significant effects over long periods of time. Roads, airports, health programmes and flood-relief schemes are common examples of the type of state expenditure to which the technique has been applied.

Now any decision-making criterion has two major components. In the first place, it formulates the question on which the decision must be made. For CBA this question concerns the preferences of society: will society as a whole be better off if this project is under-taken? Second, the decision-making criterion provides a set of rules with which that question can be answered. Essentially, CBA suggests that the answer is provided by an aggregation of all the costs and benefits to individuals over the expected life of the project, with these costs and benefits expressed in terms of amounts of money.

It will be the contention of this chapter that the questions asked by CBA have no relevance for understanding state expenditure decisions. Mooveover, even if societal preferences were relevant, the claim that CBA provides objective rules for deriving those preferences has no validity. The numbers produced within a CBA require a series of illogical leaps of faith within the problematic of neoclassical economics.

The evaluation of CBA cannot, however, remain simply a task of noting the absence of theoretical foundations to the method. It also has to explain why the practitioners of neoclassical economics and the state apparatus which they serve have been forced to attempt such an exercise. The discussion here will be concerned with state expenditure in capitalist societies.

The usefulness of CBA is a controversial issue; many people have a jaundiced view of it. And, paradoxically, many protagonists of the method are also at the forefront in pointing out is weaknesses, at least in their theoretical discussions (Dasgupta and Pearce, 1972). Most criticisms of the methods of CBA concern, however, only the problem of how to derive accurate measures of society's preferences. They consequently do not question the overall objective of CBA, only certain issues of feasibility. Many of these difficulties, moreover, only require, so it is claimed, value judgments to be made at various stages in the analysis. And it is argued that value-judgments are necessary for any economic policy statement, so the problem is hardly unique to CBA. This question of value-judgments will consequently be considered first. In this context, it is perhaps appropriate to start by assuming that the question CBA asks is valid, that societal preferences should be the determinant of state expenditure. It is then possible to consider whether the evaluation rules provided by CBA can give a guide to those preferences. Having done this, the question itself will be considered and the use of CBA evaluated.

2   A SIMPLE EXAMPLE OF COST–BENEFIT ANALYSIS

Before embarking upon an examination of the theoretical issues underlying CBA, a simple example will highlight the main principles of the approach. Consider the case of an addition to a mass-transit system by the construction of a new underground railway.[1] The system is operated by a public utility which charges fares to passengers, and whose investment criterion, in the absence of CBA, is the profitability of the new route. On that criterion, the expected net cash flow of the projected railway has to be calculated for each year of its planned operation. These estimates are then to be discounted to give a net present value (NPV), using a rate of discount which reflects the cost of borrowing the funds to finance the investment. If the NPV is positive the project goes ahead; otherwise it is dropped.

On the revenue side, there will be the flow of income from fares paid by passengers using the tube; on the cost side will be the cost of constructing and operating the new link, and the revenue effects on the rest of the system. If passengers using the new tube had previously travelled on other routes, those routes will face a reduction in revenue. If fares are set broadly on a distance travelled basis, and the new link results in shorter journeys, the utility will lose revenue as a result of passengers switching their travel patterns. This revenue effect could be offset by additional passengers using the mass-transit system but, given high installation costs, the additional traffic generated will have to be very large to justify the project solely on the criterion of commercial profitability.

CBA would argue that the simple criterion of commercial profitability ignores many of the economic effects of the proposed investment for society as a whole. The shorter journeys for passengers previously using other routes, for example, might reduce the revenue of the utility, but they also confer substantial benefits to those passengers. In the jargon, those passengers enjoy a consumer's surplus which should be taken into account when evaluating the benefit to society of the proposed investment. Moreover, the existence of the new link will divert passengers from the roads of the city on to the tube, reducing city-centre congestion. Road users will have shorter journey times, and noise and air pollution will be lessened. So all who frequent the central city area will derive benefits from the new tube. Indirect benefits such as these are part of the overall economic effect to society of the proposed project, and CBA has developed a set of guidelines for their inclusion in the evaluation of projects (see Prest and Turvey, 1965). Furthermore, the rate of discount used by the utility only reflects its costs of borrowing. This rate of interest might be higher than society's true preferences for consumption now as compared with consumption in the future. The social rate of discount might in consequence be lower, increasing the probability of the project being a net benefit to society.

In summary, CBA attempts to evaluate the total economic effects to society of public investment projects by extending the criterion of financial profitability to encompass elements which a commercial calculation alone would not consider.

3   THE PREFERENCES OF SOCIETY AND CBA

3.1   THE PROBLEM

The basic principle of CBA is that the monetary calculation of the overall social benefits and costs of a particular project will give a rule by which it is possible to decide what society prefers. If CBA is used to evaluate economic actions by the state, a strong assumption is consequently being made about the purpose of state activity. A utilitarian view of the state is being adopted which asserts that the goal of the state should be to maximise the happiness (be it called happiness, pleasure or utility) prevalent within the nation. In Section 4, it will be argued that it is impossible for the state to operate on this utilitarian criterion. But for the present it is useful to remain within the bounds of the utilitarian assertion to see whether it is possible for economists using CBA to discover what society prefers.

The utilitarian conception of maximising human happiness gives no rules as to how that maximisation can be achieved. CBA is claimed to provide such rules. The results are presented as a product of an objective analysis. Society (alias a politician) can go against the con-clusion of a cost–benefit analysis because it has a strong value-judgement about, say, the preservation of some irreplaceable amenity. But CBA has essentially presented the decision-maker with an objective evaluation of the additional cost to society of choosing that option. Unfortunately for CBA, however, there is no easy, unassailable link between the method of CBA and the ideal of a measurement of social preferences.

CBA is based upon certain theoretical propositions of neoclassical economics. But in order to implement that theory as a basis for the measurement of social preferences a series of strong assumptions have to be made. All of them are necessary to justify the use of that theory but, obviously, none are validated by the theory itself. The polite way of describing this procedure is to say that each of these assumptions requires a value-judgement to be made. More impolitely, but also more correctly, each assumption can be viewed as an arbitrary assertion; ones which are nevertheless both politically and ideologically loaded.

This section will consider these assumptions and show that they are inconsistent, invariably dubious as statements of 'real-world' behaviour, and often adopted simply to enable the neoclassical model of the market economy to be used. At two major stages of the cost–benefit procedure are such assumptions required. Initially they are necessary to justify the use of its criterion of social benefit against which social costs (i.e. negative social benefits) are compared. They are then necessary to derive a set of prices with which these benefits and costs can be assessed. The two aspects will consequently be dealt with in that order.

3.2 SOCIAL PREFERENCE

Neoclassical welfare economics has tried a number of ways of deriving rules for deciding what society prefers. One of the most famous is the social welfare function. The latter is, however, only a formal statement that the object of the analysis is to find out what society prefers. It gives no rules by which to derive the actual parameters of the function. Attempts to derive such rules have proved controversial, as they all depend upon questionable value-judgements.

Arrow's (1951) development of the Impossibility Theorem, for example, attempted to demonstrate that democratic voting procedures cannot be relied upon to produce a statement of social objectives which reflects the will of the majority. This conclusion was reached after consideration of whether decision-making procedures could be devised which satisfied certain initial conditions and axioms. It was found that a non-dictatorial decision-making rule was impossible. Subsequent debate pointed out, however, that this conclusion was entirely dependent upon the initial conditions imposed. Those conditions were the product of Arrow's own assumptions, and others were equally plausible if different value-judgements had been made. Nevertheless, whatever the conclusions of 'social choice' theory, the definition of social objectives must remain somebody's value-judgement. Social welfare functions cannot help in providing the rules for deciding what society prefers (see Dobb, 1975, ch. 6).

CBA is unabashed by such difficulties in defining social welfare functions. It simply asserts that social preferences can be measured by *willingness-to-pay*. If aggregate willingness-to-pay is greater than total social costs, society is claimed to prefer the new situation to the old. Implicit within this claim, of course, are a host of assumptions.

In the first place, only individual preferences are assumed to count. What society prefers can be derived solely from a summation of individual preferences. But there is no reason why society should just be treated as a summation of individuals. Rules are imposed which might be in opposition to the majority of individuals' preferences, but are necessary for the continuation of that society. Similarly, once it is accepted that individual preferences are determined to a great extent by the social conditions in which those individuals exist, the argument becomes tautological. It is no longer possible to impute causality in a linear way from individual preferences to social ones.

Willingness-to-pay also implies that individual preferences should be treated as independent entities. If only one person gains from a project, and that person's gains outweigh others' losses, society is supposed to prefer implementation of the project. In part, this assumption relates to the question of distribution. The person gaining could be a multi-millionaire, while the losers were in abject proverty. It is not, however, simply a distributional question. Whatever the distribution of income, costs and benefits would still be treated as being independent of each other. Envy, emulation or straightforward social conflict between groups or classes are not supposed to influence anyone's utility function. If they did, it would not be possible to aggregate individual preferences in order to discover what society wants.

The importance of the so-called value-judgement that individual preferences are independent is not really a question of ethics, as is implied by the term 'value-judgement'. Instead, it is required to create a set of initial conditions in which a cost–benefit exercise is feasible. Conclusions about social preferences become predetermined by the decision to use the CBA approach to 'derive' those preferences.

Cost–benefit does more than simply assert that only individual preferences count and that they are independent. For it deals only with preferences that are expressed through the market-place. Where activities are not exchanged in a market, they are treated as if they were. Social preferences are in consequence derived from the individual preferences of the *sovereign consumer*. Individuals choose to choose in the market. Social preferences are consequently claimed to be derived from an aggregation of market demands. Willingness-to-pay, moreover, implies an ability-to-pay. There is consequently a built-in bias in CBA towards those groups with the greatest ability-to-pay: those individuals with higher incomes and business firms. Within its own terms of reference distributional questions should consequently be of paramount importance for CBA. But they are not. Most CBAs have ignored distributional questions and those that have not have considered them only sketchily (see Weisbord, 1968).

The criterion of willingness-to-pay as an indicator of social preferences also contains another implicit assumption of crucial importance. It assumes that the form in which any activity is provided does not affect the pleasure derived from that activity. This assumption is necessary in order to be able to reduce preferences to the uniform measure of a monetary calculation. The reduction of preferences to a monetary form, once this assumption is made, can consequently be treated as just a form of presentation; a way of comparing preferences.

Two related points are raised in this assumption. In the first place, it is assumed that whether an activity is actually priced or not does not affect the pleasure derived from its consumption. Art connoisseurs are indifferent to the fact that the object they are viewing cost a million pounds. Conversely, health-service patients are unaffected by the principle of socialised medicine, but only by the price they have to pay and the quality of the service. Difficult questions indeed, but they cannot simply be assumed away.

The second problem that is raised by the reduction to a monetary calculation is that this form of measurement will determine the intensity of preference measured. Can that diverse, psychic entity called 'pleasure' be encapsulated and quantified simply by asking 'how much are you prepared to pay for it?'? Such metaphysical questions are, of course, unanswerable. But CBA by the very nature of its method is forced to pretend that it has the answer. CBA claims to consider, at least in principle, all the economic conditions which affect social welfare. And the attempt to encompass all those affects on social welfare through a reduction to a monetary magnitude must influence the intensity of preference revealed, for the latter will not be independent of the manner in which it is measured.

This point is of vital importance for activities which do not involve a simple market exchange. In the parlance of cost–benefit, they are called 'intangibles'. They include such diverse elements as the value of time, life and environmental amenity. And intangibles invariably represent the majority of benefits in a cost–benefit calculation (even though most CBAs ignore many intangibles). If the form of measurement does affect the intensity of preference that will be recorded, it makes the whole attempt to measure individuals' preferences for intangibles through a monetary measure a highly dubious procedure. It is simply not possible to reduce many of the preferences CBA claims to measure to the criterion of willingness-to-pay.

Within the context of measurement in the market-place, only *marginal changes* are being evaluated. It is necessary to assume, therefore, that substitution between entities can be continuous and infinitely small, both in terms of production possibilities and individual preferences. 'Trade-offs' between two states can then be evaluated in terms of determinate exchange-ratios, in which incremental losses can be compared with incremental gains. But there is no reason to suppose that such continuous substitutions are feasible representations of real-world processes, either in production or consumer behaviour. Yet CBA has to assume that this is so. It must be possible, for example, to compare the effects on consumer preferences of the cost of an incremental loss of life and limb with the benefit of saving a few minutes on a trip to the seaside. If such continuous trade-offs are not possible, neither is cost–benefit analysis. Once again, the world has to be claimed to operate on the basis of the assumptions necessary for internal consistency within the neoclassical model in order that a cost–benefit result can be achieved.

Even if the criterion of willingness-to-pay is assumed to measure social preferences, strict application of the principle would still wreck most CBAs. So that criterion must itself be bent in order to enable the evaluation to proceed. Let us take an example of a good that is actually purchased through a market exchange: housing. A new project, a road or an airport, will result in certain owner-occupier households having to move, for they live on a site required for the project. Their losses are argued to consist of three elements. The first two are the price of the house and the resultant moving costs. They can easily be calculated and often the household will receive monetary compensation for these losses. A third element remains however to be evaluated.

It is highly probable that the household was willing-to-pay more than the market price for the house; in other words, they were enjoying a consumer's surplus. The procedure of cost–benefit would try to elucidate this surplus using the principle of compensating variation (the notional sum of money which will compensate an individual for their loss of an activity). In the United Kingdom the Roskill Commission on the Third London Airport adopted this approach. The compensating variation can be found, it is claimed, by appropriately worded consumer interview questionnaires. Roskill asked the following question: 'Suppose your house was wanted to form part of a large development scheme and the developer offered to buy it from you, what price would be just high enough to compensate you for leaving this house and moving to another area?' (Roskill, 1970, p. 381). Subtracting the market price for the house from the figure obtained from this question should leave an amount equal to the consumer's surplus (plus the individual's estimate of their own removal expenses).

Even if it is assumed that individuals can seriously ponder over such a hypothetical calculation and come up with an answer that reflects their willingness-to-pay, for CBA some will invariably give an awkward answer: no amount of money would induce me to leave. In fact, 8 per cent of respondents gave this answer to Roskill. For these people the compensating sum is consequently infinite. So the cost of the project is infinitely high. No more calculations are required, the project must be rejected on the criterion of willingness-to-pay. The minister must be informed and an announcement must be made that the government has just spent £1.25m. (the cost of the Roskill exercise) on finding out something that was obvious to all before the Commission started its evaluation; that some people will not move voluntarily from the proposed sites for the Third London Airport.

This, of course, was not the path taken. The embarrassment of the cost–benefit analyst was avoided by arbitrarily assigning a mere £5000 consumer surplus to those who claimed an infinite sum. It could be argued that such a reduction is merely another value-judgement, in which case the true power of value-judgements is revealed. They enable any rules to be altered at will to enable the desired result to be achieved.

The procedure of deriving preferences through individual behavioural responses in the market-place also comes into direct conflict with the dominant democratic ideology within bourgeois societies. This ideology recognises that individuals will inevitably be unequal economically within capitalism. It, in fact, approves of this state of affairs for such inequality creates the 'incentive' for people to work and thereby increase the wealth of society as a whole. The most liberal formulation of this doctrine argues for equality of opportunity while abhoring the thought of genuine economic equality. For others the invisible hand of the market alone will do the job. Whatever the divergent details within the formulation of the ideology, it is appreciated, nevertheless, that some individuals have more money than others. Their exists, in other words, differences in individual abilities to express preferences in the market-place.

The argument continues, however, by suggesting that this economic inequality is not reproduced at the political level. With universal adult suffrage, each citizen has an equal influence on the policial process. Moreover, it is argued that economic inequality is subordinated to the power of the state. The state can intervene in and control the economy. So, as state policies are argued to be determined by the democratic voting process, the current economic system and its inherent inequalities express the will of the majority. Bourgeois democracy is thus claimed to be profoundly democratic.

This dichotomy between the political equality of individual voter-citizens and their inequalities as economic agents cannot be sustained, as Section 4 will show. The distinction between the way in which CBA argues that society's preferences can be measured and the way in which bourgeois democracy claims they are expressed is nevertheless obvious. For the latter each member of society has only one vote of equal weight, for the former preferences are weighted by economic power. Both claim to measure the preferences of society, and yet they are mutually exclusive. Belief in the bourgeois democratic process, therefore, is in contradiction with the claim that CBA measures the preference of society.

3.3   THE MEASUREMENT OF COSTS AND BENEFITS

Having decided upon a procedure for deriving social preferences by aggregating total individual costs and benefits in a monetary calculation, the problem of value-judgements unfortunately (for CBA) does not cease. Costs and benefits are a series of statements about monetary amounts which are the products of a set of quantities multiplied by their relevant prices, either at the margin or as market aggregates. The problem arises of which prices are relevant. Rules (and therefore value-judgements) are necessary to determine which prices should be used.

Controversy rages within the cost–benefit literature over the merits of particular sets of accounting prices. The problem of the valuation (or price) of intangibles immediately comes to mind. What is the 'price' of an hour's worth of travel time? But debate has extended to virtually the whole set of accounting prices to be used. In the case of Third World countries, for example, should world market prices be used or domestic prices? These two price sets can be very different. Alternatively, what rate of discount should be used? For neoclassical economics regards the rate of interest as simply another 'price'.[2]

These controversies, however, all operate within the narrow confines of neoclassical economics and the dominant welfare conclusions that have been derived from within it. All the debates about accounting prices are couched in terms of the relationship to the conditions necessary for Pareto optimality. This section will therefore consider the relationship between CBA and Pareto optimality. Unfortunately, that relationship is not clear-cut and is often confusing as it operates at a series of blatantly contradictory levels. They can be broadly divided into the issues of the 'ideal state' and feasibility. The argument will consequently be structured upon that basis.

3.3.1   The General 'Ideal' Pricing Rule

Cost-benefit tries to use current market prices whenever possible. In certain circumstances, however, market prices might not reflect the true social opportunity cost of the provision of that commodity. In general, consequently, the pricing rule of cost-benefit is that of marginal social cost (i.e. adjusted current market prices, where markets exist, and the calculation of 'shadow prices' which reflect marginal social cost for activities where markets currently do not exist).

The adoption of this pricing rule is derived from a particular set of theoretical conclusions of neoclassical economics concerning the operation of decentralised competitive market mechanisms. Using the market behavioural assumptions of neoclassical economics, it can be shown that a model of a perfectly competitive economy in equilibrium satisfies tautologically the conditions necessary for Pareto optimality. Pareto optimality is defined as a state in which no one can be made better off without someone else being made worse off. A corollary of Pareto optimality is that resources are efficiently allocated, such that a reallocation of resources cannot increase total output. Each item produced consequently reflects its true opportunity cost, and goods are priced at marginal cost.

Recourse to the notion of Pareto optimality gives the cost-benefit analyst a theoretical anchor on which to tie the derivation of accounting prices.[3] It appears to be a very convenient anchor, for it enables current market prices to constitute their basis. Accounting prices consequently become computationally feasible: adjustments only have to be made to existing prices where they exhibit effects of market imperfections (monopoly, unemployed resources, externalities, etc.); and shadow prices for intangibles are calculated through the use of surrogate market models. The final Paretian price set is not easy to derive, nor will it be uncontroversial, but all attempts at it are treated as approximations to the Paretian ideal. Everyone understands the characteristics of the ideal set, and it is assumed that the market mechanism has done most of the calculation. The prices to use can be treated as empirically given by the market, although some prices will require empirical research to discover their magnitude (see, for instance, the survey of empirical work on the price or value of travel time in Harrison and Quarmby, 1969).

Unfortunately for CBA, however, the notion of Pareto optimality gives no theoretical justification for the use of adjusted (or derived) market prices. Adoption of the latter can only be done by assertion and, as that is the case, any set of prices could equally be used in CBA. Each set of prices would, of course, produce a different result for a cost–benefit calculation, so every project can have an infinite number of benefit–cost ratios. As there is no objective basis to choose between those results, choice can only be on the basis of assertion. CBA is reduced to being an expensive, time-consuming irrelevance, even if acceptance is given to all the value-judgements necessary to relate willingness-to-pay to social preferences.

3.3.2   CBA, Welfare and Pareto Optimality

The first point at which an assertion must be made is when Pareto optimality is adopted. Like any welfare rule, Pareto optimality is only a value-judgement. For it requires, among other things, the assumptions necessary to equate independent, individual preferences with the preferences of society outlined in Section 3.2. This value-judgement is well known and frequently commented upon in the literature (e.g. MacKean, 1968). It is none the less never made explicit in the results of CBA, and the mere recognition of it as an assumption does not negate the fact that its adoption is entirely arbitrary. In addition, a series of logical inconsistencies result from its use.

A strange paradox arises with Paretian pricing rules in CBA. Contradictory rules are being used when designating what should be measured and how it should be measured. The assertion that social preferences are the aggregation of individual costs and benefits implies that a social state is preferred if the gainers 'outbid' the losers. Yet the accounting prices, in which the gains and the losses are calculated, rest upon the Paretian assertion that a social state is preferred only if no one loses.

A way out of this difficulty has been attempted by claiming that the willingness-to-pay criterion corresponds in a particular way to Pareto optimality. This is done by suggesting that in CBA the straight-forward Pareto rule is replaced with one that says that the project should go ahead if it creates the possibility of a *potential* Pareto improvement. Some people might lose out from the implementation of a project but if the total net social gain from the project is positive it is hypothetically possible for the gainers to compensate the losers and still be better off. A potential Paretian improvement is consequently said to exist if such a redistribution is possible, *even though it does not occur*. This is the Kaldor–Hicks compensation principle, and it is often claimed to the theoretical justification from welfare economics on which CBA is based (see Layard, 1974).

The paradox appears to have been solved, but this has only occurred through posing a *different* question. Instead of asking 'Has a Paretian improvement been achieved?' the question is transformed into one of 'Could a Pareto improvement potentially be achieved?' This reformulation is valid only if both questions have the same answer, which is not the case. They (obviously) have different distributional implications and thus produce distinct results. The reformulation has failed and the inconsistency remains.

There is, furthermore, no guarantee that a positive net present value in cost–benefit implies a potential Paretian improvement would result. It is not the case, for instance, if society is assumed to consist of more than simply its current members: in other words, if some attempt is being made to evaluate the effect on future generations. For it is not even hypothetically possible for future generations to compensate the present generation. Yet, many would claim that such long-term effects fall within the ambit of the cost-benefit approach.

Even limiting the concept of society to the existing population does not make recourse to the Kaldor–Hicks compensation criterion unambiguously correct. Two temporal states are being compared: one before the implementation of the project, the other after the project has been completed. Scitovsky (1941), and others, have pointed out that relative prices might alter between the two. Such price changes could reverse the preference of society for the project, so the project is accepted at the original set of prices, while at the new prices it is rejected.

In face of this logical difficulty, a defence of the use of Kaldor–Hicks in CBA has been mounted upon the following lines. If it is assumed that society is at a Pareto-efficient point in both states, a change in relative prices can only be produced by the changes in income distribution that arises from implementation of the project. The distributional effects of most projects will be small, so the Scitovsky result is unlikely to prevail. But cost-benefit is operating in a real, non-optimal, world. It cannot consequently be assumed that relative prices remain the same, far more will change between the two states than simply the effects on distribution of the project.

This point, however, raises a wider question concerning the necessity for CBA to assume that relative prices generally remain constant. Once this assumption is made the project can essentially be treated as an independent entity within the economic system. The partial approach of CBA is then possible: distributional effects can be regarded as minimal, and the rest of the economy assumed to be in equilibrium with invariant relative prices. These assumptions do not, however, accord with any notion of reality. The real-world economy, even for neoclassical economics, is not in a state of permanent equilibrium. Dynamic processes are at work and relative prices change. The assumptions necessary to claim an unambiguous potential Pareto improvement are therefore patently false.

3.3.3   Accounting Prices and Pareto Optimality

The problem of inconsistent welfare criteria does not end the pricing problems faced by CBA. Another fundamental assertion is required to make the concept of Pareto optimality a practicably operable one: efficiency must be assumed to be independent of distribution. If this procedure is not adopted, the 'correct' pricing conditions to apply to any evaluation exercise become essentially incalculable.

There are an infinite number of possible Pareto-efficient points for the economy of the neoclassical model. Attainment of any of them depends on the initial distribution of resources between individuals in the economy. For each of these infinite number of Pareto-optimal points, there consequently corresponds a different set of 'efficiency' prices. Prices derived from the Pareto criterion therefore depend on the initial distribution of income. Pricing and resource allocation can thus never be separated from income distribution. To take current market prices and adjust them for 'distortions' in the market so that they reflect marginal costs in the hope that they will represent allocatively efficient prices in the Paretian sense consequently requires assertions with enormous implications. It must either be asserted that allocation efficiency and distribution are separable, which is untenable within neoclassical theory,[4] or it must be assumed that society actually prefers the current distribution of income. Evaluation procedures, like CBA, which use Pareto efficiency as the basis of their accounting prices must consequently become justifiers of the present *status quo*, and of any change that its dynamic produces, with a vengeance.

The issue of Pareto pricing rules has been the subject of considerable debate within the literature; particularly concerning the infeasibility of the Pareto conditions in the real world. Although marginal cost pricing is a corollary of the neoclassical theoretical model of Pareto optimality, the application of marginal cost as a practical pricing rule has been subjected to severe criticism within neoclassical economics (e.g. in Graaf, 1971, ch. 10), primarily on grounds of feasibility. To derive this pricing rule for a decentralised market economy, even if capitalist markets are regarded as operating upon the basis desired by neoclassical economics, highly simplified market structures have to be assumed. Markets have to be perfectly competitive, perfect knowledge has to prevail, and external effects and non-convexities must be absent. In order to use marginal cost pricing CBA has to assume that this is true in the real world if it is to avoid the charge of faulty logic. On these grounds alone, the charge must stick.

Even if CBA resolutely ignores these difficulties, the question of feasibility arises again over the problem of institutional constraints. These constraints are erroneously assumed to be exogenous to the economic system but they generate some damning points, in that they produce two crucial effects for the application of the Pareto criterion. In the first place, society might desire some distribution of income which, given the current array of institutions, does not enable a Pareto-efficient point to be reached. A point within the production possibility frontier is consequently desired on distributional grounds: a point at which the marginal equivalences of Pareto efficiency do not hold. Marginal cost pricing becomes irrelevant.

A similar result holds with what is known as the 'second-best' problem. Here, institutional constraints such as monopoly mean that the first-order pricing conditions of Pareto optimality cannot be achieved. New first-order conditions have to be computed, taking into account these additional constraints upon the maximisation of the objective function. The prices that are derived once again do not produce the marginal equivalences of Pareto optimality.

3.3.4   Which Accounting Prices?

CBA has no justification for the use of marginal cost pricing, nor even of adjusted market prices, when trying to assess benefits and costs. To avoid logical inconsistency they have every incentive to use neither. What price set can be used?

Ideally, to conform to its view of how social preferences are expressed, the desired optimal state has to be specified first, with its particular allocation of resources (but, of course, here we are back in the game of social welfare functions!). Having specified this in physical terms, the price set can be calculated. This is, however, computationally and logically impossible. It is not, moreover, even sufficient to calculate this (impossible) plan, it has to be put in practice and achieved in full. An omnipotent central planner is required for these tasks; one with superhuman powers of knowledge, foresight and control. This is, after all, the neoclassical economics ultimate condemnation of socialism. For it regards socialism as constituting solely centralised planning with a surrogate market model. In any case it leaves CBA in ruins, for CBA's deductions about the determination of social preferences leaves it no possibility of producing a logically consistent price set.

The CBA exercise cannot proceed. The world consequently is teleologically assumed to operate like the Pareto model. This contradicts the whole objective of CBA, which is the comparison of non-Pareto states where some people lose while others gain. The method is irrevocably, internally inconsistent.

3.4   SOCIAL PREFERENCES AND THEIR MEASUREMENT: CONCLUSIONS

This section has demonstrated that CBA's claim to measure the preferences of society is untenable. It has been achieved mainly by operating within the terrain of neoclassical theory. Most of the points can be found within the standard welfare literature, and some have even drawn the obvious conclusion that CBA is non-operable. CBA is an ideology in the sense that it cannot be an objective, scientific method of investment appraisal (as Tribe, 1972, has concluded). Innumerable value-judgements have to be made at each stage of the analysis. Often they are not explicit and they frequently contradict others that have previously been made.

The value-judgements of CBA are not a device for calling into the analysis the pronouncements of a moral philosopher. They are, instead, arbitrary assertions required to sustain the exercise. Assertions, none the less, which have important political and ideological implications, as the Section 4 will show. Numbers produced on the basis of such a method are essentially numbers drawn out of the air. There is no basis to justify their validity. This effect is often clouded within the subtleties of the cost–benefit method, but sometimes it is even blatant. Space has meant that the lengthy discussion in the literature over the choice of the rate of discount for use in CBA has not been considered. But the conclusion of that debate is that no unique rate of discount can possibly be derived. A guess has to be made, drawn out of nothing, but one which vitally affects the relative importance of specific costs and benefits, and the overall 'social profitability' of any project.

If so many value-judgements have to be made within CBA to derive any notion of what society prefers it might not seem unreasonable to ask why anyone should bother with CBA in the first place. An initial guess at what society prefers would be much easier and cheaper. That guess could itself be called a grand value-judgement and the number would be just as valid as a statement of social preferences as that provided by CBA. But CBA is not just a theoretical exercise, it has real effects. It is to these effects that the argument must now turn.

4 THE IDEOLOGICAL AND POLITICAL EFFECTS OF CBA

The argument of the previous section examined CBA in terms of one theoretical question: the claim that CBA measures the preferences of society. It was demonstrated that this claim was false. But analysis cannot remain solely at this level. To treat CBA simply as being non-scientific cannot explain why CBA and other similar techniques (such as systems analysis and operations research) have been adopted by the state apparatus in many advanced capitalist countries; nor why they play a role in the so-called development programmes of capitalist-oriented countries of the Third World.

To remain upon the terrain of this question alone can, moreover, lead to a number of incorrect conclusions. It can, for example, imply that all governments and agencies using CBA have simply been hood-winked by faulty economic analysis. Or, alternatively, that other measures of social preferences must be derived. In this context, there has arisen the debate between bourgeois economists and political scientists over the role of representation within the political system. This debate is couched in terms of rational economic calculation versus consensus arrived at in a pluralist manner between competing political pressure groups and agencies (see the critiques of CBA by Self, 1970, and Wildavsky, 1966, and the reply by Williams, 1973). A Marxist analysis, however, does not remain upon this terrain. Historical materialism does not only point out the inconsistencies within bourgeois theory but also explains the historical and political conditions within which bourgeois theory arose and the use to which that theory is put. The task of this section, therefore, is to subject CBA to such an examination. (For a further discussion of the role of ideology in economics, see Chap. 9.)

CBA has been developed as a technique for appraising state expenditure since the 1940s; in other words, in an era during which the economic functions of the state in capitalist societies expanded considerably. This expansion has been in two predominant forms. First, the economic activities directly provided by the state have substantially increased; ranging from the provision of 'welfare' facilities, such as income supplements or health care, through to the provision of a basic infrastructure network, like roads and airports. Second, it has been an era dominated by an ideology which claims that the state can manage the economy; represented most forcibly by Keynesian theory. This ideology operates from a notion that the state is above society so that it can harmonise the conflicting interests of groups within that society (e.g. big business and trade unions) in a way which brings the overall interests of that 'society' or 'the nation' into dominance. Armed with the tools of economic management, the claim is made that the state can ameliorate the worst effects of capitalist crises, guide the economy towards economic growth, and subordinate the demands of specific groups to the 'interests of the nation'. The use of CBA is a particular expression of this notion of economic management by the state.

Mutually antagonistic classes exist, however, within societies dominated by capitalism. Marx's analysis in *Capital* shows that two antagonistic classes exist within the capitalist mode of production. The exploitation of the working class through the appropriation of surplus value by capital, structures that class relation and the dynamic of capital accumulation. Other classes, moreover, can exist in similar contradictory relations, particularly in societies where capitalism has yet to dominate all spheres of economic activity. The existence of classes consequently means that there must be contradictory economic interests. Interests which cannot be summed to produce a consensus of opinion in the form of a 'preference of society'. Class societies are, by their very nature, societies dominated by class-struggle. Social harmony is impossible. The search by CBA for such a harmony is therefore futile; a non-question *par excellence.*

Class-struggle exists at the political as well as the economic level. The state apparatus and actions by the state are consequently a site of class-struggle. The state is therefore not above the class-struggle, orchestrating conflicting interests in the name of society. It is an arena for that struggle. Political class-struggle, however, does not take place in the form of clearly specified and articulated economic interests of antagonistic classes. Instead, it takes place within specific forms of political representation of interests that have been formulated within terms of particular ideologies.

In order that capitalist relations of production can remain dominant it is imperative that political struggles take place within ideologies that can ensure the reproduction of capitalism. The mass of the exploited classes must ideologically accept that the current social order is inevitable. In conditions where this is not achieved, where the masses are won over to the proletarian ideology of the necessity of socialism, the continued existence of capitalism comes into question. The ideological notions of bourgeois right (equality before the law, bourgeois democracy, etc.), and the 'interests of society' can, if they dominate the terrain in which political struggles take place, help to ensure the continued reproduction of capitalism. They can facilitate the subordination of the working class to the needs of capital accumulation. Drastic cuts in the living standards of the working class can be imposed, and broadly accepted, as long as bourgeois ideology is dominant. For then such responses to the crises of capitalism can ideologically be presented as being in the 'interests of the nation' rather than what they really are: necessary for the continued accumulation of capital.

4.2   THE USE OF CBA

The rise of CBA as a method of economic appraisal can now be examined in greater detail. Given what has just been said, it comes as no surprise that the modern cost–benefit technique was developed in the context of a piece of substantial state expenditure: flood-control programmes instigated by the U.S. government in the 1940s. The aim of the projects was to reduce the costs to farmers of periodic flooding. Many schemes were possible, not all of which could be encompassed by the funds available. The cost–benefit procedures developed could both justify the money allocated to those schemes and provide a criterion for selecting which of them to undertake. The affected parties, farmers, were a politically important group but selection of the schemes without the semblance of an objective assessment of need could lead to justifiable claims of political bias.

CBA fitted the bill. It enabled a ranking and justification of projects strictly on the basis of the capitalist criterion of profitability. Profitability not to the agency providing the flood-relief schemes but to the recipients of the economic gains from the projects: the farmers. The relative economic gains to farmers could be compared, dressed up in the guise of being gains to the nation.[5] U.S. farmers are, of course, capitalists operating within agriculture. CBA, in this context, enabled the effects of federal expenditure to be evaluated in terms of their impact on capitalist profitability. All within the framework of an ideology of gains to society.

This use of CBA has been extended to other spheres of state expenditure, especially transportation infrastructures in advanced capitalist countries. Capital accumulation requires such facilities, but they often cannot be effectively provided on the capitalist criterion of profitability. The state has either to subsidise them (e.g. railways) or to provide them free (e.g. most roads). CBA enables a framework for ranking such projects in terms of their economic effects, for instance, with road systems it facilitates assessment of relative traffic flows. These economic effects, however, do not relate to the needs of society but to the requirements imposed by the accumulation of capital.

Now CBA is not the only possible method of assessment of such effects: operations research or systems theory would be just as feasible. But the latter approaches do not necessitate calculation on capitalist criteria. Evaluation could instead be in terms of physical measures (e.g. vehicles per hour) and some notion of need which is at variance with the notion of comparative profitability. CBA, however, brings state expenditure decisions into conformity with the capitalist notion of need, which is profit. The contradiction between the necessity of state provision outside the direct process of capital accumulation and that accumulation process itself appears at an ideological level to be resolved. Both are made to appear to be driven by the same need: profit. 'Society' 'profits' from state expenditure in the same way as capitalists profit from their own investment of capital. The absence of such an ideological congruence could lead to a questioning of the capitalist ideology of profitability as being the motor-force for the maximisation of human welfare. CBA can extend the notion of profitability through its use of willingness-to-pay and monetary calculation to ensure that capitalist calculation can be all-pervasive.

Take the example of railways. They are necessary for the efficient spatial movement of commodities (and, in some countries, passengers). They consequently aid the accumulation of capital. But railway systems have an unfortunate tendency to lose large sums of money. Most advanced capitalist countries have railway systems which only survive through substantial state financial support. The existence of such a permanent loss-making activity could question the efficacy of profitability as the criterion for provision. Some other criterion, such as that relating to a socialist society, might seem ideologically to be in operation. If this is true for this activity, why should not the same apply to all activities? Well, CBA shows that railway systems are not really making a loss when the wider economic effects of railways are brought into the calculation. Society makes a profit out of them because they, for example, reduce congestion on the roads. The loss is only an apparent one in the accounts of the railway corporation; in the reality of CBA they are making a 'profit'. This same criterion, which justifies the existence of the rail system as a whole, can also be used to close down individual lines once they are no longer shown to make a 'social profit'.

In summary, CBA enables state expenditure projects to be evaluated in terms of the effects upon the accumulation of capital and it does so in a way which reinforces the dominance of bourgeois ideology. At this stage, a number of qualifications are perhaps necessary. In the first place, the argument above does not imply that all state expenditure is simply enacted to facilitate the accumulation of capital. It is not the purpose of this chapter to explain the determinants of state expenditure but only to consider the role played by CBA. But it is obvious that to claim that all state expenditure immediately benefits the accumulation process implies that the state is simply an instrument at the disposal of the capitalist class, and not a site of class-struggle. Like all other aspects of its activity, state expenditure will be influenced by that class struggle. It is a struggle, however, which is structured by the dominance of capitalist relations of production, so the conditions in which it exists are vastly more favourable to bourgeois interests than to those of other classes. Nevertheless, state expenditure has contradictory effects for capitalism. Sometimes expenditure is undertaken by the state in response to the political demands of non-bourgeois classes, even though it is at variance with the short-term economic interests of capital.

In a similar way, CBA can be contradictory in its effects. The appeal to the interests of the nation contained with the CBA approach can place limits upon the operations of private firms or upon particular forms of state expenditure which facilitate industrial development. CBA could demonstrate that the 'social costs' are too high. This is one of the attractiveness of the method to certain of its supporters, who see it as a way of diminishing the importance of private profit while enhancing the consideration given to wider social issues. Alternatively, rigid application of its criteria could justify state projects which were to the short-term detriment of the accumulation process. The restructuring of state-owned capital, for example, could be slowed down by a consideration of the wider social and economic costs of, say, the closure of out-of-date plants. CBA could be used to keep those plants open when the criterion of company profitability alone would necessitate their closure.[6]

These potential contradictory effects give CBA greater ideological acceptability, for it appears to favour no vested interest. The preferences of society, not those of particular groups, are its concern. These potentially adverse effects for capital, however, are severely limited. The rationale of CBA does after all stem directly from capitalist ideology: the notion of profit as the guide to beneficial social action.

CBA is, furthermore, judiciously used. It rarely plays a part in the broad strategic choice of state expenditure, but is used to justify specific projects (often *ex post*). In addition, its role is limited to particular types of expenditure. State handouts to industry, for example, are seldom subject to the scrutiny of the cost–benefit procedure; their benefits to society are 'too obvious' to require it.

The criteria in CBA of willingness-to-pay, monetary calculation, and social profitability themselves imply that in CBA the effects on the accumulation process will be paramount. The implication of CBA is that economic effects in terms of profitability are the arena of debate, as has been argued above. Section 3.2 also pointed out that willingness-to-pay gives dominance in CBA calculations to those with the greatest market power. Most of the benefits from road investment projects, for example, are savings in travel time, and willingness-to-pay evaluations show that business travel time is much more important than mere leisure time (see Harrison and Quarmby, 1969). Cost–benefit calculations value the former at three or four times the value of leisure time, in which case it is hardly surprising that the benefits to capitalist enterprises come to the fore. Such effects, moreover, are compounded by the general approach in CBA of ignoring distributional effects.

These factors perhaps explain the enthusiasm of international agencies, such as the World Bank, for cost–benefit appraisals of projects in Third World countries. CBA becomes a good ideological weapon in determining that the capitalist road to, economic development will occur. Exploitation of the mineral resources of such a country by a multinational corporation will, after all, show a much greater CBA 'social return' than improving the lot of a subsistence agriculture sector.

The dual economic and ideological effects of CBA were heightened during the late 1960s in advanced capitalist countries by a growing recognition of the undesirable effects imposed by capitalist development. This found expression in the form of the environmental lobby. Petty bourgeois liberal ideology in this form come into contradiction with the accumulation of capital. Growing political resistance developed to the irreversible environmental consequences of industrial growth. Struggles in particular centred around the continued expansion of multi-laned highways, and new international airports. The intangibles in the cost–benefit calculation began to assume greater importance.

CBA, however, once again structured the ideological terrain of this struggle. In Britain, groups in opposition to new motorways had to question the details of cost–benefit calculations in attempts to prove that society did not prefer these new routes. Traffic forecasts become the area of debate. While this has enriched innumerable expert witnesses at planning inquiries, it has deflected the issues away from the fundamental one of the nature of the economic system that requires such developments. It, moreover, reinforces the ideological notion of the state being above society, for government and ministers can ponder over the values of intangibles and reject, in the name of society, the recommendations of the cost–benefit analyst. In Britain, for example, over £1.25 m. was spent on a cost–benefit analysis of the site for a proposed Third London Airport in the early 1970s. The decision of that analysis was rejected after a long debate in the Houses of Parliament. 'Democracy' was seen to prevail over the hard-headed economist.

To an extent, CBA has failed as a form of representation of bourgeois ideology. Few people, apart from economists, place much faith in the detailed calculations produced of social costs and benefits. Much of this disenchantment has centred on the valuations of non-market items, the intangibles of a cost–benefit calculation. This is not surprising given some of the estimates that have been used. The official figure in Britain for the value of a life in the early 1970s was around £9000. The absurdity of such a number is readily apparent. A plane carrying 100 passengers is, on this evaluation, transporting a cargo 'worth' £900,000. The jet aircraft, on the other hand, has, say, a replacement value of £2 m. Imagine that this aircraft, while airborne, suddenly develops mechanical failure. The pilot is faced with the choice of irreparable damage to the aircraft in order to save the passengers, or jettisoning the passengers in mid-flight in order to save the plane. The pilot consults the cost–benefit manual to find out what society would prefer. After safely landing the now lightened aircraft, the pilot explains the absence of the passengers by reference to the mechanical difficulty and the cost–benefit manual. Heroes, it seems, can come in many different guises, particularly if you believe in cost–benefit analysis.

Practitioners of CBA are, of course, well aware of such difficulties. In face of such criticisms, a retreat is made from the position that cost – benefit produces an exact measure of society's preferences to the argument that cost–benefit clarifies the issues around which decisions have to be made. 'Well, there is quite a lot wrong with it, but it isn't bad when you consider the alternative', claims Williams (1973) in defence of CBA; quoting that well-known philosopher and entertainer, Maurice Chevalier. This chapter has shown the opposite to be true. CBA poses the wrong question and makes innumerable and unsustainable assertions in order to justify that its method can answer that question. By doing so it enables the effects of state expenditure on the accumulation of capital to be assessed in an ideological framework which diverts class struggle away from the real issues. In the name of clarity all that is reproduced is the hegemony of bourgeois ideology and of the dominant class in capitalist societies.

NOTES

1. An example of the use of cost–benefit for this particular type of project can be found in Foster and Beesley (1963), which describes a cost–benefit analysis of the Victoria Line underground railway constructed in London in the late 1960s.

2. For a discussion of these issues, see the Introduction to Layard (1974).

3. A detailed criticism of neoclassical economics will not be undertaken in this chapter. Only the relationship of CBA to that theory

will be considered. Certain pertinent criticisms of neoclassical economics, particularly of its theory of price determination, are discussed in F. Green and P. Nore (eds) *Economics: An Anti-Text* (London: Macmillan, 1977), in the essay by S. Mohun.

4. Many of the assertions about the link between society's preferences and individual choice in the market-place also collapse once inter-generational factors are brought into consideration.

5. Political factors were, of course, not entirely divorced from this federal expenditure simply by the use of CBA. They determine the use of federal funds for this type of expenditure in the first place. In addition, they still affected the ranking of schemes, and continued to do so. Over half of the water-resource projects approved in 1960 (i.e. $69 m. out of a total of $133 m.) were found by Haverman (1965) to have been approved contrary to what pure cost–benefit criteria would have selected. Projects from particular geographic regions seemed to be selected in spite of relatively low measures of efficiency. This can be interpreted as implying that the Federal government was concerned with distributional questions (as Weisbrod, 1968, has claimed). It does not require much cynicism, however, to produce a different interpretation: the importance of political considerations in the allocation of the Federal budget.

6. The Beswick Report (1975) on the restructuring of the British Steel Corporation employed the broad notions of cost–benefit to justify the continued operation of plants British Steel wanted to close- thereby avoiding a massive confrontation with the steel union, something which was politically unacceptable at the time.

REFERENCES

Arrow, K. J. (1951) *Social Choice and Individual Values* (New Haven, Conn.: Yale University Press). 1973. (Originally published in 1951.)

Dasgupta, A. K., and Pearce, D. W. (1972) *Cost–Benefit Analysis* (London: Macmillan).

Dobb, M. (1975) *Welfare Economics and the Economics of Socialism* (London: Cambridge University Press).

Foster, C. B., and Beesley, M. E. (1963) 'Estimating the Social Benefit of Constructing an Underground Railway in London', *Journal of the*

Royal Statistical Society, **126**. (Reprinted in D. Munby (ed.) *Transport: Selected Readings*, Harmondsworth: Penguin, 1968.)

Graaf, J. de V. (1971) *Theoretical Welfare Economics* (London: Cambridge University Press).

Harrison, A. J., and Quarmby, D. A. (1969). The Value of Time in Transport Planning: a review in *Theoretical and Practical Research on an Estimation of Time-Saving*, European Conference of the Ministers of Transport, Sixth Round Table, Paris, 1969.

Haverman, R. (1965) *Water Resource Investment and the Public Interest* (New York: Vanderbilt University Press).

Layard, R. (ed.). (1974) *Cost–Benefit Analysis* (Harmondsworth: Penguin).

MacKean, R. N. (1968) 'The Use of Shadow Prices', in S. B. Chase (ed.) *Problems in Public Expenditure Analysis* (Washington: Brookings Instituion).

Prest, A. R., and Turvey, R. (1965) 'Cost–Benefit Analysis: a survey', *Economic Journal*, **75**.

Roskill Commission (1970) (formally called: Commission on the Third London Airport), *Papers and Proceedings* (London: H.M.S.O.).

Scitovsky, T. (1941) 'A Note on Welfare Propositions in Economics', *Review of Economic Studies*, **9**.

Self, P. (1970) 'Nonsense on Stilts: the futility of Roskill', *Political Quarterly*.

Tribe, L. H. (1972) 'Policy Science: Analysis of Ideology?' *Philosophy and Public Affairs*, **2**. (Reprinted in *Cost–benefit and Policy Analysis* (New York: Aldine, 1972.)

Weisbrod, B. A. (1968) 'Income Redistribution Effects and Benefit-cost Analysis', in S. B. Chase (ed.) *Problems in Public Expenditure Analysis* (Washington: Brookings Institution).

Wildavsky, A. (1966) 'The Political Economy of Efficiency: cost -benefit analysis, systems analysis and program budgeting', *Public Administration Review*, **26**

Williams, A. (1973) 'Cost–Benefit Analysis: bastard science? and/or insidious poison on the body politick?', in J. N. Wolfe (ed.) *Cost Benefit and Cost Effectiveness* (London: Allen & Unwin).

CHAPTER 4

Oil and Contemporary Capitalism[1]

Petter Nore

It is by now 'conventional wisdom' in the West that the world is living through an 'energy crisis'. It is furthermore claimed that in the absence of serious countermeasures such a 'crisis' will mean the disruption of Western civilisation as we know it. In order to understand to what extent, if any, such a 'crisis' actually exists (the term is normally defined in a very imprecise way), we must turn to a closer analysis of the concept of energy. Because 67 per cent of the world's energy needs are satisfied by oil, this means we must examine the commodity oil (here meaning both crude oil and gas).

Sections 1 and 2 try to show why a full understanding of oil *cannot* rely on an explanation which is founded on an orthodox micro-economic market model for oil. The main reason for this shortcoming is not that these instruments of analysis are logically wrong, but rather that such a conceptual apparatus will largely be *irrelevant* for understanding what is happening in the oil industry today.

Section 3 will analyse and criticise, albeit in less detail, the other main school of thought which has been brought to bear on the question of oil; the ecological perspective. Ecologists claim (among other things) that the world will quickly run out of fossil fuels, and that our primary task is therefore to cut down the use of energy.

The shortcoming of the orthodox and the ecologist theories is only an indication that a more in-depth analysis is needed. This is the task we set out to accomplish in Section 4, where an understanding of oil as a commodity is primarily linked to the conditions of accumulation in the Western societies. This is not an easy task, partly because of the strength of the ideological misconceptions related to oil and partly because there are shortcomings in the Marxist concepts dealing with oil.

This chapter is more than an intellectual exercise. The political attitude taken towards the international oil companies depends upon an adequate materialist understanding of their main product, oil.

1   THE ORTHODOX APPROACH

It is more difficult to talk about one coherent conceptual apparatus being shared by all orthodox oil economists than in other fields of economic analysis. There is in particular a main distinction between what I would label the 'institutional' school and the 'market' school of oil economists.

The basis of the more orthodox 'market' school analysis of oil is that there is nothing special about oil as a commodity. Hence it follows that oil, with a few suitable extensions, can be subject to a traditional micro-economic analysis. It is the proponents of this school like Adelman (1973), Dam (1976), Robinson and Morgan (1976a, b), and Jacoby (1974) whose analysis we will present and criticise in this section.

The 'Institutionalists', on the other hand, emphasise the more political and historical elements of the situation in the oil industry at the expense of more formal micro-economic thinking. Among its leading proponents are Penrose (1968, 1971), Rafai (1975) and Odell (1973, 1975, 1977). In attempting to incorporate a historical method-ology they have a valid starting-point of analysis which stands in contrast to the ahistoricism of neoclassical theory. However, their approach will be subject to criticisms in Section 4. It should also be pointed out that some members of the 'institutional' school share a number of micro-economic foundations of analysis with the 'market' school, so the distinction we have made is not one of a total segmen-tation. To the extent that they overlap, the following discussion is also relevant for some members of the 'institutional' school.

We will first show how the market framework has been applied to oil. Within this framework the price of oil is, as for any other good, determined by demand, supply, and the degree of monopoly in the market. While this general pricing formulae has been supplemented by a number of more subtle refinements (Adelman, 1973, for example, specified as late as 1972 that the price of crude would gravitate towards the marginal replacement cost of producing one barrel in the Persian Gulf, 15 cents per barrel), this extension nevertheless was clearly derived at within the context of an orthodox micro-theoretical analysis. Based on the above discussion the degree of monopoly seems to be one possible way for the orthodox economists to explain the apparent contradiction between their own predictions about the price of oil and the actual OPEC price, which turned out to be about a hundred times as high as Adelman's prediction. A constant high degree of monopoly could thus, at least initially, 'explain' the contradictions between the 'observed' and the 'real' (even though it would leave orthodoxy without an explanation of why there has been such a constantly high level of monopoly in the industry). But orthodoxy has not taken this way out. It maintains that 'the oil industry is basic- ally a competitive industry' (Jacoby, 1974, pp. 5–6) where over time there is a tendency towards the erosion of monopoly power. Hence the number of very confident assertions made from 1973 onwards from this group of economists that the OPEC cartel would break up due to the 'inevitable' tendency towards free competition within the oil industry. This vision was at the time very influential among a number of Western policy-makers, when it was thought that a 'firm' line from the consumer countries would bring about the disintegration of OPEC according to the principles of neoclassical theory. This was one of the factors behind the formulation of the International Energy Agency (IEA) in 1974.

A spin-off from this way of thinking relates to the existence of 'rent' or excess profits (defined as a rate of return in excess of the 'normal' rate in the economy). If one thinks as Jacoby (1974) then it follows that there will be a tendency for the removal of this rent by the process of competition. The companies will end up with a 'normal' rate of return, while the producer states will appropriate the rent involved. The rent can be removed by means of taxation or as proposed by Dam (1976) by a system of sealed bids. This procedure, which is normally used in the United States and which was used on one occasion in the British sector of the North Sea, is the ultimate way of trying to apply the market mechanism to the oil industry. Within this system sealed bids are given to the landlord (in Europe the nation state) indicating how much the company in question would be willing to pay in order to obtain the concession. In addition the companies pay all 'normal' taxes. The system can also be modified to submit bids for sliding royalty rates, size of work programs or any other specific aspect of the oil-production process. The idea is that the different companies in a competitive process would 'outbid' each other and ultimately be content to be left with the 'average' rate of profit.

Within this orthodox framework of analysis there is also another reason why monopolies are not likely to last and which then would mean that the earning of 'excess profits' would be expected to be of relatively short duration. In the wake of OPEC's increase of prices a shift would take place towards the consumption and production of other sources of energy exerting a downward pressure on the price of oil and tending to weaken the monopolistic OPEC structure. In short the substitution of oil with other forms of energy would operate.

This vision of a smooth transformation and relatively effortless adjustment process also lies behind the final feature which characterises the 'market analysis' of the world's oil market; the implicit assumption of a 'well-behaved' supply function of oil which predicts that an increase in the price of oil will bring about a corresponding increase in the production of oil. U.S. policy-makers especially tend to rely on such an assumption. Both 'Project Independence', drawn up by the Nixon Administration after the 1973 oil crisis to increase U.S. production and make the country more self-sufficient in energy, and the present lobbying by the industry to raise energy prices have relied on this assumption.

Only on one point has neoclassical theory been forced into some theoretical advances when confronted with oil. This is in relation to the property of oil as a 'non-renewable' resource. The normal micro-economic assumption that a given optimal price–quantity decision taken by a firm can be maintained indefinitely must be modified. Even if the basic analytical framework was laid down as early as 1931 by Hotelling, depletion did not become a major theoretical issue until after 1973 when it was fully realised that it might not be optimal for a number of the producer states to maximise their output of oil. The problem of the rate of depletion is crucial for oil producers because so many organisational consequences follow from it. If, for example, a country decides to implement a slow rate of depletion this may mean more time to build up a national oil expertise and thus rely less on the international oil companies. The rate of depletion is also important in deciding the exact nature of the accumulation process in each producer state. A rapid rate of extraction in a country with absorption problems will push an important part of the rent into the international financial system rather than finance an internal industrialisation process.

Neoclassical theory, once aware of the problems within its own framework, had relatively few difficulties in dealing with the concept of an optimum rate of depletion. Hotelling (1931) showed how a micro-economic market equilibrium with respect to depletion rates could come about through the operation of the market. For a given reserve of a non-renewable good the optimum rate of depletion is established when the increase of the profit margin of extracting oil (and hence of price, if the marginal cost remains constant) equals the rate of interest. This is because the extra future income a producer would get from leaving the natural resource in the ground is equal to the extra income that can be generated from extracting the oil and investing the proceeds at the going interest-rate, i.e. the marginal revenue of following both courses of action is equal.

According to Hotelling (1931) there is a natural tendency towards an equilibrium in this situation. If the rate of extraction is less than the equilibrium rate, supply will decrease and prices will rise, encouraging a higher level of extraction. If the rate of extraction is greater than the equilibrium rate the reverse will hold.

The main problem when we extend this optimal depletion theory to the case of monopoly arises because a monopolist might use a higher rate of interest with which to determine the equilibrium path of extraction and subsequently increase the current rate of extraction compared with a competitive 'path'. This higher rate of interest may result from the higher rate of return that a monopolist can earn elsewhere, and thus would be likely to counteract a monopolist's tendency to restrict output.

According to neoclassical thinking such a discrepancy between the competitive and monopolistic optimum rates of output can then be adjusted on the micro level by taxes, or on the macro level by controlling the rate of new concessions.

A number of extensions can be made to these simple cases, the most important of which involves the introduction of uncertainty with respect to technological progress which affects the substitutability between non-renewable resources and manmade capital goods (Dasgupta and Heal, 1974).

Neoclassical theory therefore treats oil in the way it treats any other commodity. The industry is basically competitive, which means that the problem of rent in the long run is not important. There exists a normal set of 'well-behaved' functions, allowing substitutability between different forms of energy. The normal process of price determination is postulated to hold for the industry even if this may be interrupted by temporary periods where a monopoly may dominate. Finally, no particular theoretical difficulties spring from the fact that oil is a non-renewable resource.

The above conclusions mean that there exists a market equilibrium for oil. This has important ideological consequences. Within the present world energy scene this fact is blatantly used as a justification by the companies to 'get on with their work' in an eternal chase for this equilibrium. For a good example of this attitude, see Robinson and Morgan (1976a and b).

2   THE CRITICISMS

The first line of criticism of the theoretical model presented above is that it is irrelevant rather than in any logical sense 'wrong' for a meaningful understanding of the present oil industry. This irrelevance stems from the special features of oil production in the contemporary world. If these characteristics (which will be discussed in more detail below) could be viewed as transitory and insignificant features of the industry then orthodox oil theoreticians would have relatively little to fear from this part of our critique. They could just claim that the situation would soon return to 'normal'. Unfortunately this is not so. These characteristics are not just temporary aberrations, but rather permanent features of oil production. As a consequence our criticism can be seen to be a necessary theoretical modification to account for an actual and permanent situation in the productive process.

We will also present a number of criticisms made at a lower level of abstraction which take as their departure the *specific* (and hence more transitory) relations of the present-day oil market. These can be said to be less damaging to the theoretical structure of a neoclassical analysis of oil production but are nevertheless highly relevant. The strength of any analytical apparatus is in the end shown in its ability to say something meaningful about the 'real world'. To the extent that we can show that the neoclassical 'market approach' is failing on this count, this will also undermine its *whole* theoretical framework.

To carry out a first criticism of the orthodox approach, we must briefly mention the special features of oil production. A more in-depth analysis follows in Section 4.

Oil production, first, gives rise to large permanent financial surpluses in excess of 'average profit', which we will label 'surplus profit'. This surplus profit is divided between producer-states who receive it in the form of rent; the oil companies which can earn excess profits; and the consumer countries that collect their share in the form of indirect taxes.

Second, the oil industry as a result of trying to control the constant threat of over-supply, has tended to be vertically integrated. Because of this threat of over-supply, as well as a consequence of the strategic importance of oil, there has,

Third, been a permenently high level of market concentration in the industry. This has meant that the major companies have historically earned a return in excess of the 'competitive' return on capital in the form of excess profit.

THE MIRAGE OF 'OPTIMAL DEPLETION'

The initial *detailed* criticisms to be levelled against the neoclassical conceptual apparatus will deal with its treatment of the optimal rate of depletion. Our charge is that there is a significant difference between the optimal private and social rate of depletion of a non-renewable resource. Theoretically this can be expressed by a difference between the social and private rate of discount. If the state has a lower rate of discount than a private company this means that the resource will be exploited at a slower rate. It also means that altogether more oil both from an oil province as well as from individual fields will be produced. The first effect will follow because a number of fields which have an expected discounted rate of return between the social and the private rate of discount would not be exploited by a private company but would be exploited by a state company operating with a lower discount rate.[2] The second effect is spelt out in detail by Odell and Rosing, (1977). Because the state requires a smaller rate of return on its investment than firms in the private sector (the logical implication of a lower discount rate), then in the concrete example of the British sector of the North Sea this would mean that more platforms would be utilised on any specific field. Final total output from each field, would as a consequence be greater. More platforms and other spin-offs would also be required, which again would have significant employment effects in important sectors of the British economy. Due to this shortfall in total production, Odell and Rosing (1977, p. 55) assess that the British Exchequer will lose £3 billion in potential tax income from the North Sea. It now must be shown why there should be an important discrepancy between the private and the social rate of discount. There are three reasons for this.

First a private company which makes a micro-economic assessment about a future investment must try to incorporate a notion of uncertainty into its calculations. For the specific firm there is a fixed statistical chance that the future level of key variables will deviate from the expected mean (even if this mean can be assumed known by the existence of future markets). To compensate for this uncertainty the firm would require a rate of return which is higher and hence use a higher rate of discount than if the future was known with certainty, or if these uncertainties did not exist. The latter situation holds if the state completely controls the whole productive output from that specific sector. In that case all uncertainties cancel out, and the state will be able to base its calculations on the mean of the future expected value of the variables in question. With respect to oil production from one oil province the most obvious risk which would cancel out in the event of full state ownership would be the geological risk and the corresponding size of the oil deposits which have been shown to be log-normal distributed.

Second, let us now assume for the sake of argument that the social rate of discount is equal to the private rate, and that the latter reflects, as is widespread practice, the opportunity cost of investment for the firm plus some kind of adjustment for 'risk'. This would in some oil projects lead to a discount rate in the order of about 30 per cent. The concrete implications of this result should on *a priori* grounds alone be extremely worrying. $1 income in ten years' time would be almost valueless to the state, being worth $1/1.3^{10} = 0.06$. While a planning horizon of ten years may sound reasonable for a private firm, it is certainly *not* adequate for the state. Note that we are making a crucial distinction between politicians' and the state's discount rates. Robinson and Morgan (1976b) may well argue that the politicians have a time-horizon which stretches no longer than to the next election. What we argue is that the state's discount rate will be lower because its planning horizon is much longer than the politicians'. This is because the state's actions is bound to the continuous and long-run functioning of the prevalent mode of production and is only marginally related to political phenomena like general elections.[3] Our discussion of a difference between the private and social rate of discount has so far been conducted at a relatively high level of abstration. We will now relate the arguments more closely to the situation in the oil industry.

The final reason why there is a discrepancy between the private and the social rate of discount springs from the fact that oil production permanently gives rise to rents. Because these rents do not correspond to the value of goods and services used in the production of oil, but rather reflect the transfer of surplus from other parts of the economic system a number of particular problems tend to arise in oil-producing states. If we talk about relatively large producers these rents may lead to important structural problems for the economies in question. These are most often described as 'absorption problems', but hide a number of different processes. Saudi Arabia, Kuwait, and the United Arab Emirates face the problem that there is not enough productive invest- ment within their own boundaries on which this rent can be spent. Since a number of other outlets for their investments are closed to them for political reasons, their social opportunity rate of return is the rate obtainable in so-called 'safe' placements in the Western finan- cial markets, normally U.S. treasury bills. This rate is certainly dras- tically different from the private oil companies' discount rate. For other countries like Norway even the *expectation* of large future rents from oil production in the North Sea has led to a generally overvalued currency and the highest production costs per unit of output of any OECD country, problems that only will increase in step with the oil production itself. These problems will in the long run bring out a structural transformation of the Norwegian economy. (See *Parliament- ary Report* No. 25, 1973/4, for a description of these expected changes.)[4] This trend is already to some extent visible in the recent drop of traditional Norwegian exports and the subsequent collapse of parts of the Norwegian export industry. Iran was until 1978 in a broadly similar situation, where agricultural production had dropped drastically as a result of the structural changes related to oil. Different societies will value these consequences of oil production differently. But our main point is that because of the characteristics of oil produc- tion (high rents) it is *in the above cases almost impossible to limit any analysis of depletion to the micro-economic depletion path of one single oilfield.* Such an exercise is largely irrelevant for the determina- tion of the 'optimal' rate of depletion, which depends much more on an analysis of the wider structural and political implications of oil production.

Having established that there is a discrepancy between the private and the social rate of discount, we shall finally show that even a mean- ingful theoretical existance of a private rate of discount in the world is in doubt. To the extent that the international oil industry is earning a rate of profit above the average rate in the economy (and there are strong indications that this has been the case during large parts of this century), then we claim there is no reason to even equate the general *private* rate of discount with the rate of return which is today required by the international companies. The companies will, for example, not develop a field in the North Sea unless its expected rate of return is between 20 and 25 per cent. This high rate of return required by the industry is nothing but a reflection of the rate of profit they can earn from investments elsewhere in the world market, even if it is claimed by the industry to be 'necessary' for a number of other reasons. The companies claim that profits must be so high in order to finance the high expected costs of finding new sources of energy. But this begs the question why the private companies for ever shall be the entities to undertake this search. The argument that, for instance, North Sea exploration is very 'risky' and hence requires a higher return also falls on closer examination. There is ample indication that the commercial find-rate in parts of the North Sea is much better than the world average (Nore, 1976, p. 11). As for the high cost of developing new deep-water technology, there is no reason why the cost of this should be carried exclusively by the North Sea governments as it is also going to benefit the companies *wherever* in the world they are going to look for oil under similar conditions. Consequently, using the private rate of discount in the real world has no theoretical foundation, but is a result of the peculiarities (vertically integrated, monopolised firms) of the oil industry. As long as the North Sea producer states do not have technologically competent state oil corporations to replace the private companies, they must accept the oil industry's private rate of discount as the 'correct' one for the very simple reason that they have no choice. But there is no theoretical justification for this. If they pressed for a lower social rate of discount the companies would leave.

The main casuality of the above discussion about the social and the private rate of discount is the micro-economic market analysis of optimal depletion rates. What becomes of prime importance is then not a minute, painstaking and often extremely sophisticated mathematical micro-economic analysis, based on the private rate of discount, but rather an investigation of what the appropriate social discount rate for oil production should be. A correct analysis, even within a neoclassical framework, *must* therefore include an analysis of the macro-economic variables which influences the social rate of discount. What goes for being the 'normal' depletion analysis is therefore largely irrelevant as it stands.

WHY OIL IS NO ORDINARY COMMODITY

Orthodox theory claims that the analysis of oil can be pursued like an analysis of any other commodity. It is our next task to show why the orthodox framework also on this count is largely *irrelevant* to an understanding of oil in the contemporary world. If at the same time we can show that a number of the 'normal' micro-economic functional relationships tend to be invalid in the case of oil, this may help to cast further doubt on the analytical validity and usefulness of orthodox theory.

(i) PRICING

It is possible to argue that the pricing of oil is mainly influenced by political considerations, and that therefore the market framework of analysis is of little value. One point needs to be clarified. When talking about the 'price' of oil we mean the overall price-level. Nobody denies that the traditional market mechanism *does* work in the oil market. But it does so only to the very limited extent of setting the prices of the 52 different OPEC crudes in relation to the price of the 34 Degree 'Arabian Light'. A country sets the relative price for its particular kind of crude. If there are not enough buyers at that price it simply decreases the price and vice versa. But when it comes down to determining the price-level of the 'marker' crude itself totally different forces are at work, one of which is the political element. Two examples will illustrate this.

The refusal by the Saudi Arabians to increase the price of oil in the winter of 1978 strongly suggests that political elements are paramount in determining oil prices. Saudi Arabia is today the producer state with the largest excess capacity and which in the present situation of slack demand has been the OPEC country which has been cutting production. They therefore hold the key to any price changes. But they are also the oil-producing state which both economically (their total investments in the United States total almost $30 billion) and politically is most closely tied to the West. The Saudi Arabian Oil minister, Sheikh Yamani, argued strongly against any price raise because of the alleged damage this would do to the Western economies–

a position he has adopted on several occasions.[5] This contrasts sharply with for example the Iraqi position, which had much less regard for the economic stability of the West. Iraq lead a group of oil-producing nations which at the time argued in favour of a price increase.

Another and equally direct example of the importance of the 'political' in setting oil prices is the background to the 1973/4 quadrupling of oil prices. At that time there was a demand coming from the producer states, the companies and the United States that the oil price ought to increase. (This section will deal with the more 'political' elements of this situation. For a full background see Nore (1978).)

The exporting countries wanted a reorganisation of the industry, which could bring about an increase in oil prices because they felt their share of the rent was too low.

Even in the wake of an increased tax-take only 8 per cent of the final cost to the consumer of a gallon of petrol was in the late 1960s made up of taxes received by the exporting countries. The search for an increased amount of oil rent was bound to be found not necessarily in an increased share of a meagre whole, but rather in the form of a policy which sought to increase the overall size of the rent that the producer states could control. The desire by some producer states to increase their share of the rent became particularly clear around 1970. The countries which initially pushed hardest for higher prices – Iraq, Algeria and to some extent Libya – were also the ones which had the most urgent need for additional oil revenues. These three countries were also the ones with the clearest 'developmentalist' ruling classes.

The oil companies also wanted an increase in the price of oil which would increase the overall amount of rent in the industry because their distributional share of the rent had steadily declined since the early 1960s. This was partly a result of a higher level of taxation by the oil-exporting countries which it was difficult for the companies to pass on to the consumers in a situation which was characterised by a global excess supply. It was also due to a threefold challenge to the major oil companies in the oil industry. This arose first out of a new situation in the international industry and in particular the rise of the 'independents' following the U.S. import quota system in 1958[6]; second, the emergence of important state oil companies in Europe like the Italien ENI, which tried to outbid the terms that the majors offered to the producer states and in general challenged the hegemony of the U.S. oil monopolies in Europe; and, third, the increase in Soviet oil exports to the West. The immediate expression of all these factors was a drop in the profit per barrel for the majors, which was only partly overcome by a sharp increase in total production.

The third 'actor' with an interest in increasing prices was the U.S. government. From 1970 onwards the United States clearly pressed for an increase in the general price-level of crude. Oppenheim (1976) shows how the U.S. government's actions were interpreted by the oil producers as a political go-ahead for higher prices, a point of view that has also been forcefully put by Chevalier (1975) and Rafai (1975). It was assumed by the U.S. government that such a rise would make a number of indigenous production wells in the United States commercially viable and therefore help the United States to achieve a higher degree of self-sufficiency in oil as well as in a direct way help the profitability of the U.S. oil companies. But the push towards higher prices was also related to inter-imperialist rivalries. The U.S. government saw how an increase in crude prices would deliver a serious blow to its industrial competitors in Western Europe and Japan.[7] The problem for the United States was that prices finally increased far more than originally anticipated, but this can to some extent be ascribed to special events, notably the Yom Yippur war in the autumn of 1973.

This general under-estimation of the 'political' also leads the proponents of the 'market school' to continuously predict the breakup of OPEC because in any cartel there are, according to orthodox theory, powerful and continuous temptations to cheat each other. This kind of argument completely disregards the political and ideological cohersion of OPEC at the same time as it disregards the extremely strong forces which originally pressed for an increase in prices.

(ii) RENT EXTRACTION

In order to implement the 'market method' of extracting rent suggested by Dam (1976, p.5) one condition in particular has to be met. The whole system of sealed bids which is meant to appropriate the rent in favour of the state can only function within a perfectly competitive framework where there is no collusion between the oil companies. If – as we argue – on the other hand there is an almost inevitable tendency towards a centralisation and concentration of firms in the oil industry, the probability that this method of rent-removal can operate under this assumption becomes much more doubtful. Furthermore this method was initially advocated not only as the most efficient, but also the politically most stable method of collecting the rent because it would take the heat out of the company/producer-state relationship by avoiding retroactive increases in taxation rates if there was an increased amount of rent to be earned. But such a solution shows a most naïve disregard for the political situation both in Western and Third World countries. It is argued by the proponents of this scheme that the number of times that average levels of bids from the companies are mistakenly too high in the long run will cancel out with the number of times when the company hits a bonanza and when consequently the bids are too low. Consequently the company will be left in the long run with an 'average' level of profit. However, what is forgotten is that the 'over' and 'under' estimation may take place in different countries. And there is not the slightest reason to believe that political opinion in a producer state will accept that a company, for whatever reason, will receive a higher amount of rents not expected in the sealed bids, just because in another country at an earlier date the company might have paid too much in a sealed bid. It therefore seems that without a truly political understanding of the situation the 'market schools' policy prescriptions which are directly derived from their theoretical framework are next to useless.

(iii) NORMAL SUPPLY

Within the present-day oil industry it is even doubtful whether a traditional supply curve for oil, which predicts that an increased price will bring about an increased production of oil from national sources holds true. While 'backward bending' supply curves of course can be accounted for in orthodox economics, their introduction into any analysis to 'save' an orthodox analysis is nevertheless problematic and indirectly tends to weaken it.

A backward-bending supply curve may first exist in a situation where a country which controls what it regards as a fixed amount of exhaustible resources aims to produce just enough oil to cover its internal consumption and to finance its export bill. In a number of countries the latter can be expected to be relatively fixed not the least because of the 'absorption problems' referred to above. A rise in the price of oil may then induce the country to extract *less* oil and not more as a 'normal' supply-curve would predict. Second, this backward-bending supply curve is also related to the fact that oil is a strategically important commodity. Lower prices may mean higher consumption with the resulting increased dependence by major consumer nations on oil imports from the OPEC countries. This may push the consumer countries towards even greater efforts to bring about increased production of oil because of the political fear on external dependency. A lower price may bring about a higher national supply.

(iv) SUBSTITUTION

One reason why the normal substitution-effect between different forms of energy may not work in the field of oil is related to another structural characteristic of the industry which we so far have ignored. This is the move by oil companies to become 'energy corporations' which has lead to extensive oil-company ownership of other energy sources like coal, atomic energy and oil shales. In the United States, where the oil companies own 60 per cent of the total coal reserves, the full implication of this structural characteristic on the rate of substitution between different kinds of energy became particularly clear when the increases in oil prices in 1973/74 did not bring about the expected switch to other energy sources. One of the main reasons for this was revealed in a hearing carried out by the U.S. Senate's Anti-Trust committee in 1974. According to Oppenheim (1976) the President of Continental Oil (owner of Consolidated Coal, the largest coal company controlled by any U.S. oil corporation), when asked whether its coal subsidiary would try to underbid Continental Oil in seeking business, from the controlled private monopolies like electricity, he replied: 'Under no circumstances.' Asked whether this held even in a situation where coal was cheaper, he flatly stated: 'We are not going to play one source of energy against another. . . We don't run our business that way.' The institutional obstacles to the operation of a micro-economic substitution-effect could not have been more clearly spelt out.

CONCLUSION TO SECTION 2

What we have shown in Section 2 is how orthodox micro theory remains relatively helpless in the understanding of the commodity of oil in contemporary capitalism. This is not so much because such a theory is logically wrong. It is rather because it is largely irrelevant as a mode of analysis.

3 THE ECOLOGISTS

The second major trend of contemporary thinking which has been
brought to bear on the question of energy and oil is that of the ecology
movement. It is difficult to define the concept of ecology in a precise
manner. However, according to one observer, ecologists concentrate
their analysis on 'the concept of mutual dependence and [of a] balance
between all inhabitants of an ecosystem' (Enzenberger, 1974, p. 3). The
main result which follows from their analysis can be summarised in the
following central hypothesis: 'the industrial societies of this earth are
producing ecological contradictions, which must in the foreseeable
future lead to their collapse' (ibid. p. 4). In this section we will concentrate only on one crucial contradiction which permeates their
analysis; the belief that the world will very soon run out of fossil-
fuels. One of the most important documents of the ecology movement,
A Blueprint for Survival (1972), states in no uncertain terms: 'If these
rates [growth-rates of energy PN] continue to grow exponentially, as
they have done since 1960, then natural gas will be exhausted within
fourteen years and petroleum within twenty years' (*Ecologist.* Jan
1972). Such sentiments have not been reserved for ecologists alone.
The *MIT Report,* 'Limits to Growth', and the *Reports from the Club of
Rome,* just to mention the most famous ones, echo the same belief
that mankind is in the process of 'running out of fuel'. Once such a
conclusion is accepted a number of extremely important consequences
follow. In simple organisational terms such an impending 'crisis' acts
as an inducement not to change the existing institutional set-up within
the industry, since it assumes the industrialised countries will have
to take full advantage of the existing expertise (the companies) in
trying to find a maximum amount of new fossil fuel as rapidly as
possible. On another level, if it is correct that industrial expansion will
stop as a consequence of the world running out of energy, this has
important consequences for how Marxists see the concept of 'crisis'.
One's whole approach to 'politics' must change if the collapse of
capitalism is brought about not by the internal contradictions of that
social system, but rather by some exogenous factor like a physical
limit of a raw material. We will then be back to a pre-Marxian notion
of crisis where it is the under-production of use-values and not the
over-production of exchange-values which will constitute the main
reason for a 'crisis'.

However, on closer scrutiny, it does look as if at least *this* aspect of the ecological analysis is seriously wrong.[8] Most alarmist conclusions are derived from the simple procedure of extrapolating current growth rates of demand for oil into the future and comparing them with 'existing reserves'. The problem with this procedure is twofold. First, simple extrapolation of demand is a doubtful analytical tool which disregards possible substitution-effects and makes assumptions about unchanged technological processes. Second, and more importantly, the concept of 'existing reserves' is itself very ambiguous.

To take an example from *A Blueprint for Survival*. The conclusion quoted above was based on 'proved reserves' which is the sum of the estimate of reserves given by the oil companies themselves. These reserves have the same status as an inventory in production theory. They are recoverable beyond all reasonable doubt under existing economic and political conditions. But the figure of reserves defined in this way will increase sharply if the price of oil increases since this will make more reserves profitable to extract. Total reserves will also increase if we add 'inferred reserves', defined as materials in yet undiscovered extensions of 'proved reserves'. The oilfields of Alberta, Canada, provide the most famous example of how the original reserves in the end drastically increased as a result of such 'inferred reserves' (Odell, 1973). Total 'proved reserves' would also increase if the present average recovery factor of 40 per cent from oil fields could increase, or if finally the rate of profit the companies require to produce oil is decreased. The companies today require a rate of return of between 20 and 25 per cent to develop a field in the North Sea. A number of additional fields would be developed if the requirement was only 10 per cent.

Estimating the total of undiscovered reserves is difficult as only a fraction of the world's sedimentary basins (the main geological prerequisite for the existence of oil) have been explored in any detail, if at all. There are huge sedimentary layers on all continental shelves, as well as in areas such as Latin America that until now have been left unexplored. On the other hand, there are areas such as the United States which have been very thoroughly explored. Of the 575,000 operating oil wells in the non-Communist world, 540,000 are situated in the United States (Foley, 1976, p. 136). While a number of these only produce a few barrels a day, and are a direct result of the archaic rules with respect to the ownership of subterranean resources in the United States, it is nevertheless a safe assumption that, if a similar exploration effort were to be made worldwide, total reserves of oil would increase dramatically. An expansion of exploration and production, especially offshore, will be expensive. But that is not the point at stake in this discussion, which deals with the *physical availability* of a given raw material.

If the situation is as outlined above, why has there been such miscalculation by so many analysts, including the ecologists? The reason must, at least partly, be found in their inadequate understanding of the institutional structure of the industry, and more specifically in the historical dominance of the major oil corporations.

Companies have a direct interest in underestimating the amount of available reserves that an oil province is expected to hold. This will strengthen their initial negotiating position in their dealings with a potential host government because they can then ask for better taxation and other operating terms than if the oil province in question is expected to be a bonanza. An analysis of the early negotiations in the North Sea bears out this point (Nore, 1978).

In addition, as profit-maximisers there is an optimum level of oil stocks or inventories that individual oil companies should hold. It might not be rational for them simply to add to their reserves beyond a stock of say fifteen years' supply. Hence if there are few new entrants to the industry one should expect the total amount of 'proven reserves', measured in equivalent of years consumption, to stay relatively stable over time. Interestingly enough the situation in the industry has, since the beginning of this century, constantly been one in which reserves have been expected to run out in fifteen to twenty years. In 1938 world production of oil corresponded to 6 per cent of known oil reserves. In 1974 this figure was less than 3 per cent (Adelman, 1975, p. 97). There is therefore every reason to believe that the world's reserves of oil are much greater than is indicated at any one moment.

However, if for some reason all the above arguments turn out to be incorrect, it is *then* true that the economic expansion of the capitalist West is threatened as the ecologists claim? Unfortunately for the ecologists not even this argument will do, because there are a number of substitutes to oil which, in the medium to long run, can be used as primary sources of energy even if oil runs out. In terms of energy content the known world coal reserves are today forty times as large as the proven oil reserves (Foley, 1976, p. 121), and, at the present level of consumption, are sufficient to last for 2500 years (ibid. p. 122). If there was a complete shift from oil to coal, total reserves would not last as long and there would also be environmental opposition to the exploitation of these reserves since the production of a large percentage of these would be by strip-mining (particularly in the United States). But even taking these factors into account, total coal reserves are of such a magnitude that they render meaningless the claim that the world is about to 'run out of energy'. Technological change could also significantly increase the importance of alternative sources of energy. Coal gasification is, for example, an excellent substitute for natural gas. And when oil can be produced at a lower cost from the huge deposits of oil shales that exist (mainly a question of sufficient research and development expenditure) the whole energy situation will change. However the world first has to overcome the structural barriers which spring from the existence of 'energy corporations' whereby a company which owns two different energy sources will not let them compete against each other (see p. 103). A solution is therefore more a question of *social* organisation and cost than any *physical* constraints to the total amount of energy available worldwide.

We have thus cast serious doubt on one of the most important building-blocks of the ecology movement: the assertion that mankind is rapidly and irreversibly in the process of using up its deposits of fossil fuel. This does not, of course, imply that supplies are unlimited. However it does have two consequences. First, it implies that there is more time available in which to take a decision about the future supply of energy to the industrialised countries; for example, the present rush by a number of vested interests in favour of extensive nuclear-energy programmes could be scrutinised much more carefully. Therefore interestingly enough the ecologists' anti-nuclear lobby would benefit from a critical evaluation of the oil companies.

Second, it should also focus our critical attention on the extremely wasteful way that Western societies have been consuming their energy resources. A social reorganisation which could decrease the total demand for energy would also contribute towards giving the West much more breathing space in which to evaluate its energy options. The stunning fact that the United States import of crude could decrease by 40 per cent were all U.S. cars to have the engine-size of European cars (Szulc, quoted in Barraclough (1975b) p. 22) is a clear enough indication of what might actually be achieved.

But it is an understanding of the relationship of the demand for oil to the capitalist mode of production and why such a dramatic decrease in energy consumption is unlikely to take place (outlined in Section 4 below) which will give an insight into the future energy demand, and *not* the ecology movement's repeated assertion that total energy consumption must be reduced 'for the sake of future generations'. Such an argument, apart from disregarding the operation of capitalism, seriously blurs one major issue: inter-generational transfers are not inherently good; we must also look at the distributional consequences of these transfers. For instance, if we assume that energy were saved today only to become the basis for a political and economic domination exercised by a tightly knit oligarchy in the future (a scenario vividly outlined by Stretton (1976)); or even barring such dramatic developments if it continued to be distributed in an increasingly inequitable manner on a world basis than is the case today, why should ecologists advocate a decrease of energy consumption today? There is nothing *a priori* desirable about conservation.

For this section we can therefore conclude that the limits to the world's energy resources are better understood in relation to the *social* organisation of oil production than in terms of any *physically given* amount of oil.

4 THE ALTERNATIVE MARXIST PERSPECTIVE AND THE PRESENT CONJUNCTURE

A Marxist understanding of oil must centre on the relationship between oil and accumulation. Only on this basis can we revert to our original question of whether the capitalist societies face an 'energy crisis'. To carry out such a task we must show in what sense oil is a special commodity.

The starting-point of such an analysis is our brief reference to the existence of surplus profit in the industry (pp. 95–6). There is a permanent surplus profit to be earned in oil production on a world scale. The reason for this is twofold. Normally in capitalist production it is the most productive of the production processes within an industry which become generalised, and in due course determines the average price of production (production costs plus the average rate of profit) for commodities in the industry. This is not the case in oil production because the most productive wells with respect to production costs, quality, and location are fixed in supply and cannot be generalised in the same way as the technologically most efficient process in manufacturing industry. There is, for example, a strictly limited number of oil wells in the world, which yield sulphur-free oil at 15 cents per barrel. We therefore need to modify the reference-point for pricing in the oil industry so that the price of production does not relate to the average production conditions, but instead to the marginal production conditions within the industry. Because marginal producers lack access to 'average' fields they would always earn less than the average rate of profit and go out of business. Social demand would as a consequence not be satisfied. This analysis therefore explains the existence of differential rent in the oil industry which originates because oil is of different qualities and is found under widely different conditions. Middle East production costs are around 15 cents per barrel, while North Sea costs vary between $2 and $6 per barrel (1977). The extra return earned by Middle East producers is differential rent.

A further modification of the notion that the price of a commodity is related to the average price of production in the industry must be made if we look at oil as part of energy measured in any appropriate energy unit such as joules.[9] In this perspective it is the marginal production unit, not of oil, but of energy as a whole,which constitutes the basis for the price of oil. The final market-price of oil (when indirect taxes are included) will therefore be above the price of production of oil, but equal (measured in BTU's) to the price of production of the marginal energy-producer on a world scale.[10] According to Masserat (1979) the marginal energy-producer on a world scale is U.S. coal production because it yields a normal rate of profit, whereas other energy-producers like European coal-mining and nuclear energy are still subsidised (and if left to their own accord would not earn a normal rate of profit). On the other hand oil producers earn a permanent surplus profit both compared with nuclear energy production and coal-mining in the United States. It is this permanent surplus profit in oil production which can yield a theoretical insight into our analysis. As stated above (p. 95), there are three groups with a claim to this surplus profit. Historically the largest share of the surplus profit has been accruing to the importing states.

The financial surplus which accrues to either the producer state or the oil companies within the oil industry can, in addition to differential rent, also take the form of absolute rent. Such rent exists when either the state as a landowner or the oil company, manage to extract rent for the marginal oil well in operation (instead of it all being taken by the oil-importing countries). The origin of this absolute rent can either be a result of the historical strength of the landowning class (in our case the state) which forces the capitalists using their land to pay a rent even for the marginal land. Or it can be due to the monopolistic stength of the oil companies so that even the firm which exploits the oil fields in the worst conditions will earn a rate of profit above the 'normal' rate. Given the high rate of profit which historically has been earned by the companies we will now concentrate our analysis on the second factor for absolute rent and ask why the process of monopolisation has been permanently more effective in the oil industry than almost anywhere else in the world economy.[11]

The monopolisation is partly explained by the peculiarities of oil production. Ever since oil was first extracted commercially in 1859 it has been possible to produce additional oil either by using existing spare capacity or by rapidly finding new oil at a cost less than the average cost of extracting oil from known reserves. Such a situation meant that the industry was under constant threat of destabilisation. A new entrant to the industry producing in these low-cost areas could undercut the price that was charged and which was necessary for the companies already operating in the industry to earn an average profit in high-cost areas. Also in an industry with heavy capital investment and a relatively low cost of producing one additional barrel of oil, there is always a temptation for producers to unload additional oil on the market as it would contribute positively to the company's short-run cash-flow. But the long-run results of such behaviour for the stability and profitability of the industry would be catastrophic. The history of the oil industry has many examples where there have been threats of oversupply. The most famous is the unregulated 'glut' in the U.S. market in the early 1930s as a result of the east Texan oil finds which brought down prices by 90 per cent in one year. Therefore, to avoid such threats to the price structure, the companies almost of necessity set up a cartel that both restricted entry into the industry and controlled production between existing firms. The history of the modern oil industry can be interpreted as a fight for the breakdown or preservation of these restrictive practices set up to deal with the natural tendency towards oversupply in the industry. OPEC becomes in this light a necessary successor to the company oil cartel – as an organisation which tried to control both prices and production of oil.

A logical and necessary corollary of exerting control at the level of production has been that the companies also exert control at all other levels of petroleum activity (refining, petrochemicals, retailing). This has historically led to an extensive vertical integration in the oil industry. From the time Rockefeller set up Standard Oil in 1890 until today, the oil industry has been dominated by vertically integrated, internationally operating companies that jointly controlled the market. Even today in the wake of the oil nationalisations a *de facto* vertical integration continues. This is accomplished by the long-run supply contracts which have been negotiated between the oil companies and the producer states.

The 'oil crisis' is much more understandable on this theoretical basis. The OPEC pricing and participation initiatives were attempts by the producer states to increase their share of the total surplus profit at the expense of the companies and the importing states.

We must now ask to what extent an increased share of the surplus profit going to the producer states can be said to constitute a 'crisis' for the orderly accumulation process in the West. Within the above framework the main result of the 'oil crisis' has been the transfer of surplus profit from one part of the world economic system to another (and partly back again through the process of the 'recycling' of petrodollars). So while the final cost of energy in the West has only increased modestly in real terms (being determined by the price of production of the marginal energy-producer on a world scale), the foreign-exchange costs of *imports* of oil to the West has increased dramatically.

The increase in OPEC's share of the surplus profit therefore threatened the importing states' and the companies' share of the surplus profit. But because the profitability of the companies has not dramatically changed since 1974[12] it has been the Western consumption states that have stood to lose most from these developments. But to the extent that the increase in the price of oil made it possible to argue for an *overall* increase in energy prices (and thus restore the state's tax margin) there has been a redistribution of the cost of increased energy prices from the state to the society as a whole.

A transfer of surplus profit on such a massive scale (in 1970 total OPEC income was $7.9 billion, in 1974 it totalled $115.8 billion) leads of course to a number of short-term instabilities and adjustments, the most important of which were to deal with the sudden balance-of-payments deficits in a number of countries. But in no sense can such a transfer be said to constitute any *fundamental* crisis for the accumulation conditions in the West. The effects of these temporary disequilibria have also been largely exaggerated (see pp. 116–17).

We will now link the discussion about the 'special' nature of oil more closely to the process of capital accumulation and in particular examine how different outcomes in the struggle for the surplus profit has different consequences for the process of accumulation. There are three such connections we can make.

First, if all surplus profit is captured by the landlord capital accumulation in the oil industry will not take place at a maximum rate. There will not be any continuous inducement for oil companies to look for the most productive sources of raw materials since all they will be left with at the end of the day is a 'normal' rate of profit as a result of the landowners' appropriation of *all* the rent. A similar barrier to accummulation can be postulated if rent has to be paid at the margin. Both these factors may make total investment in the industry less than what it otherwise would have been. This methodological orientation is important because it goes beyond rent as a distributional category.[13]

But even if all surplus profit is initially transformed into rent a second barrier to accumulation can be postulated. Accumulation of social capital on a world scale is slowed down when the rent is neither used internally nor externally as investment in productive industries.

Third, accumulation will take place under suboptimal conditions for the system as a whole if a commodity is produced under high-cost conditions when there is a possibility of producing the same good under more favourable cost conditions. This barrier may be a result of monopoly owership of natural resources, or represent a conscious political choice either by the companies or their home governments not to produce in certain areas.

To what extent can the above barriers to accumulation be said to exist today? The first barrier does not seem to be of decisive importance because not all the surplus profit is transformed into rent. Even if the oil-producing states from 1 Janurary 1975 instituted a very modest fixed profit margin of 22 cents per barrel, there are strong suggestions that the realised upstream profit for the companies is much higher (Odell and Rosing, 1977, p. 52). There are also important differences *between* producer states on this count.

To clarify the importance of the second barrier to accumulation, mentioned above, we must first distinguish between different OPEC countries. Saudi Arabia, the United Arab Emirates, and Kuwait use a large percentage of their oil revenues on luxury imports, on investment in property and Western treasury bills, and on arms. None of these ways of spending the oil revenues will in any direct way increase the total social capital in these countries. This use of the oil rent is a reflection of the development of the productive forces as well as of the composition of the ruling classes in these three countries.[14] For instance the reluctance of the Kuwaiti ruling class to industrialise fully reflect their fear of the political consequences of such a process. The need to import non-Kuwaiti labour from the Middle East, in particular skilled Palestinian labour, could in the long run upset the Kuwaitis' own political power. That a policy whether to industrialise or not is not merely related to physical and geographical reserve and absorption characteristics of the producer states (both Kuwait and Saudi Arabia are, for instance, 'excess supply' countries) is shown by Turner (1976), who, in the case of Nigeria, convincingly argues that the lack of Nigerian industrialisation is related to the class composition of the Nigerian ruling class.

Iraq and Algeria are the most typical representatives of another set of countries for which the oil revenue will almost totally be invested in development projects. This will tend to increase the amount of social capital. This 'developmentist' policy which expresses itself through an industrialisation process undertaken almost exclusively by state enterprises is again a reflection of the correlation of forces within such countries and the aims and aspirations of a 'bonapartist' ruling class which itself (especially in the case of Algeria) has emerged from an anti-imperialist struggle. Whether the present situation constitutes a barrier to accumulation therefore depends on the division of oil revenues between these different state types.

THE STATE AS CAPITALIST

Extrapolating into the future let us now regard the state *not* as a rent-receiver, but rather as an entity acting as an individual capitalist. The basis for this assumption is the emergence of numerous state oil corporations in producing countries. Consequently the confrontation in the oil industry is no longer mainly between capitalist and landlord, as we so far implicitly have assumed, but rather between state and private capital. One consequence of this approach is that our former discussion about barriers to accumulation outlined above must change and that new contradictions may consequently emerge.

If these state oil corporations are allowed to operate as if they were private units of capital (the Brazilian state oil corporation Petrobras, which is diversifying internationally, is only one example), then capital accumulation would not be affected. The only novel element in such a situation *might* be that the surplus profit will remain within the nation state and in this way support a process of 'modernisation', either directly by positively discriminating in favour of national suppliers of 'spin-offs' in the oil industry, or indirectly by the use of oil revenues for the purpose of industrialisation.

If on the other hand, severe restrictions were put on the operations of such state companies, either by limiting their access to capital or by forbidding them to operate internationally, then barriers to accumulation *would* result.

The final outcome of such a choice would again in each case depend upon the specific historic circumstances of each producer state and in particular on the strength of a technical–administrative sector in the state apparatus which might gain from the existence of an 'unconstrained' state oil corporation. But there is no easy conclusion to be drawn about the present trend towards the state acting as capital constituting a 'barrier' to capital accumulation.

WHY CRISIS?

So far our analysis seems to conclude that there is no reason to describe the present situation in the energy industry as a 'crisis' for the West. It is only by concentrating on the third barrier to accumulation that we can see how the developments in 1973/4 *potentially* could constitute such a crisis. The inroad to such an understanding springs from the assessment that oil is no ordinary commodity. It is the most important source of energy in capitalist societies and therefore plays a distinct and crucial role in the process of capital accumulation. From supplying 21.5 per cent of the world's energy supply in 1940, oil accounted for 67.2 per cent in 1974 (Foley, 1976, p. 64). It is, indeed possible to argue that the post-war boom has been based on the fact that ample supplies of cheap energy was widely available for the reconstruction after the war. As Barraclough (1975a) says: 'If communism . . . equals Soviet power plus electrification, neo-capitalism equals US power plus oil'. One set of figures is sufficient to indicate how the accumulation process during the post-war became increasingly energy intensive, which meant an increasing reliance on oil. Whereas between 1870 and 1950 GNP *per capita* rose sixfold for a mere doubling of *per capita* energy use, between 1950 and 1973 energy growth *per capita* actually exceeded the *per capita* growth in production (Ford Foundation Report, quoted in Barraclough, 1975a, p. 22).

The operation of the whole capitalist system in thus totally dependent in the short to medium run on a steady supply of oil because of the way capital accumulation takes place in capitalist economies.[15] A total cut-off of oil would bring the accumulation process to a halt with the same certainty as if the supply of labour-power was withdrawn. It is for these reasons that we label oil a 'strategic' commodity. Based on this we claim that analytically speaking not all goods are equal. A commodity which is an input to more than a critical number of goods at the same time as not having any short or medium-run substitutes must be categorised as a different kind of commodity; a strategic commodity. It is our assertion that the state takes a particular interest in 'strategic' commodities because of its central role in the accumulation process. A capitalist state, preoccupied with supporting the process of 'capital accumulation', has little choice but to ensure the 'security of supply' of such a good. Therefore to the extent that the 'oil crisis' threatened to cut off the supply of a strategic good, can we claim that the 'oil crisis' of 1973/4 fundamentally threatened the accumulation process in the West. With hindsight and given the close relationship between the United States and the Saudi Arabian governments (the latter being the largest and politically most influential oil producer) it is easy to see that such a cut-off was never on the cards in 1973/4 (see also Stork, 1975, ch. 9). On the other hand one should not underestimate the long-run political impact of the events of 1973/4. The OPEC price rise, the corresponding reorganisation of production and the brief oil embargo was the first major decision about the development of the world's economic and political system which for at least two centuries was *not* taken either in Europe or in North America. It signified an important shift in political power on a world scale, a factor which initially made the Western states extremely uneasy about the whole situation. And even if, as mentioned, the immediate threat of a supply boycott receded, the reaction in the West emphasises and makes clear how the political stability and process of accumulation of the West was seen to rely on a steady supply of oil. The 'energy crisis' can then be redefined as a momentary realisation on behalf of the Western ruling class that this model of accumulation might not be viable for ever. It would not come to an end because the world was about to run out of energy, nor because prices had increased. But it might stop because the oil-producing state might not see it in their interest to deplete their oil reserves at a pace which was determined by the logic of capital accumulation in the West. The temporary, and very inefficient, embargo during 1973/4 took place even when the main

OPEC countries were closely linked to the West. The realisation of what would happen to the nature of accumulation and the political stability within the Western capitalist system if countries like Iraq became dominant within OPEC, not to mention if a revolutionary government was installed in Saudi Arabia, was the basis for the momentary panic in 1973/4.

Partly as a result of the factors just outlined, and partly because tax regimes are not uniform worldwide, the oil companies have since 1973/4 drastically stepped up their search for oil supplies in politically 'safe' high-cost areas like Alaska and the North Sea. Simultaneously Western states have initiated a nuclear programme which both in terms of cost per energy unit produced and in terms of safety seem madness to embark upon when compared with other existing energy sources. But the latter decision is also related to a desire that the future supply of a strategic good like energy should be insulated from the threat of working-class action; in particular from the organised strength of coal-miners.

The increased costs to the capitalist system as a whole of following such policies (which again is undertaken because oil and energy is a strategic commodity) can now finally be related back to the third 'barrier' to accumulation we listed above. For example by looking for oil in the North Sea rather than trying to extend the vast reserves which still exist in the Middle East and North Africa imposes a direct additional cost on capital accumulation in the West. Once the threat of a supply embargo had faded, this is the only sense in which the events in 1973/4 could be said to have permanent effects on the process of capital accumulation in the West, and hence warrant the characterisation of a 'crisis'.

THE IDEOLOGICAL DIMENSION

Given that the one serious effect on capital accumulation we have identified in the wake of the events of 1973/4 does not seem particularly dramatic and mainly will be of a long-run importance, we are left to speculate as to why Western public opinion continue to refer to the existence of an 'energy crisis'.

It is possible to claim that the common Western interpretation of the increase in oil prices, the strengthening of OPEC, and the restructuring of the world's energy industries all have been partly ideological in character. We take this to mean that this reaction represents an *external* explanation to the world crisis that got under way in 1973/4, instead of rooting such an explanation in the internal contradictions of the Western capitalist system, where it belongs. As an example of this attitude consider the comment made in the *New York Times* to the effect that the 'sudden and massive transfer of income, wealth and power to the small group of oil-exporting countries', was propelling the world towards 'the double threat of world inflation and world depression' (22 Sep 1974). Contrary to such a view it is possible to argue after a close scrutiny of official sources that the changed situation in the oil industry only contributed marginally to a crisis that was already under way before the autumn of 1973.

According to IMF 'a slowing down of economic expansion in most industrial countries was already in process in the course of 1973, prior to the sudden emergence of energy-problems later in the year' (IMF, *Annual Report 1974*, pp. 5–7). The energy 'crisis' was also made responsible for the world inflation which started to accelerate in 1973/4. In this way the reason for the current world inflation was pinned on an 'exogenous' factor. For that reason the large drop in the British and other European workers' real wage administered and backed up by a plethora of official and unofficial incomes policies, were described as 'inevitable'. But again such 'explanations' were seen to be more ideological than anything else. The OECD *Economic Outlook* (July 1974) claimed that the increased oil prices had only added 'one-fifth of the overall rise' in the inflation rate; incidentally a view when presented by OPEC in the winter of 1974 was ridiculed by Western observers and described as pure propaganda.

This erroneous analysis by Western politicians and media must nevertheless not be seen as a crude 'conspiracy' to fool the Western populations. They are rather an expression of the more deep-seated and commonly held view that a 'crisis' *by necessity* has to be caused by an exogenous factor, because to admit anything else would be to question the existence of the capitalist system. But, whatever the reason for such views, the existence of such an exogenous factor luckily was at hand at the very time when Western governments needed some justification for the harsh deflationary policies deemed necessary to overcome the crisis. The oil 'crisis' performed this role perfectly.

NOTES

1. I would like to thank Alison Johnson, Pat Clawson and the other contributors to this book for helpful comments and suggestions.

2. This assumes that a firm will invest in a project as long as its expected internal rate of return is larger than the discount rate used in the investment analysis.

3. For a further discussion of why there should be a conceptual difference between 'the state' and 'politicians' see ch. 12 of Green and Nore (1977).

4. The fact that 1977/8 saw a temporary reversal of this trend due to the relative slowness with which oil was coming ashore, and the continuation of the world economic crisis, in no way negates these long-term trends in the Norwegian economy.

5. During OPEC's meeting in Vienna in March 1974 Yamani blocked a further price increase for the same reasons. According to the *New York Times:* 'On the major issues of the embargo and the oil prices decided here, Saudi Arabia virtually imposed conditions that were closely in line with American desires.' (20 Mar 1974, quoted in Stork, 1975, p. 243.)

6. In 1958 the United States imposed import quotas to protect its national oil industry. A number of U.S. corporations such as Occidental, which had just started to produce oil outside the United States, therefore effectively had their access to U.S. markets blocked. As a consequence, these companies (also called 'independents') had to unload a large part of their production in Europe, thereby undercutting the going price.

7. According to *The Economist* (7 July 1973) the United States accepted a higher price of oil because it saw such a policy as a way of slowing down the Japanese economy, 'which would be more hurt by rises in oil prices than any other nation'.

8. Note that we say nothing about the ecologists' legitimate fears about the safety of the nuclear 'option', which is also very much part of their energy analysis.

9. 1 joule (J) = 1 newton meter (Nm). Another unit which is much used is kilowatt-hour (kWh). 1 kWh = 3.6×10^6 J.

10. This calculation is not straightforward, as due consideration has to be paid to the value of by-products of oil and the energy content of converting one kind of raw material into energy. For an empirical investigation into the level of oil prices in the post-war period, see Masserat (1979).

11. Note that to explain the existence of absolute rent with reference to monopoly is controversial within the Marxist tradition. Marx relied on the low organic composition of capital in agriculture to explain the existence of absolute rent. To generalise such an argument to the oil industry, which has an extremely high organic composition, is problematic.

12. If anything company profits have increased slightly as a consequence of the move downstream in the wake of the oil nationalisations. For an overview of company profits in the post-nationalisation era, see Nore (1978).

13. We do not claim that a distributional perspective is superfluous; our analysis of the background to the 1973 events showed that this is not so. But a distributional perspective has to be seen, together with other perspectives.

14. See Halliday (1977) for an analysis of the industrialisation process in the Persian Gulf.

15. This does *not* contradict what we have said about the abundance of substitutes for oil which today exist, but which are difficult to develop within the present organisational set-up of the industry.

REFERENCES

Adelman, M. (1972) *The World Petroleum Market* (Baltimore: Johns Hopkins University Press).

Adelman, M. (1975) 'Amerikanske Synspunkter pa Norsk Oljepolitikk', *Bergens Privatbank Kvartaltidskrift,* no. 3.

Altvater, E. (1973) 'Notes on Some Problems of State Interventionism', *Kapitalistate'* no. 1 and 2.

Barraclough, G. (1975a) 'The Great World Crisis: I', in *New York Review of Books,* 23 Jan.

Barraclough, G. (1975b) 'Wealth and Power: The Politics of Food and Oil', *New York Review of Books,* 7 Aug.

Chevalier, J. M. (1975) *The New Oil Stakes* (London: Allen & Unwin).

Dam, K. (1976) *Oil Resources: Who Gets What How?* (Chicago: University of Chicago Press).

Dasgupta, P., and Heal, G. (1974) 'The Optimal Depletion of Exhaustible Resources', in *RES* (op. cit.).

Enzenberger, H. M. (1974) 'A Critique of Political Ecology', *New Left Review,* no. 84.

Foley, G. (1976) *The Energy Question* (Harmondsworth: Penguin).

Green, F., and Nore, P. (1977) (eds) *Economics: An Anti-Text* (London: Macmillan).

Halliday, F. (1977) 'Migration and the Labour Force in the Oil-producing States of the Middle East', *Development and Change,* no. 8.

Hotelling, H. (1931) 'The Economics of Exhaustible Resources', *Journal of Political Economy,* vol. 39, no. 2.

Jacoby, N. (1974) *Multinational Oil* (New York: Macmillan Co.).

Masserat, M. (1979) 'The Energy Crisis', in Nore and Turner (op. cit.).

Nore, P. (1976) 'Six Myths of British Oil Policies', *Thames Paper in Political Economy* (Summer).

Nore, P. (1978) 'Oil and National Economic Development: The Case of Norway', in S. Picciotto and J. Faundez (eds) *Nationalisations of Multinationals in Peripheral Countries* (London: Macmillan, 1979).

Nore, P. and Turner, T. (eds) (1979) *Oil and Class Struggle* (London: Zed Press).

Odell, P. (1973) 'The Future of Oil: A Rejoiner', *Geographical Journal* (June).

Odell, P. (1975) *Oil and World Power* (Harmondsworth: Penguin).

Odell, P., and Rosing, K. (1977) *Optimal Development of the North Sea's Oil Fields* (London: Croom Helm).

Oppenheim, V. H. (1976) 'The Past: We Pushed Them', *Foreign Policy* (Autumn).

Penrose, E. (1968) *The Large International Firm in Developing Countries: The International Petroleum Industry* (London: Allen & Unwin).

Penrose, E. (1971) *The Growth of Firms, Middle East Oil and Other Essays* (London: Cass).

Rafai, T. (1975) *The Pricing of Crude Oil* (New York: Praeger).

Review of Economic Studies (RES) (1974) 'Symposium on the Economics of Exhaustible Resources.'

Robinson, C., and Morgan, J. (1976a) 'Depletion Control and Profitability', *Energy Policy* (September).

Robinson, C., and Morgan, J. (1976b) 'Economic Consequences of Controlling the Depletion of North Sea Oil and Gas', *Trade Policy Research Centre Guest Paper.*

Stork, J. (1975) *Middle East Oil and the Energy Crisis* (New York: Monthly Review Press).

Stretton, H. (1976) *Capitalism, Socialism and the Environment* (London: Cambridge University Press).

Szulc, T. (1974) *The Energy Crisis* (New York: Watts).

Turner, T. (1976) 'Multinational Corporations and the Instability of the Nigerian State', *Review of African Political Economy*, no. 5.

PART C

Issues in Economic Theory

CHAPTER 5

The Role of Money in the Economy

Laurence Harris

Money's importance for capitalist economies cannot be hidden, for the
process of buying and selling, the process of exchange of commodities,
is fundamental to capitalism and money is fundamental to exchange.
Goods are not exchanged directly for each other (such exchange would
be called barter), but, instead, the process of exchange, when looked
at from the point of view of an individual who has something to sell,
is that he first sells it for money and then at a different moment he
may use the money for the purchase of other goods. Exchange under
capitalism involves money and from the little that has already been
said it can be seen that monetary exchange (as opposed to barter)
implies, first, that only money can be used to purchase goods (other
goods cannot); second, that therefore the exchange of goods is indirect;
and, third, that purchases and sales are separated in time. This much
is now acceptable to both orthodox monetary theorists and their
critics (Marxist or otherwise), although the study of orthodox monetary theory reveals many important instances where these principles
have been forgotten so that theories have developed in such a way
that they implicitly (and sometimes explicitly) deny them. But agreement that money has this role, its function as *medium of exchange*,
is not the same as agreement on every aspect of its role, for there are
differences over, first, the *basis* of the medium of exchange role (what
enables money to act as medium of exchange) and, second, the *effects*
and *implications* of money's existence as a medium of exchange.
  This chapter is primarily concerned with both of these areas of

disagreement, and the two are not unrelated. Thus we are concerned with whether money's existence causes it to have a role in matters such as the determination of the price level, output and employment, what the limits are to such a role, and how it comes about.

1 ORTHODOX MONETARY THEORY

Orthodox monetary theory has many variants, but what unites the different schools is more significant than what divides them. Although I shall briefly examine the distinctions between the various versions of orthodox theory I am, in the main, concerned with its common aspects. There are two in particular. The first is that an economy which uses money is compared with a barter economy, and the latter differs from the former only in the one respect that money is not used. On the basis of this comparison it is concluded that exchange is conducted with less cost in a monetary economy, and that this explains the existence of money. This aspect of orthodox theory will be considered and criticised in Section 2. The second common aspect is that economic fluctuations are seen as determined by fluctuations in the demand for commodities and that the stock of money is a (or, in some cases, *the*) prime determinant of this demand. In this section this central idea is elaborated.

It is now second nature for economists and laymen alike to think that the physical amount of output is determined by the demand for it and therefore to think that money can have an effect on the level of output if it can affect that demand. But this is not the only way to conceive of the economy. Indeed, before Keynes wrote his *General Theory* (1936) and popularised the idea of effective demand it was unusual for orthodox economists to think in this way; it was more common to think that the level of output (supply) determines demand. On that view, since the level of physical output is determined independently all that changes in the stock of money could do was affect the price of that output and, although pre-Keynesian writers did not always make clear how this effect on prices occurred, implicit in several of their arguments was that an increase in the stock of money would increase the demand for commodities and, in that way, push up the price of the given supply. Now, however, all orthodox monetary theorists, (except, as we shall see, for those who develop the logic of monetarism to its limits, argue that money may at times have an effect on physical output and at times on its price, and that changes in the stock of money affect these variables by affecting the demand for output, for commodities. This immediately raises the question of *how* the money stock affects the demand for commodities. For over a century and a half monetary theorists have considered two mechanisms which may enable money to have this effect, a direct mechanism and an indirect mechanism. In modern interpretations, both are based on the assumption that individuals have a stable demand function for money in accordance with which the amount of money they choose to own is determined.

For the *direct mechanism* the theory of this demand function concentrates on the idea that, for any given flow of nominal income or consumption, individuals choose to hold a definite stock of money; if your salary goes up you will, it proposes, want to hold a larger value of wealth and, assuming for simplicity that money is the only form of wealth, this means a desire to hold a larger stock of money. If there is a demand function for money of this form (income determining the demand for money) then the converse is also implied, if the stock of money is determined exogenously it affects income. Suppose that the stock of money is initially that which is demanded at the going level of income (the demand f)r and supply of money are in equilibrium) and then the money stock is increased by the government printing more notes and distributing them in subsidies (like pension and other welfare payments); individuals will be holding a greater stock of wealth than they desire at the existing level of income and will therefore try to get rid of this excess wealth (money balances) by increasing their demand for the flow of commodities. The raised demand causes either an increase in output or an increase in its price, and since the value of output is, in national income accounts, identical with the value of national income the latter increases so that in the new equilibrium the rise in the value of income will have induced a rise in the demand for money sufficient to match the increased stock of money. This direct mechanism underlies simple versions of the pre-Keynesian Quantity Theory of Money. Postulating that the desired stock of money is a given proportion, k, of nominal national income, py, the demand function is:

$$M^D = kpy.$$

Postulating that equilibrium is achieved only when the demand for money equals the existing stock, $M^S = M^D$, equilibrium requires

$$M^S = kpy.$$

In consequence, if the money supply increases, nominal output and national income (*py*) must increase proportionately (since *k* is assumed fixed). The mechanism which moves the economy towards the new equilibrium is an increase in the demand for output. However since in simple versions of this it was not thought that demand affects the physical amount of output produced or, in other words, real national income, *y*, the required increase in the value of income was attributed entirely to an increase in the price level, *p*. This direct mechanism, the idea that the demand for commodities is directly affected by the stock of money (as a counterpart to the dependence of the demand for money being a function of the flow of income and output) is sometimes known as the real balance effect, Pigou effect, or wealth effect.

For the *indirect mechanism* the theory of the demand function concentrates not on the choice between holding a stock of wealth as money and purchasing a flow of commodities, but, instead, on the choice between holding a stock of wealth as money and holding it in other financial assets such as bonds. Because bonds pay their holder an interest yield, *r*, whereas money balances do not in general do so, there is an incentive for individuals to hold their wealth in the form of bonds rather than money. There are, however, disincentives, too. Keynes, in his theory of liquidity preference, emphasised that the risk to the holder of bonds of suffering a capital loss when they are sold will deter individuals from holding all their wealth in the form of bonds; they will hold some money and the amount they choose will depend on the extent to which the interest yield on bonds offsets their disadvantages. With a given amount of wealth, the higher is the interest yield the higher will be desired bond holdings and accordingly the lower will be the demand for money. In functional notation:

$$M^D = f(r).$$

If we combine this demand function with the condition that, for equilibrium, the demand for money must equal the existing stock, $M^D = M^S$, we have

$$M^S = f(r)$$

in equilibrium. In other words, if the stock of money is increased the new equilibrium of the economy will be one where the rate of interest is lower than previously, for a fall in the interest rate would be necessary to induce individuals to raise their demand for money to match the increased stock. This fall in the interest rate is crucial for the indirect mechanism, for it is postulated that it causes an increase in the demand for commodities and thereby induces a rise in either their output or price. The fall in the interest rate is thought to increase demand because it encourages capitalists to increase their rate of investment – or, in other words, purchase more investment goods such as machines, factories and inventories of finished goods in each period – and it is thought to do this by making it cheaper for capitalists to borrow money.

The direct mechanism is the idea that a change in the stock of money directly leads to a change in demand for commodities; the indirect mechanism is the idea that it indirectly has the same effect via interest-rate changes. Both, in their modern formulations, postulate that these effects occur on the basis of a stable demand function for money with individuals choosing to hold monetary wealth as against carrying out expenditure on commodities (in the theory of the direct mechanism) or choosing money as against other forms of wealth (in the theory of the indirect mechanism). Both, in their most general forms, suggest that the resulting change in the demand for commodities may affect *either* the supply of commodities (physical output and real national income) or its price. What is important is that output, measured at current prices, py, is affected irrespective of which component, p or y, alters. This requires some explanation, for particular monetary theories do deviate from this general formulation and concentrate on the idea that a change in demand affects only p or only y. The simple Quantity Theory, as we have seen, conceives of the effect of a change in demand as falling entirely on the *price of output* since the physical amount of output is seen as being determined independently by the forces of profit maximisation and free competition unaffected by the demand for output. By contrast, Keynes and his early interpreters conceived the effect of a change in demand as falling upon the *physical level of output* and, since a particular level of output requires a particular amount of labour, upon the amount of employment. The distinction between these emphases arose partly because Quantity Theorists were concentrating upon long-term effects and abstracting from the fact that in the short term physical output is variable and may be affected by demand, whereas Keynes was explicitly concentrating upon short-term phenomena.

The modern debate between Monetarists and anti-Monetarists concerns issues which are wider than the question of whether demand influences output, prices or both (although that remains one of the central questions which divides the factions). There is a fundamental similarity and unity between Monetarists and anti-Monetarists. It is more significant than their differences but before elucidating let us consider the antagonisms and reflect on the ideological significance of the debate. All writers have difficulty in summarising the debate and pinpointing its main points because even the protagonists disagree over which issues are the ones which divide them and the issues which cause the journals to be filled with controversy change from time to time. Much of the debate concerns the question of whether the money supply alone systematically affects the aggregate demand for commodities or whether demand could also be reliably influenced by pure fiscal policy defined as changes in government expenditure and taxation which do not affect the money supply (although it is recognised that such changes do usually affect the money supply).

The argument primarily concerns empirical results rather than fundamental differences in competing theoretical models. Monetarists and anti-Monetarists alike employ models where the nominal value of output is determined by demand which, in turn, is determined by the supply of money. Both postulate that the direct effect and the indirect effect operate, although it must be said that there is some confusion over this since at times each side has said that the fault with the other is that it ignores the indirect mechanism. Tobin, a leading anti-Monetarist, has stated that the distinguishing features of Monetarism is a postulate that the demand for money is not a function of an interest rate. This would, indeed, given Monetarists a model where pure fiscal policy is ineffective since it would imply that the *LM* curve is vertical so that shifts in the *IS* curve affect only the interest rate, but it is not a postulate which has been put forward by Monetarists. On the other hand, Friedman has stated that the distinguishing feature of Keynesianism is a belief in the existence of the liquidity trap (a horizontal section of the *LM* curve) so that changes in the money supply have no effect on the interest rate, investment or demand, but in fact all orthodox anti-Monetarists argue that money does have an effect and none advance the thesis of a liquidity trap.[1]

Although their basic theoretical models are not substantially different, Monetarists and anti-Monetarists claim to have obtained radically opposed empirical results. Even here, however, the differences are less substantial than they at first sight appear to be, for both agree that a systematic relationship between the money supply and nominal income is suggested by empirical data. The disagreement concerns only the Monetarists' conclusion from empirical studies that government expenditure itself (or the budget deficit) has no such systematic relationship, with its corollary that Keynes's theory of the effectiveness of fiscal policy is thrown into doubt. Anti-Monetarists refute this argument by demonstrating that different econometric results are obtained if the variables are measured in ways which are more consistent with their theoretical categories and if more 'reliable' econometric techniques are employed. But although the Monetarists' emphasis on the impotence of fiscal policy is the most prominent aspect of the debate it is by no means the whole of their argument, for the Monetarist view of policy goes one step further; not only is fiscal policy to be eschewed, even monetary policy should only be pursued in an inactive manner. It should be restricted to control of the money supply instead of intervention to influence interest rates or the availability of loans (two types of policy which, although criticised by Monetarists, are widely used) and the more extreme forms of Monetarism argue that this control of the money stock should follow a rule such as 'let the money supply grow at a steady 6 per cent per year' rather than causing the money stock to fluctuate in attempts to counter unemployment in one period and excess demand in another.

In their academic writings Monetarists, therefore, not only put forward the argument for which they are famous – that fiscal policy should be abandoned – but also argue that active (discretionary) monetary policy should be given up. The argument against fiscal policy is that its effects on the level of effective demand for commodities are too weak. That against monetary policy is more complex. For many years the argument was that changes in the money supply have such a strong effect on demand that any error in its application will *de*-stabilise the economy. And related to this is the view that without government intervention (except intervention to *prevent* sharp changes in the money supply which arise exogenously) the capitalist economy is inherently stable around a point at which all who want to work are employed (those who are registered as unemployed being voluntarily unemployed while they search the job market). Now the argument is somewhat more sophisticated. It is that (especially if no 'error' is made in the application of policy) monetary policy, like fiscal policy, will have no effect on the level of output or employment. The theoretical model underlying this conclusion is based on the assumption that all individuals have 'rational' expectations in the sense that they have perfect knowledge of the underlying systematic behaviour relations in the economy and of the past and present values of all variables. They are therefore able to perfectly predict the future variables of the economy in the sense that they accurately predict all except random changes *and* that means they are able to predict monetary policy itself and its effects on the economy. Accordingly, individuals are able to make decisions in the light of these accurate predictions and, with the basic assumption that such decisions lead to economic stability, stability is the necessary result. More specifically, supposing that the price level is a function of money supply, individuals are able to accurately predict the rate of inflation and the price level among other variables. Nominal wages are therefore adjusted to ensure that real wages are at that level at which the demand for labour equals the supply so that there is no involuntary unemployment. This adjustment is made whatever the level of the money supply (except for random fluctuations) so monetary policy is unable to affect the level of employment, or output or other real variables. It can, however, affect the price level and rate of inflation; indeed, since output is seen as being automatically at its full-employment level a rise in the money supply above the rate of growth of capacity output must have an effect on prices unless k in the Quantity Theory equation (see p. 127) rises to compensate. The argument that changes in the money supply have no effect on output, therefore, takes us a step closer to the old Quantity Theory argument that increases in the money supply merely produce inflation.

The upshot is that Monetarists ascribe a minimal role to state intervention in any form, and that according to them a positive macro-economic stabilisation policy in the form of either fiscal or monetary measures is of little use; the capitalist economy will tend to stability at full employment in any case.

The place of such a conception in bourgeois ideology is easy to see; it is merely another example of the idea, so pervasive in orthodox economics, that the capitalist economy is a harmonious self-regulating system. We have encountered that idea elsewhere in this volume. But the other aspect of Monetarist ideas has an even more crude and direct role to play in bourgeois ideology. That is, the idea that the money supply's rate of change is the primary determinant of inflation is one which is employed to great effect by right-wing parties in their campaigns to limit state expenditure. Playing on people's fear of inflation, 'Control the Money Supply' is inscribed on their banners, and their leaders explain that this means that public expenditure must be curtailed because it is this expenditure which makes governments print money at too fast a rate (or raise loans which enables the banks to create money). The Monetarist emphasis on control of the money supply, therefore, gives academic respectability to politicians' calls for a decrease in public expenditure: a TV newsreader saying 'the money supply over the past year has risen too fast and the authorities have decided to limit its growth to 6 per cent next year' in order to restore its target long-run growth rate will undoubtedly cause less disquiet and provoke less disruption than one saying 'the urban aid programme and all educational spending are to be drastically cut next year'.

It remains the case, however, that while Monetarism is an argument against state intervention in macro-economic processes while its opponents (loosely classified as Keynesian) are more tolerant toward the expansion and 'perfection' of the state's role, the underlying theory of money is essentially the same in each case. In each the essential idea is that individual agents, households and firms, have a demand function for money and when these are aggregated over the whole private sector we obtain a stable demand function. In its independent variables this stable function includes interest rates and either wealth or income (the choice being relatively unimportant since in orthodox economics income is treated as the return on wealth and hence as a proxy for it). Because of this stability of the aggregate demand function changes in the supply of money lead through the direct or indirect mechanism to changes in nominal expenditure on commodities, and thereby to changes in either prices or output.

From within bourgeois economics there is remarkably little criticism of this consensus, although from time to time alternative views are expressed. They are critical only in a limited sense, arguing that the supply of credit, loans, rather than the supply of money determines nominal expenditure. In terms of the essential elements of orthodox monetary theory enumerated in the last paragraph this is framed as a rejection of the assumption that the demand for money is a stable function of interest rates and income (or wealth). Look at it from the point of view of an individual and contrast this credit hypothesis with the idea underlying the direct mechanism of monetary theory. There the idea was that the demand for commodities is determined by the individual's stock of money balances because he attempts to maintain a stable relationship between the two. Under the credit hypothesis it is assumed that the demand for commodities is determined by forces other than a desired relationship between money balances and expenditure (thus implying that the demand for money itself is not stably related to national income or expenditure) and the individual's money balances do not even act as a constraint on his expenditure. Instead, he is constrained by the availability of credit so that when the supply of loans is decreased, so is expenditure and, on an aggregate scale, national income. The credit hypothesis has never been carefully formulated as an alternative to the mainstream of bourgeois monetary theory and is now largely ignored in theoretical writing. But much of the monetary policy of capitalist states since the second world war has been based upon it: attempts to restrict expenditure have involved restriction of the availability of credit (consumer credit, bank loans to industry) instead of restriction of the supply of money.

2   MARXIST CRITIQUE

All the elements of orthodox monetary theory are at variance with Marxist theory. Most fundamental is the difference in the conept of causality: the direction of causality and also the very nature of causality itself. Whereas bourgeois economists see fluctuations in production, national output and income as determined by fluctuations in the demand for commodities with the latter determined by the money supply (and other variables), Marxist economics treats the fluctuations in capitalist economies' output as ultimately determined by capitalist methods of production themselves. Demand for commodities, money and other elements of exchange do have an effect on fluctuations, but they are secondary to and themselves determined by the variations in production. This difference in the direction of causation can be seen in quite concrete terms if we consider the explanation of the severe recession of the 1930s in the United States. Monetarists have argued that the collapse in output and employment was caused by a collapse in the money supply which resulted from a series of bank failures, whereas the Marxist approach sees it as resulting from the fact that production in the United States and other capitalist economies had to be reorganised in order to permit future profitability. On that view, crisis and unemployment with the concomitant bankruptcies and break-up of operating units had the function of causing the decline of some unprofitable industries, the restructuring of others on a profitable basis and the building of new industries with the resources released in the depression. The cause of the depression ultimately lay in the need for the changes in production which underlay this process and while monetary factors did have a role to play in precipitating the crisis they cannot explain its depth and duration.

To say that production rather than exchange categories such as money are fundamental determinants of fluctuations in capitalist economies does not mean that we can ignore money. For one thing, to say that money is not a fundamental determinant of fluctuations is not to deny that money does play an important intermediate role in fluctuations, affecting the timing of crisis and booms as well as their form. And if we consider how to analyse that role we are forced to ask whether there are alternatives to the bourgeois approach, or are we to adopt the theory of the direct and indirect mechanism with its basic assumption of individuals having stable demand functions for money (merely amending it by warning that production is somehow the fundamental determinant)? To see how the Marxist approach differs from the bourgeois let us begin by seeing how it conceives of the role of money in economic crisis and since these are crisis of capital we have to start with the concept capital. The economic process without which no others can exist under capitalism is the circuit of industrial capital, a movement in which the source of profit, surplus value, is generated and realised and in which capital is constantly being transformed: the capitalist first exchanges money for raw materials, the hire of machines and men's ability to work for a 'week'; these are then set to work and capital is transformed into finished commodities which are then transformed back into money. Thus, capital at one point in its circuit exists in the form of commodities, in another it exists in the form of money, and at another it exists as productive capital, the factory in motion. For the circuit of capital to proceed smoothly definite proportions between its different forms must be established and maintained, but there are no mechanisms which automatically ensure this balance. On the contrary, capitalism continually tends to disrupt this internal balance, causing production to get out of step with exchange, or causing money capital to be swollen or shrunk to proportions which are not consistent with the level of production. These dislocations between the spheres of activity, and disproportionalities between the forms of capital, at times become so great and severe that they can only be resolved by a break in the circuit of capital, a crisis.

All this is discussed in Chapter 7 on crises and inflation (p. 174

below). For the present, two aspects of it are significant. First, one factor in the disproportionalities which precede a crisis may be an over-expansion of the money form of capital and in this sense fluctuations in the volume of money capital may precipitate crises. But fluctuations in the volume of money capital are by no means the same thing as fluctuations in the volume of money. Not all money is money capital and this is an important point to which we will shortly return. Second, the source of the disproportionalities between the forms of capital and the tensions between exchange and production is not to be found in individual decision. It is not because individuals choose to hold a certain amount of money or commodities that disproportionalities arise; instead, it is because the accumulation of capital over the cycle necessarily gives rise to a complex interaction in the development of the rate of profit, the mass of profit, the value of wages and other variables, that disproportionalities necessarily arise. For example, the production of a mass of surplus value too low to enable the accumulation of industrial capital may give rise to a speculative boom in land, commodities or shares as capitalists compete for profits which capital as a whole cannot achieve (because of the low amount of surplus value) but which each capitalist can attempt to gain at the expense of the others through speculation and capital gains. Such a speculative boom generates an expansion of money capital as an increased amount of money is thrown in to the search for profit, but it is an *over*-expansion and the speculative boom necessarily ends in crisis since the basis of the expansion of exchange, its basis in the production of surplus value, is not sufficient.

From what has been said so far we can already identify two essential aspects of the difference between bourgeois theory and Marxist theory in their approaches to the role of money in the economic fluctuations of capitalism. Whereas the former is concerned with the money supply and the demand for it, the latter is concerned with money primarily to the extent that it acts as capital; and whereas bourgeois theory takes individual decisions as central in these fluctuations, Marxist theory treats the movements of the economy as the outcome of the impersonal forces of capital. These ideas are difficult for those of us trained in bourgeois economics to assimilate. Let us explore them more carefully, and let us do so by concentrating upon the distinction between *money as such* ('the money supply', 'the demand for money') and *money capital*.

Money as such is a concept which relates to the exchange of commodities and although capitalism is a system in which exchange is generalised to its greatest degree, exchange is more widespread than capitalism; it exists in pre-capitalist societies and in socialist societies. And the exchange encountered in reality is invariably monetary exchange. Whereas barter exchange would involve the direct exchange of commodities for commodities, $C-C$, monetary exchange involves in essence the sale of commodities for money, $C-M$, and, in a separate transaction, the purchase of other commodities with the money, $M-C$, so that in total it involves the indirect exchange of commodities, $C-M-C$. The fact that monetary exchange involves this use of money as an intermediary is very important for both Marxist and bourgeois economics (although, as will be seen, in different ways for each). Its emphasis by recent bourgeois writers leads them to argue that the basic function of money is this one of being a medium of exchange; and it also enables us to realise the integral connection that exists between this function and money's role as a store of wealth, for the essential feature of monetary exchange is that the act of selling goods, $C-M$, is distinct from purchase, $M-C$, so it is necessarily separated in time and money as a medium of exchange is held as a store of wealth in between ('temporary abode of purchasing power' is an apt and widely used expression). These concepts, medium of exchange and store of wealth stemming from the nature of monetary exchange, are all that are needed by bourgeois economics to understand money as such, for on the basis of them bourgeois economics is able to build its theory of the demand for money. Since money is held between sales and purchases we can derive a demand for transactions balances. Since any individual need not purchase as much as he has sold (causing his $(M-C)$ to be less than $(C-M)$) he may build up a hoard of 'idle balances' and, in analysing the factors which determine whether the individual holds the hoard in the form of money or bonds, bourgeois economics arrives at its theories of the speculative and precautionary demands for money; 'liquidity preference'. Thus bourgeois economics develops its central concept, the individuals' demand for money, from the concept of money as such or, in other words, from the nature of monetary exchange. And there, more or less, it stops.

The Marxist theory of money does not stop there, nor, as we shall see, does it start at the same place. In unravelling the role of money under capitalism it goes further than the concept of money as such to the concept of money as capital. This is associated with the fact that the concept of monetary exchange, $C-M-C$, does not in any way describe the whole of capitalism's economic processes, nor even the most fundamental part of the whole. The Marxist theory of the capitalist economy has as its centre the concept of the circuit of capital which was briefly described three paragraphs ago. In symbols, the circuit is described by:

$$M_1-C_1 \; - - P_1 \; - - C'_1-M_2-C_2 \; - -$$

If the capitalist is envisgaged as starting with money, M_1, he uses it to buy commodities, C_1, in the form of raw materials, the service of machines, and workers' ability to work. These are set in motion, the workers and machines working on the raw materials under the direct or indirect control of the capitalist so that his capital takes the form of productive capital, P. This process produces new commodities, C'_1, which are sold for money, M_2, and a new circuit (with subscript $_2$) is started. Writing the circuit in symbols does not by itself tell us anything, but it does help to isolate the main features of the concept of capital and to identify what distinguishes M in this circuit from money as such. The first point is that the formula for monetary exchange, $C-M-C$, appears in this series of circuits as merely one part, $C'_1-M_2-C_2$, of the whole. The second is that the whole circuit is a circuit of *capital* only because surplus value is produced and realised as profit. The operation of the factory, P, leads to commodities being produced, C'_1, of a greater value than the commodities, C_1, which entered into the factory; the money with which the first circuit ends, M_2 is therefore greater than that with which it started, M_1, the difference being the capitalist's profit. The third is that the surplus value or profit which is the hallmark of capital's circuit is produced in the process of production, between C_1 and C'_1; it is not generated by the exchange of commodities for money even though that exchange is a necessary part of the whole circuit.

From this consideration of the circuit of capital we can immediately see that not all money is money capital. M_1 and M_2, money held by capitalists and capitalist institutions as part of the continuing process of making profits, is money as a form of capital. If, however, M_2 were to be withdrawn from the process of profit-making rather than thrown into the succession of capital's circuits – if it were paid out as dividends to capitalists intending to use it for consumption – it would not be money as capital. It would be called 'money as revenue'. The same name is given to the money received as wage revenue by workers, for they themselves do not after receiving that money spend it again in a process which makes profit for them. The example of money as wage revenue helps to make clear the distinction between money as such and money capital. Workers engage in monetary exchange and therefore use money as such. They sell their ability to work as a commodity and with the money received they buy food, housing and other commodities, so the formula $C-M-C$ applies. But money is by no means capital in this process, whereas it is, as we have seen, when money is in the hands of capitalists so that $C-M-C$ is part of the whole circuit of capital.

Of course, money is in reality always moving from one category to another and back again. Workers receiving money as revenue spend it on commodities so that it is received by capitalists in the process of profit-making; it returns to its role of money capital. Also workers save their money revenue by depositing it in a bank or savings institutions; they do not therby own capital or become capitalists but when the bank uses that money for profit-making what was money as revenue for the worker becomes money capital for the bank. But despite this movement of money between its roles as capital and as revenue the roles are conceptually quite distinct and a theory of money based on the distinction is quite different from one which ignores it. To see how, let us consider the three problems which we have identified in the context of orthodox economics: the effects of an increase in the money supply, the nature of the credit system and the relationship between money and barter.

'The effect of an increase in the money supply' is a formulation of a problem which makes sense only within orthodox economics and this for several reasons. First, it is posed in isolation from the problem of what induces the increase and from what the underlying situation of the economy is. The Marxist theory that the movement of the economy is determined by fluctuations in production means that the effect of an increase in the money supply cannot be separated from its source in these fluctuations; the booms and slumps which result from capitalism's fundamental relationships *cause* fluctuations in the stock of money and the extent to which these monetary factors react back on to the business cycle depends on these underlying causal forces. If production is not generating sufficient profit for growth and accumulation of capital the money supply will not be increased through the banking system lending to firms (since accumulation will not be proceeding and will not require such loans), and if it is increased through the state's activities in connexion with capital accumulation and the business cycle it will not be able to stimulate accumulation for which the fundamental conditions do not exist. Orthodox economics is able to pose the question of an effect of an increase in the money supply as if the latter is exogenous only by ignoring the fact that the banking system and the state are not exogenous but have an effect on the money supply which is determined by their own situation in relation to capital and capitalist accumulation. Second, and related to this, the concept of an increase in 'the money supply' ignores the distinction between money as capital and money as revenue. If the underlying determinants cause an upturn in the accumulation of capital and this causes an increase in the money supply through the banks lending to firms, it is money as capital which is being increased. In such circumstances, the 'effect' of the increase in the money supply is merely to ensure that capital in the form of money increases concomitantly with commodity capital and productive capital. If, on the other hand, the business cycle is at a point where the accumulation of capital is interrupted the state will increase its expenditure (on unemployment pay and perhaps other items) and may finance this by directly or indirectly increasing the supply of money. Such an increase is money as revenue, but it does not remain isolated from the circuit of capital. As the recipients buy commodities with it the money enters the circuit and becomes money capital, but because its growth was stimulated not by an expansion of capital but by its opposite, an interruption of accumulation, money capital becomes too large in relation to other forms. Inflation which reduces the 'real value' of this expanded money capital is a process which develops in such circumstances to restore the correct proportions between money capital, commodity capital and productive capital.

'The nature of the credit system' is a problem which bourgeois economics can only consider to a very limited extent. Money as such, monetary exchange, permits the development of the credit system since it permits the splitting of sale and purchase into the two parts, $C-M$, $M-C$. On the one hand this split enables individuals to hoard money and therefore lend it out (thus not completing the second part), on the other it enables individuals to reverse the order of the two parts, borrowing so that the purchase, $M-C$, occurs first and the sale to obtain money to repay the loan occurs second. At any time, in consequence, some individuals (lenders) hold financial assets and some (borrowers) hold financial liabilities. This is the essence of the bourgeois theory of the credit system; it is concerned with how individuals and financial institutions make choices about the proportions of different assets and liabilities held at any time and it explains these choices in terms of preferences for yield and certainty. The Marxist theory, as in previous examples, moves beyond the concept of money as such and, from the concept of money as capital, develops the idea of credit as capital. Thus, capitalists obtain money capital not only through the sale of commodities but also by borrowing from other capitalists and this is a form of credit (interest-bearing capital) which cannot be understood by referring only to individual choices as to how to order the transactions, $C-M$, $M-C$. First, its very existence depends on the fact that the borrowing capitalist is to use the money capital to make a profit and is therefore able to pay interest. The relevant circuit, therefore, is not the circuit of exchange, but the whole circuit of capital, $M_1-C_1--P_1--C'_1-M_2$. It is only because capital completes that whole circuit, going through production as well as exchange, that profit is generated. Second, the amount of borrowing which is done depends upon the conditions of accumulation. If the accumulation of capital is proceeding smoothly the amount of interest-bearing capital expands, together with the other forms of capital. Third, the credit we are concerned with here is credit from one capitalist to another. It is quite distinct from the credit given by workers to capitalists (that is, workers' savings in banks, pension schemes and other institutions) and from the credit given by capitalists to workers (consumer credit). These latter forms of credit are not themselves capital; they have entirely different functions in the economy, although their functions too can only be understood by studying their relation to capital, a relation in which they are always subordinated to the movements of capital.

While this is clearly of interest at an academic level, it also has implications which have a more direct impact on our understanding of the world about us. For one thing, the idea of credit's role and money's role as capital and their relation to other forms of capital as being central to their position under capitalism enables us to understand how the capitalist class is divided into fractions according to their control over different forms of capital. Those fractions which control interest-bearing capital and those which control industrial capital have interests which at one level coincide (since each depends upon the production of surplus value for the existence of interest and industrial profits respectively), but at other levels come into conflict with each other. At times these conflicts become intense and are even reflected in political struggles with one party representing the immediate interests of finance ('a bankers' ramp') and another the interests of the industrial and other fractions of capital. In practice it is not always easy to identify these distinct political fractions within the ruling class but even in such a case the distinction between financial capital and industrial capital has important economic effects. The development of financial capital has given it a position, since at least the end of the nineteenth century, where it greatly influences the operation of industrial capital. Capitalist competition requires that capital moves from industries with low profitability to those with high. In the absence of a credit system such movement is difficult but with well-developed stock exchanges, banking institutions and money markets, capital – financial capital in the form of credit –moves from one industry to another with great flexibility, thereby perfecting the mechanisms of competition. This flexibility means that financial capital is, in a sense, able to subordinate industrial capital to itself for the possibility of withdrawal of credit from an industry means that each industry is subject to the criteria of the credit system. Academically it is an interesting paradox: financial capital is completely dependent upon industrial capital for without production the surplus value which is the foundation of its dividend and interest receipts would not be generated, yet industrial capital is dependent upon and subordinated to financial capital. Outside of academic riddles, though, there is a harsh reality: the flexibility of financial capital means that industries which are relatively unprofitable can be shut down overnight and workers thrown into unemployment by a completely invisible hand. All this is the effect of credit under capitalism which, in turn, is based upon money as capital and ultimately upon monetary exchange and money as such. It is, therefore, an aspect of money's role in the economy which is not considered in bourgeois economics, for the latter does not have any concept of money as capital.

The final problem which enables us to examine the distinction between bourgeois and Marxist approaches is 'the relationship between money and barter'. It is a problem which bourgeois monetary theory takes as fundamental, but it analyses it in a manner which prevents it from coming to grips with historical developments. Bourgeois theory is concerned with the puzzle of whether a monetary economy is different from a barter economy. It faces the problem by supposing that the barter economy consists of profit and utility-maximising individuals and firms, and that exchange is so generalised that all goods are produced for the market. There is even a 'market for labour' so that wages are paid and a 'market for the services of machines' so that profit is received (as a reward for the ownership of machines). This is compared with a model of a monetary economy where exchange between maximising agents is equally general, but where money acts as a medium of exchange. It is easy to show that the existence of money facilitates exchange at a lower cost than is possible under barter. In both old discursive and modern mathematical writings it often comes down to the idea that under barter the exchange of one commodity for another requires a search for an individual willing not only to sell what you want to buy, but also to buy what you want to sell. This problem may be reduced under barter by the establishment of shops specialising in the purchase and sale of particular commodities, but these shops are themselves costly to run. Under a monetary economy, by contrast, trade requires the agreement of two parties concerning only *one* commodity at a time since sellers are always (and only) willing to accept money in exchange. The difficulty of, and the costs involved in, searching for other agents willing to carry out exchange are therefore reduced; alternatively, fewer specialised shops are required since a shop which specialises in selling, say, apples is always ready to receive money for them whereas under barter there is one specialist in selling apples for shoes, another selling apples for bread and so on. An extension of the conclusion that a system of monetary exchange is less costly for society than a barter system yields an explanation of how a particular commodity such as gold comes to be differentiated from others and used as money, a medium of exchange. For it is argued that, under barter, exchanges become increasingly indirect: an agent who wishes to sell apples and buy shoes will have an incentive to sell the apples for an intermediary commodity and then sell the intermediary for shoes. Some commodity such as gold comes to be used increasingly as an intermediary because it is cheap to store, transport and exchange and because its quality is known with relative certainty. As such indirect exchanges become universal a monetary economy develops from barter.

Compare that bourgeois conception with the theory of money implied by the Marxist theory of capitalism. The bourgeois conception gives us a comparison between money as such and barter, with the idea that both the monetary economy and the barter that supposedly preceded it are based on universal exchange. The Marxist approach also sees universal exchange as one basis of money as such, *but* it denies that this system emerged out of a barter system which itself involved universal exchange. Instead, it emerged from a system where goods were not produced for exchange. To be more specific, capitalism is a system where all goods are produced for exchange and where even people's work is only possible through exchange – through them selling for a wage their ability to work. In this system, money as such exists and so does money as capital. What preceded the transition to capitalism (at least in Western Europe) was feudalism. It was not a system where a mass of individuals produced goods for exchange and carried out their trades by scurrying around looking for partners willing to barter. And it was most certainly not a system whose essential feature was that individuals were hired for wages so there was no 'labour market'; equally there was no market for the services of machinery and tools, for the means of production were owned by the direct producers themselves. Under feudalism goods were produced for the use of the producer and for the non-working classes (the landed aristocracy and related groups). The latter obtained their share of production not through buying and selling and receiving profits but through more direct methods to ensure the extraction of rent payments. Money did exist under feudalism but its role was peripheral until almost the end of that system. Thus, for Marxism, the question of the emergence of a monetary economy – an economy where money is central – is the question of the emergence of capitalism; it is the problem of how a system of universal exchange emerges from one where exchange was peripheral. And this is a question of class conflict, a question of how peasants were forced off their land and forced to seek work for wages in the factories owned by the developing class of capitalists. It is not a question of individuals, already engaged in exchange, buying and selling goods and working for wages, deciding that indirect exchange is less costly than barter.

The Marxist critique of the bourgeois comparison between monetary exchange and barter is illuminating. We have already seen that orthodox economics is restricted to the analysis of money as such, and is unable to consider the role of money as capital under capitalism. Now we see that it even fails to understand money as such for it fails to understand that monetary exchange is the only form of universal exchange and the latter is historically specific to capitalism. Barter capitalism is a myth of orthodox economics. The corollary is that money as such can only reach its full development when capital exists; money as such can only be understood, therefore, if it is understood in its relationship to money as capital. When money acts as money as such in the occasional exchanges which occur under feudalism it and the exchange relationship differ from money as such under capitalism for there it is a fundamental aspect of the economy.

To conclude this consideration of the orthodox 'money and barter' problem, it is interesting to note another way of presenting the above argument. Under feudalism labour's primary dimension is a specific type of labour (a cobbler is distinct from a blacksmith) and its product was produced for its specific usefulness (as a shoe or plough). Under capitalism labour's most important aspect is its undifferentiated nature. A worker in a car factory is not employed for his specific car-making skills but for his work in general (work which could equally well be performed in another industry) – his 'abstract labour'. And the car which he produces is not produced directly because it is useful but because the firm can sell it and make profit. Thus, under capitalism commodities have a common characteristic in that they are produced for exchange and that the labour which produces them is 'abstract' in the sense that its important aspect is its universality. This sharply distinguishes capitalism from pre-capitalist systems. It also corresponds to the role of money as such under capitalism. For under capitalism money as such is a medium of exchange *because* it is universal, because when a commodity is sold for money it is exchanged for something which is universal and exchangeable for all commodities. Money enables commodities' common characteristic of exchangeability to predominate over their specific usefulness. But commodities can only be generally exchanged for this universal equivalent, their exchangeability can only come to the fore, because there is already something universal which is inherent in commodities produced under capitalism; it is the universal, abstract (non-specific) labour which goes into producing them. Since this non-specific nature of labour is what distinguishes capitalism from pre-capitalist systems, the full development of money as such can only be understood in its relation to capital (and, thus, money as capital). In consequence orthodox economics is unable to develop that understanding since it has no concept of capital or money capital. Its failure on this score is illustrated by the fact that orthodox economics takes money as such and the medium of exchange function of money as its starting-point, whereas Marxist economics sees the existence of generalised monetary exchange as itself dependent upon the existence of abstract labour.

3 CONCLUSION

The examples we have considered make clear that the Marxist theory of money is quite different from others in that it is able to formulate and also go beyond the theory of *money as such,* and it constructs a theory based on *money as capital.* It is a theory developed in the light of capitalist economic relations: it enables us to go beyond the idea of individuals' behaviour to the idea of a distinction between capital and labour in their relations to money and credit. Orthodox economics, too, can make a distinction between individual agents and it does offer us a theory of firms' demand for money distinct from the theory of households'. But within orthodox economics the distinction is arbitrary; it is not the same as the Marxist distinction between workers and capitalists because the latter is based on the different relations of the classes to capital. In the Marxist conception the monetary aspect of their lives is a product of those relations and it cannot be treated as the outcome of different demands for money.

In this chapter we have considered money's role in the *capitalist* economy. From what has been said it is easy to see the fallacy in one utopian view, the idea that money is the 'root of all evil' and that its abolition is the precondition for the abolition of capitalism. Under capitalism it is not money as such which determines economic events, nor is it money as capital, it is the existence of capital itself and money as capital is merely one of the forms which capital takes. The construction of socialism, therefore, involves the abolition of capital and of money as capital; it does not necessarily involve the abolition of money, but does involve its transformation. This conclusion gives an insight into the function that monetary theory has within bourgeois ideology. Limiting itself to the analysis of money as such, and without even understanding how money as such itself has a different significance under feudalism, capitalism and other systems, orthodox monetary theory is not able to compare money under capitalism (money as capital) with socialist or pre-capitalist monetary arrangements. Instead, it is constantly making comparisons between money as such and non-money, putting monetary exchange against a mythical barter economy, and it is thereby able to demonstrate the superiority of money (because of the way in which it facilitates exchanges) without once having to cast a shadow by noting that money *as capital* bears all the stigmata of capital in general plus a few more tricks of its own.

NOTE

The references to Tobin and Friedman relate to J. Tobin, 'Friedman's Theoretical Framework', and M. Friedman, 'Comments on the Critics', both published in *Journal of Political Economy*, **80** (1972). The idea that Monetarism is based on the postulate of an interest-inelastic demand for money (vertical *LM* curve) gained currency largely as a result of Friedman's article, 'The Demand for Money: Some Theoretical and Empirical Results', *Journal of Political Economy*, **69**, 327–57 (1959), where he claims to find that observable interest rates have little or no effect on the demand for money. His claim, however, is rejected by all other Monetarists and is now not emphasised by Friedman himself. See D. Laidler, *The Demand for Money*, for a discussion of this.

FURTHER READING

A good orthodox textbook which explains the theory's reliance on the individual's demand function for money and which touches on the Monetarist debate is: D. Laidler (1969) *The Demand for Money* (Scranton, Penn.: International Textbook Co.).

One which gives an antagonistic summary of the Monetarist argument against fiscal policy is: V. Chick (1973) *The Theory of Monetary Policy* (London: Gray–Mills), while F. Modigliani (1977) 'The Monetarist Controversy or Should We Forsake Stabilization Policies', *American Economic Review*, **67** (Mar 1977) 1–19, surveys the whole Monetarist debate.

T. M. Havrilesky and J. T. Boorman (eds) (1976) *Current Issues in Monetary Theory and Policy* (Arlington Heights, Illinois: A.H.M. Publishers) is a collection of easily read articles many of which are on the Monetarist controversy. An orthodox appraisal of the Monetarist theory that changes in the money supply caused the 1930s depression is found in P. Temin (1976) *Did Monetary Forces Cause the Great Depression?* (New York: Norton).

For a presentation of one version of orthodox theory's 'credit theory' alternative see R. S. Sayers (1960) 'Monetary Thought and Monetary Policy in England', *Economic Journal*, **70** (1960) 710–24.

One introduction to the Marxist theory of money is H. Ergas and D. Fishman (1975) 'The Marxian Theory of Money and the Crisis of Capital', *Bulletin of the Conference of Socialist Economists*, 4, II (June 1975). Another, which is not at all easy to read, is: S. de Brunhoff (1976) *Marx on Money* (New York: Urizen).

Both differ in significant ways from the interpretation presented here.

The Marxist concept of credit is discussed in L. Harris (1976) 'On Interest, Credit, and Capital', *Economy and Society*, 5, no. 2 (May 1976), and the circuit of capital is elaborated in B. Fine (1975) 'The Circulation of Capital, Ideology, and Crisis', *Bulletin of the Conference of Socialist Economists*, 4, 12 (Oct 1975).

Finally, B. Fine and L. Harris (1979) *Rereading 'Capital'* (London: Macmillan) discuss the circuit of capital (chap 1), the development of the capitalist credit system (chap 7) and the relationship between money, inflation and the business cycle (chap 8).

CHAPTER 6

Growth and Reproduction

Sue Himmelweit

This chapter will look at a method by which orthodox economics tries to theorise historical change. It will not survey all orthodox theories which incorporate changes through time; for example the vast area of development economics will not be touched, nor will Keynesian short-run macro-dynamics. Instead, I shall concentrate on neoclassical growth models and only on the most basic of these, because it is with these models that orthodox economics tries to use its *own* methods to talk about change in the purest way. These methods can be summed up in the two words: individualism and equilibrium. Other parts of the attempts of orthodox economics to theorise historical change either do not hold to both these methodological postulates in their entirety or add something else to them. Thus Keynesian macro-dynamics does not fully hold to individualism; it allows statements about the movement of macro-aggregates without necessarily making explicit the individual behaviour that underlies the movement of the aggregates.[1] And development theories are eclectic, adding bits from a massive variety of disciplines; in no sense can the field, or rather fields, of development economics be located purely within mainstream orthodox theory.

In a chapter in an earlier book,[2] I talked about individualism; in this one I will concentrate on equilibrium. While this chapter should be relatively self-contained, reading that other chapter would be helpful because it does point to why exploring change is central to any critique of orthodox theory. In this chapter I will use this centrality of questions of change in the following way. The first section will discuss the orthodox method of equilibrium analysis in general and will look at the justifications orthodox theory gives for its use. I will then go on, in the second section, to show how this method is applied when theorising 'change' to create growth models and evaluate its success in this field. The final section will show how an alternative systematic approach to that of equilibrium analysis can get to grips with more substantial concepts of change when not bound by the necessity of explaining everything in equilibrium terms.

1   THE METHOD OF EQUILIBRIUM ANALYSIS

Equilibrium analysis is the theorisation of a system of variables by the specification of conditions such that the values of the variables can be simultaneously determined when all the stated conditions are satisfied. For example, equilibrium in the market for one commodity is specified by the condition that supply and demand are equal; more complicated types of equilibrium can be specified by requiring more such conditions to be satisfied.

This is what a mere formal description of equilibrium analysis tells us; the content lies in the definition of the *conditions* to be satisfied, and the *interpretation* to be given to these conditions. In general, though this is not definitionally required, the conditions will be able to be specified as equations which allow of an interpretation as the balancing of two sets of forces. In the example of market equilibrium for one commodity, the condition can be interpreted as the balancing of supply and demand for the commodity. When these two forces are unequal the variables of the system (in this case the price and quantity exchanged of the commodity) will not be fixed: only when supply equals demand do the conditions specify what the (equilibrium) price and quantity will be.

This is all equilibrium analysis claims to do. Why then does it play such an important role in orthodox economic theory, and what are the reasons that justify its use? One answer is that it is just a first step; formulating questions and answering them in an equilibrium framework may be relatively easy yet may point to how the analysis may be taken further. And this indeed is what has happened. The history of economic thought is littered with examples of previous relatively simple formulations being replaced by more complex models as the subject grew and what was previously taken to be *ceteris* no longer assumed to be *paribus*. Ricardo's consideration of the effects of variations in the durabilities of capital on the value of commodities, through Walras's extension of the analysis of the forces of supply and demand to encompass his conception of the economic system as a whole in general equilibrium analysis, to most recent attempts to analyse the behaviour of individuals faced by uncertain prices and constrained by liquidity before income, all provide examples of how economic theory has rejected its own previous conditions of equilibrium and has extended its analysis to previously untheorised areas. Nevertheless, very little of this extension has been outside the equilibrium framework. The introduction of heterogeneity to exogenous variables previously considered to be homogeneous, such as Ricardo's durabilities of capital, changes the results but not the methods of previous analysis. The extension from partial to general equilibrium analysis *à la* Walras makes previously exogenous variables endogenous (prices of all commodities are to be determined simultaneously rather than the price of one to be considered an exogenous variable in determining that of another) but again does not change the method. And even modern 'disequilibrium economics' uses equilibrium methods but requiring different forces to be balanced, e.g. supply to equal effective demand rather than notional (planned) demand.

So, although it is a perfectly respectable reason to do equilibrium analysis because it is easy as a first step and leads on to other things, these other things turn out not to be so different after all; that is, they are not outside the basic equilibrium framework. So the respectable reason is in fact only an internal reason; it explains why certain questions are looked at within equilibrium analysis before others: it will not do as a reason for the concentration on equilibrium analysis altogether.

To the extent that orthodox theory makes clear its epistemology it displays a vague commitment to empiricism. That is to say it is supposed to be developed in such a way that the results it comes up with can be rejected by comparison with observed facts. Any part of theory which has not been so rejected can stand; the body of economic theory consists of all such not yet rejected parts. This is not the place to go into the criticisms of this methodology as an ideal practice, nor into whether orthodox theory indeed lives up to this ideal (for this see Chapter 2). But from within orthodox theory empiricism gives us an answer as to why, and indeed which, equilibrium states should be studied; we should study those and only those whose conditions correspond to the observed facts. Thus, for example, the concentration on equilibrium conditions in the study of commodity markets can be justified by pointing out that (at least some) markets do clear.

But though reference to the world of empirical facts is sometimes made to justify certain theories, mainstrain economists often prefer to produce their justifications from inside the theory itself. (Note that such an internal justification can never, for an empiricist, be a substitute for correspondence with the facts. Orthodox economists' preference for purely theoretical validation must be seen as demonstration of their lack of wholehearted commitment to empiricism. In attempting to copy the natural sciences, orthodox economics has shown a preference for the former's mathematical systematisation over its empirical methods.) Now, since the definition of an equilibrium, is simply the statement of certain conditions to be fulfilled at that equilibrium, such a statement cannot in itself give any theoretical reason as to *why* those conditions should be fulfilled. So any such reason must come from more than mere consideration of the equilibrium state itself. This can be done by consideration of what happens when the system is not in equilibrium. Which way do the variables more? Or, if we think of equilibrium in terms of the balancing of forces, what happens when the forces do not balance? To answer these questions, we need more theory, theory about what happens out of equilibrium. If this theory tells us that when the system is out of equilibrium it will move towards an equilibrium then this equilibrium is called a *stable* one. To have a theory within which equilibrium is stable is sufficient reason for studying that equilibrium. For the stability of the equilibrium means that if the conditions for equilibrium do not hold at any point in time they will eventually; the system is always either in or moving towards equilibrium.

There is a third possible explanation of why orthodox economics concentrates on equilibria. This explanation is not a justification that orthodox economists themselves could use; rather it is a way that by standing outside the theory we can explain why it takes the form it does. That is, it is an explanation of economic theory as ideology, ideology whose function is to explain the current economic system as natural and inevitable. This means that it will not look for explanations of how capitalism is transformed into some other economic and political system, but rather for reasons why it will not change structurally. The concepts of equilibrium and stability are clearly very useful in this task; indeed, it is difficult to see how theory which eternised the *status quo* could be developed without them. Because chapter 9 of this book deals with the ideological status of orthodox economics I shall not say much more about this aspect in Section 2, concentrating instead on the validity of the orthodox justifications by stability or empirical accuracy of equilibrium-based growth models.

2 EQUILIBRIUM AND GROWTH MODELS: STEADY-STATE GROWTH

The method of equilibrium analysis, the specification of equilibrium states and the investigation of the conditions of their stability, would appear to be suitable to deal with only static questions and the explanation of the magnitude of variables that are constant. In essence this is correct, most of equilibrium analysis is concerned with the derivation of such quantities as the level of GNP, the level of demand for a certain commodity or the share of profits in national income not as changing quantities, but as fixed magnitudes dependent on the magnitude of other exogenous variables (called 'parameters'). Nevertheless the method can be and is applied to what are essentially dynamic questions; questions such as: How does GNP grow?, What is the rate of increase of the demand for a certain commodity? and How does the share of profits in national income change through time?

How is that possible? How is it possible to theorise dynamic variables using an inherently static method, one which is concerned to find states in which variables do *not* change rather than talk about how they do? The way that orthodox economics overcomes this limitation of equilibrium analysis is to restrict the range of questions that it can ask about dynamic variables to ones that can be answered by saying that although the magnitude of the variable itself is changing its rate of growth is constant. It can then use its static method concerned with the nature and properties of equilibrium on the rates of growth of variables rather than the variables themselves. The method it uses is no more dynamic than formerly, it is just that the variables that are to be unchanging in an equilibrium state are now rates of growth rather than the absolute levels of GNP, demand or the capital – output ratio. The results of this method are called 'steady-state growth paths', the method itself 'equilibrium dynamics'. And just as constant equilibrium values can be compared by comparative statics, so comparative dynamics compares steady-state growth paths. The terminology that orthodox economics uses here is commendably accurate, qualifying the use of the word 'dynamic' to show its restricted context.

This rules out of consideration changes in certain variables, for example one of the examples given above, the share of profits in national income. The share of profits in national income is a proportion: its value must therefore lie between zero and one. Now a variable that has a constant rate of growth grows exponentially; that is, in proportion to the magnitude of the variable itself and so will increase faster and faster (Positive rate of growth) or decrease slower and slower (negative rate of growth) or not change at all (zero rate of growth). Now the only one of those things that a proportion can do is to stay constant, for if it were to increase faster and faster it would eventually become greater than one, while if it were to decrease the remaining proportion (in this case the share of non-profit income in total national income) would grow and would have to grow exponentially to satisfy equilibrium conditions, thus eventually becoming greater than one. Since a proportion cannot be greater than one, we have to rule out both of these possibilities forcing us into the position that the only allowable rate of growth within a steady-state model for any proportion which represents a share is zero; that is, no change at all.

So the restriction of only considering equilibrium states, where equilibrium here means constancy of rates of growth of variables, is not just a quantitative approximation, it actually restricts qualitatively the types of change that can be considered. This is not a trivial point. It is well recognised by orthodox economists and their critics alike. Why then are steady-state growth models the foundation of all modern orthodox growth theory?

As we saw in the previous section, one possible answer to this question, at any point in time, is simply that we are still on the first step, we cannot investigate disequilibrium without knowing about equilibrium first. And it is true that the mathematics of models in which at least the rates of change of variables are constant is easier than those of models in which rates of change themselves can change. Indeed the mathematics of the latter is in some cases not only difficult but incapable of analytic solution. In others, the difficulty renders it a subject for the high theorists but not for the ordinary economist, student or policy-maker. But that, as we saw, cannot be an eternal justification for the continued use of these models. The two acceptable justifications for orthodox economics are either the stability of the growth paths or their empirical validity. Either justification clearly begs the other question; given the correctness of the theory, if steady-state growth paths are stable, they must be what we observe and, if they are what we observe in general, we must have some stability argument to explain their ubiquity. Theorists have differed in which they have taken as the reason and which as the question. Before we turn to these distinctions let us first take the common ground and examine what are the assumptions necessary within orthodoxy for a steady-state growth path to result.

THE CONDITIONS FOR STEADY-STATE GROWTH

Two early papers which looked at this question were the famous ones of Harrod and Domar,[3] which have been fused together (though they were actually very different) in the popular view of the history of economic thought into the 'Harrod–Domar model'. The answer of this model to the question, 'Under what circumstances will an economy follow a steady-state growth path?' is straightforward: 'Only if $s = vn$'; that is, only if the saving rate is equal to the product of the capital/output ratio and the rate of growth of the labour-force. On the assumption of a fixed technology, and bearing in mind that if the ratio of two variables is fixed those two variables must grow at the same rate, it is easy to see why this condition must hold. For we then have a constant capital/labour ratio and so capital stock and the labour-force must grow at the same rate because otherwise one or other factor would be unemployed and our stationary state would then not be an equilibrium. Now the rate of growth of capital stock is given by investment (i.e. savings since we are in equilibrium) as a proportion of existing capital stock. But s, the savings ratio, is savings as a proportion of output, so we only have to divide it by the capital/output ratio v to give us the rate of growth of capital stock. And this growth rate as we have seen must equal that of the labour-force for our steady-state conditions to be fulfilled. So we must have $s/v = n$, giving us immediately the condition we stated above, $s = vn$.

Now there are certain things to note about this condition. First, if it is satisfied not only are all variables either constant or growing at a constant rate, but those that are growing are all growing at the same rate. We saw above how the constancy of the capital/labour ratio implied that the capital stock and the labour-force had to grow at the same rate; the same assumption of a fixed technology which gave us the constant capital/labour ratio, gives us constant capital/output and labour/output ratios and so implies that output is growing at this time rate too. And the constancy of the savings ratio, means that this growing output results in savings and investment growing at this constant rate too. So we have divided the variables of our model into two sets: those that are growing at the same constant rate, which are, labour-force, capital stock, output, savings and investment; and those which are constant, which are, the rates of change of the growing variables, the savings ratio, and the technological ratios relating output, capital stock and the labour-force.

This is one feature of this model which it is important to note when we come to look at the question of its empirical justification. It is not, however, a universal feature of equilibrium dynamics. More complicated models can be built in which variables grow at different rates. There are, however, still necessary relations between these rates. For example, if we allow for technological improvement such that the amount produced by each worker (the output/labour ratio for productivity) grows, the requirement for a steady-state growth path becomes $s/v = n + t$, where t is the rate of growth of productivity. But technical progress does not necessarily only change productivity; it can also change the capital/output ratio. In the latter event steady-state growth paths do not exist[4]. But if the capital/output ratio remains constant the results are modified. The rates of growth that are now equal are those of output, capital stock, savings and investment, and all of these are equal to the sum of the rates of growth of the labour-force and productivity. So while we should not see all the specific requirements of the Harrod–Domar model as necessary to all steady-state growth paths, we must recognise the general type of requirement on growth rates and the restriction of the applicability of the whole class of models to worlds in which certain sorts of variations just do not happen.

There is, however, one feature of the Harrod–Domar model which does carry through to its more complicated generalisations. This is the famous 'knife-edge' problem which Harrod introduced in his original article. Strictly this is not a problem for neoclassical growth models in their own terms, where savings and investment are automatically equal. But once one considers the adjustment of investment to capitalist expectations, under one set of plausible behavioural assumptions, instability immediately arises.

To see this, let us call s/v the 'warranted rate of growth'. This is the rate of growth that the technology, giving v, and savings behaviour of the population, giving *s*, requires. The problem is getting investors' behaviour to fit in with this. Now, making the Keynesian assumption that capitalists' expectations are determinant, the higher investors think the rate of growth is going to be the more they will invest and therefore the higher will be the actual rate of growth. Harrod shows that if investors' expectations are of a rate of growth higher than the warranted rate the effect of these high expectations will be to create a rate of growth yet higher than that which they expected. So the investors who expected too much will *think* that they expected too little. Similarly, if they anticipate a growth rate lower than the warranted rate of growth, the actual rate of growth will fall short of their expectations, and so the investors will *think* that they expected too much rather than too little. So assuming investors act on their 'corrected' expectations they will exacerbate the situation. For if planned investment was higher than that 'warranted' by savings before, planned investment will then become higher and diverge yet more from savings. So once off the steady-state path, Harrod's argument is that the economy moves further and further away from it. The steady-state growth path is therefore unstable if investors behave in this way.

This instability is potentially there in any neoclassical growth model; that is, in any growth model that does not take explicit account of the different mechanisms that determine savings and investment. This means that some *ad hoc* assumption has to be brought in, for example that government intervention ensures that planned savings equal planned investment. That is, the government has to ensure that investors are never wrong, for if they were they would render the stationary-state model irrelevant. One of the most prolific of growth theorists put this *ad hoc* assumption as 'either that the authorities have read the *General Theory* or that they are socialists who don't need to'.[5] Alternatively, a retreat can be made, and it can be admitted that all steady-state growth models can do is trace out full-employment growth paths.

This retreat just leads us back into another area of orthodox theory, the haven for those theorists who do not claim any causal validity for their models. They do not claim that steady-state growth tells us anything about what actually happens but rather that they are descriptions of the consequences over time of the maintainence of full-employment and the fixing of certain exogenous variables (presumably by the government). In that sense, they would claim that growth theory is a part of normative rather than positive economics. Such theorists are always safe from logical inconsistencies in their own arguments. Nevertheless, their continued acceptance as 'economists' rather than 'storytellers' depends on the existence of other, far larger school of economists, the school which justifies its use of equilibrium methods by the belief that they tell us more about how the world is than how it is not.

By considering problems like this, which result from the instability of capitalists' expectations, we are straying from the world of neoclassical equilibrium dynamics into that of Keynesian short-run macrodynamics. As noted in the Introduction, while the latter is an important area of modern economics it is not purely based on individualism and equilibrium analysis and therefore its criticisms of steady-state growth models are not central to the theme of this chapter. It is to the criticisms that come from inside neoclassical theory and to the responses to them that we now turn.

JUSTIFICATION BY STABILITY

For equilibrium economists, as we saw in an earlier section, the only ultimate *theoretical* justification for studying equilibrium states is that they can be shown to be stable. But our steady-state growth model has required the fulfilment of a condition $s/v = n$ which we have, as yet, no reason to assume will be fulfilled. If the variables involved in the equation are naturally (n), or technologically (v) or behaviourally (s) given, then if the warranted rate of growth, s/v, equals the natural rate, n,[6] it is only by fluke. But then steady-state growth would be a rare occurrence, not justifying the expenditure of thought, paper and ink that its study has generated.

Orthodox economics reacted very well to this criticism. It disclaimed its constants, one by one, and made them variables. It found equilibrating mechanisms for each in turn and discussed the relative merits of each. To let the rate of population be the dependent variable would have been the solution of classical economics.[7] If the rate of population growth is below the warranted rate of growth, a labour shortage will arise, wages will rise, more of the children of the working class will survive and so the rate of growth of population will rise. Conversely too high a rate of population growth relative to the warranted rate of growth will cause unemployment, low wages and a high death-rate in the working class. Modern orthodoxy prefers, quite appropriately, equilibrating mechanisms that work faster than can adjustments in the population size.

One of the other possibilities is to let the savings ratio do the equili-brating. This is the argument of some of the non-neoclassical orthodox economists concentrated on Cambridge. They argue in different forms that the working class and the capitalist class can be distinguished by their savings behaviour; workers have a lower average propensity to save than capitalists and that the average propensity to consume of the economy as a whole is therefore a weighted average of those of the two classes taken separately. Propensities to save are ratios of income and therefore the weights used to calculate this average must be the share of each class in total national income. Now let us suppose that the warranted rate of growth is above that of the natural rate; as we have seen above this means that labour is in short supply, real wages rise and the share of wages in national income should rise while that of profits should fail. This means that the weights used to average the workers' and the capitalists' average propensities to save shift more towards the workers'. So the overall average propensity to save, the savings rate s, becomes more like the workers' propensity to save and less like the capitalists'; that is, it becomes lower. So by this mechanism a warranted rate of growth higher than the natural rate results in s being lowered, and a converse argument would show that if the warr-anted rate of growth were higher than the natural rate, then the savings rate would rise. But these changes in the savings-rate change the war-ranted rate of growth and change it in the required direction. When the warranted rate of growth is too high it is lowered, and vice versa. So provided nv does lie somewhere between the capitalists' and the workers' savings ratio, we have here another stabilising mechanism that can explain how the conditions for steady-state growth can obtain other than by pure chance.

But even this stabilising mechanism is not that preferred by main-stream orthodox economists, the neoclassicals, who prefer to introduce their favourite tool, the neoclassical aggregate production function. In this way they let the capital/output ratio be the equilibrating variable. Too high a warranted rate of growth increases wages and causes a shift to more capital intensive production methods thus lowering v and the warranted rate of growth. Conversely a warranted rate of growth lower than the natural rate is raised by a decrease in capital intensity.

Now much of neoclassical growth theory is concerned with the implications of the relaxation of the requirement of a constant capital/output ratio – more and more complicated models can be built by allowing different types of production functions. We shall not be concerned with these here; what is more interesting is the general structure of the theory of steady-state models that has been developed. We can summarise it in the following recipe:

1. Specify what is meant by equilibrium, i.e. which variables are to be constant. (In growth models, as we have seen, this means deciding which variables are to have constant rates of growth and which are to be themselves constant; in other words, which rates of growth are to be constant and which are to be zero. As we have seen, the nature of some variables rules out their being allowed to change at all in any situation that could possibly be described as an equilibrium.)
2. Work out what the conditions on other variables (parameters) for this equilibrium are.
3. Find an explanation as to why those conditions should be satisfied by turning one or more parameters from exogenous variables into endogenous ones.

Contrast this with the justification of the use of equilibrium models by their stability that was outlined in the previous section. There when theory gave us stable equilibria such equilibria were worth study because, *by the theory*, the states they represented were ones into which the system represented by the theory tended. But the development of theory that we have analysed above points in quite the opposite direction. It is not that those equilibria are studied which can be shown to be stable; rather, having specified the equilibrium path to be of interest, theory is adjusted in order that the equilibrium be stable.

Such adjustments to theory, of course, are not purely Machiavellian. Indeed, if we were to accept the empirical justification for the use of equilibrium analysis, rather than that above we would indeed require of our theory that it show why equilibria persist. So while the criticism of this section shows that orthodox economics cannot claim that its practice has lived up to its purpose if that purpose was to give *a priori* theoretical justification for the use of steady-state models, it does not rule out the possibility of empirical justification. It is to this possibility that we now turn.

EMPIRICAL JUSTIFICATION

Some orthodox economists do indeed claim that the growth paths of real economies display the characteristics of steady-state models.

Following Kaldor, the economist talks about 'stylised facts', things which are broadly supposed to be true of all advanced industrial economies. These stylised facts can be summed up as follows:

(I am giving Solow's version here,[8] there are many others)

1. Real output per man has a constant rate of growth.
2. The stock of capital has a constant rate of growth.
3. Real output has a constant rate of growth equal to that of the stock of capital.
4. The rate of profit on capital is constant.
5. The rate of growth of output per man can vary from country to country.
6. Across countries, higher share of profit in income go with higher ratios of investment to ouput.

Before we examine what is meant by calling these statements stylised facts, let us recall from our initial discussion of the Harrod–Domar model that allowing real output per man to grow as in (1) and (5) above is not a major modification of the basic model. Now from this modification, the first four stylised facts are exactly what a steady-state model would have told us; some variables are growing at one rate and some are constant and which ones are doing which is just as we would have predicted. The last two stylised facts simply point out that the class of steady-state models as a whole is useful because economies are on different such growth paths and that within this range growth paths can be ordered in the way that the models predict.

Now let us examine to what extent these stylised facts are 'facts'. To what extent can orthodox theory justify its concentration on steady-state growth on empirical grounds? I shall examine the two most central of the stylised facts; 'fact' 3 that real output and the stock of capital grow at the same constant rate of growth and 'fact' 4 that the rate of profit on capital is constant. These are central facts in that given the assumptions of the model they are sufficient to specify that the growth path is a steady-state one. If one looks at a study like that of E. F. Denison's *Why Growth Rates Differ*[9] for the period 1950–62, we find that in some countries (the United States, Denmark, Norway and the United Kingdom) the capital/output ratio has been rising; that is, capital stock has been growing at a faster rate than output, while in others (Belgium, France, Germany and Italy) output has had a higher growth rate than capital stock. As far as the rate of profit goes, those countries whose capital/output ratio had been rising as well as the Netherlands (which was the only country surveyed whose capital/output ratio remained relatively static) showed a falling trend in their rates of profit. In other countries there was no clear evidence about tendencies in the rate of profit in that period. We do not here have to take any position as to whether this 'evidence' supports or refutes the stylised facts. We can, however, note with some amazement that it has been used by some (e.g. Solow[10]) to argue that not only does it provide a justification for *interest* in steady-state models, but indeed imposes the *requirement* that any realistic model must explain the stylised facts.

Denison's study did not take a long enough period to be able to examine the basis postulate of steady-state growth, that growth rates *over time* are constant. Feinstein's studies[11] of the U.K. economy find a rising capital/output ration from 1856 to 1899 and from 1924 to 1937, a falling one in between and a roughly constant one since the Second World War. This certainly means that not both output and capital stock can have been growing at steady rates; that is, that the most we can say is that growth rates may have been stable within certain periods, but they have varied considerably over the past century. Similarly with the rate of profit, it was probably rising during those periods when the capital/output was falling, falling slightly perhaps in between and certainly in the later part of the post-war period. Again, constancy is only within certain periods not overall.

This means that however good a representation the steady-state model may be of growth paths within such periods it does not constitute a complete theory. For if we were to have such a complete theory it would not only say something about what happened within these periods but also about what determined what those periods were. That is, it would explain the *structural* changes that lead to the economy shifting from one growth path to another.

But equilibrium analysis cannot do this. Its content is the explanation of how things stay the same rather than how they change. The ideological importance of this aspect was indicated by the way that when stability as an attribute of the steady-state models could not be demonstrated it was constructed. A steady-state growth path is not one that ends in disaster for capitalism; it is not even one that brings it into question. It displays capitalism as a smoothly running system to which crises if they occur are but accidental jolts to the system which has no *inherent* reason not to be stable and smooth-running.[12] Any political questions are thereby reduced to the choice of *which* steady-state growth path the economy should follow: a restriction of options indeed.

3 THE MARXIST ALTERNATIVE

By contrast, Marxism is primarily concerned with the transformation of economic systems into one another. But in order to do so it has to be able to characterise what can be meant by 'structural change'. It has to be able to say which features are fundamental and which can be expected to change without undermining the whole structure of society. Another way of phrasing this whole question is to ask for a method by which to periodise history. For to divide history into periods is to state which changes are to be considered fundamental; those are changes in those features that distinguish one period from another. Changes that do not affect the determinants of the periodisation are those that do not in themselves undermine society. Orthodox theory does not consider the question of periodisation, because it does not consider capitalism as a system in the process of change into something else. The changes that it does look at are precisely those that would be considered non-fundamental in the Marxist periodisation.

Marxists recognise the conditions under which people live as the most important elements in determining their history. Thus history can be periodised by the material conditions under which people in a particular epoch live out their lives. This means looking at how people live, eat, produce and have children. The interesting question is not whether these things go on but *how*. To carry out these 'relations with nature' people set up relations with each other; these social relations are the determining force of history. These 'relations with nature' indeed become completely encompassed within the social form under which they take place (the relations between people). Marxism denies any validity to theories based on 'human nature' instead social relations form the basis of its theory of history. They are not simple to study because they are continually in a state of change and forcing further change (another way to put this is that they are contradictory), but they are the basis of our characterisation of any society. Because these social relations are continually changing, any society therefore is in a state of transition, it is in the process of becoming another type of society.

Now again this is very different from orthodox theory, which instead of trying to capture how society is changing captures just how it is staying the same – that as we saw is precisely what equilibrium analysis is all about. So, not surprisingly, both the methods used and the questions asked by Marxists are different from those of orthodox economics.

In order to characterise an epoch of history, we must specify the material relations of that epoch. This means specifying how production is carried on, but not only that, also how the existing production relations both do and do not re-create the conditions for their own continuation. That is, in what ways they are also relations of *reproduction,* and in what ways such relations are contradictory. In the remainder of this chapter I will attempt to do this for capitalist production relations and show why this constitutes the basis for an alternative theory of growth; a theory which is based on a recognition of the fundamental types of change that must be theorised and not on any attempt to trivialise any potential change into the sort that can be incorporated into an equilibrium framework.

CAPITALIST PRODUCTION

The fundamental production relation of capitalism is the relation between capital and labour. Capitalist society is a commodity-producing society; that is, all production is of things for sale. Now this is clearly not true of all societies, in many economies peasants have and still do produce most of their own subsistence requirements, without any need for the intervention of the market. Indeed, it is not even completely true of capitalist societies; certain production does go on that is not the production of commodities, for example housework or much labour employed by the state. We will return to these other contemporary forms of production later, the relevant point here is that these other forms of production are not necessary to our specification of the basic capital/labour relation. Indeed we shall be able to show why they are necessitated by the contradictions generated by the capital/labour relation. For this reason, following Marx's method of explaining rather than explaining away contradictions, we build up theory from basic abstractions, developing their implications in such a way as to get beyond them, rather than throwing in all at once everything that we wish to explain.

The abstraction that we start with now is that everything is produced as a commodity. This means that in order to live people have to sell things to get the money to buy their means of subsistence. Those people who do not own any means of production (tools, raw materials, land, etc.) are not in a position to make anything to sell. They therefore have to sell something which is not produced and, unless they happen to be the owners of some vast holding of natural resources which can be let or gradually sold off to keep body and soul together, this leaves them but one thing to sell – their ability to work, which Marx called their labour-power. This is what constitutes the working class in capitalist society, those who have nothing to sell but their labour-power. Those who purchase labour-power must be able to make some use of it; that is, they must be able to put the worker to work and to do this they must own, or be able to buy, the means of production. Those who have access to the means of production constitute the capitalist class. Our definitions of the two classes is by their relation to each other in production. The definitions are abstract ones, the people who fit within these categories are therefore just there at this abstract level of discussion as representatives or personifications of the relations of production.

To make this clearer, let us look at how the whole system works. We know why the worker has to sell his labour-power; he needs to in order to survive. The capitalist, however, is not purely philanthropic in purchasing it; he does so in order to make a profit. This profit, surplus-value, comes from the capitalist buying labour-power for less than the worker produces. This is not an unfair exchange, for labour-power is bought at its value; exploitation occurs in the process of production for it is there that the worker *produces* more than he is paid.[13] So the purpose for the capitalist is the expansion of the value that he owns, by continual increments of *surplus-value,* occurring through the worker continually producing more new value than he or she takes home in the form of wages.

But what appear as subjective motivations of the individual worker or capitalist are really the *raison d'être* of the whole system. Both worker and capitalist are representatives of the two sides of the capital – labour relation. To remain a worker, a worker must have the desire to eat and to remain a capitalist; a capitalist must have the desire to get richer, but whether or not an individual worker or capitalist continues to feel these desires does not alter the fundamental relation at all. Even though the relation can only exist in some personification or other, we can conceptually make a distinction between the people involved and the relation itself.

Having now this very abstract characterisation of how the system works, we can look at the basic question we saw that we had to ask about its growth and change. How do the relations of production reproduce themselves?

CAPITALIST REPRODUCTION

We can look at this question in three parts: the reproduction of the means of production, the reproduction of the producers, and the reproduction of the relations of production themselves. The last is both a part and the whole of the question of reproduction. We can rephrase the whole question as one of how the capitalist system reproduces itself, but since our characterisation of the system is by its relations of production this boils down to the same thing.

The reproduction of the means of production is important because they are clearly essential to the continuation of production. We know that because, in order to characterise the capitalist mode of production, we had to specify that the means of production were owned by a class other than the class which used them in production. This means that means of production are a necessary part of the capitalist production process. We therefore have to explain how they are reproduced. Sticking to our very abstract level at which all we have specified is the capital/labour relation, we can still get quite far in explaining how the means of production are reproduced. The answer is quite simple; since all products are commodities and means of production must have been previously products themselves, the means of production by workers for the capitalists as commodities. Another way to put this is that a portion of the commodities produced ends up being consumed in production as means of production (as opposed to being consumed individually in personal consumption).

The reproduction of the producers is not quite so simple. The capitalist buys from the worker only that which is necessary to production; that is, the worker's labour-power. Now, to some extent, capitalist production relations reproduce the worker's labour-power. For the worker is paid a wage and his means of subsistence are produced as commodities under capitalist relations. So, as far as his day-to-day living requirements are concerned, all that is necessary is that these wages are exchanged for means of subsistence which are subsequently consumed by the worker. But while this process may, at this very abstract level, sufficiently explain the reproduction of one worker's labour-power it does not explain the reproduction of the working class as a whole. For this, as we shall see, we have to go beyond the capital/labour relation alone.

Finally, the relations of production themselves have to be reproduced. This means that we have to examine not only how the means of production and the producers are reproduced, but also how they are reproduced as part of capitalist production relations. This relates to the separation we made earlier on between the capital/labour relation itself and its personification in people who are capitalists or workers. What we are concerned with here is the reproduction of the relation itself. The worker as we have seen is paid wages which he spends on his subsistence; this reproduces his labour-power but it does more than that. It reproduces the worker in the same class position as he was before, with nothing to sell but his labour-power. Similarly, the capitalist is reproduced in his class position since he owns the commodities produced which he sells giving him sufficient money after paying for his personal consumption to be able to buy means of production and labour-power again. So not only are the worker and the capitalist reproduced, they are reproduced as *worker and capitalist.* And this is the crucial point, for it is in this way that the capitalist system both reproduces itself, as we have seen, and the conditions for its own downfall.

This is because the capital/labour relation, on which the system is based and which it reproduces so carefully, is an antagonistic relation. It is the relation around which class-struggle takes place. For the capitalist class extracts a surplus from the working class in the form of surplus-value (the difference between what the worker produces and what he is paid). It is over the terms of this surplus extraction and ultimately over its very existence that class-struggle takes place. The forms that the struggle takes and its outcome depend on the stage of development of the capitalist mode of production and of the two classes, but that it continues to exist is ensured by the reproduction of capitalist production relations.

To characterise the ways in which the class-struggle changes as capitalism develops, we have to examine how capitalist relations of production are developed and changed. For what we have looked at up to now is merely a self-reproducing system in which the possibility that things just carry on year after year is not explicitly ruled out. But the extraction of surplus-value is not a process that is limited by the existing scale and methods of production. In subjective terms, for the capitalist, as personification of capital, this means that his primary motivation is to increase as much as possible the amount of surplus-value extracted. There are two ways to do this, either he can increase the amount of his capital or he can increase the amount of surplus-value he extracts on his existing capital.

The most obvious way to increase the amount of surplus-value extracted without increasing his capital is for the capitalist to increase the length of the working day. This means that each worker creates more new value so, assuming the value of his labour-power has not changed; that is, that he is still paid the same wage, there is more left for the capitalist as surplus-value. This is what Marx called the extraction of absolute surplus-value, because it was an increase in surplus-value due to an increase in the absolute amount of value produced by each worker. It is in fact, the very basis on which the capitalist mode of production was established; for the establishment of the wage-labour system depended on requiring people who had no other means of support to work longer hours than those necessary to provide for their own subsistence. Initially, it would have been operated on the basis of pre-existing techniques of production (carried over from previous modes of production), specifically *capitalist* methods of production not yet having been established. At this stage, the class-struggle would take place mainly over the length of the working day as the newly created working class attempted to prevent capitalist attempts to extract absolute surplus-value. As capital displaced people from other means of existence it did not automatically provide them with jobs. In such circumstances the struggle against the extraction of absolute surplus-value would have been extremely difficult, for capital would have been very successful in forcing those who did have jobs to work longer and longer hours for fear of losing jobs. But even in this initial period capitalists did not only look to their existing workers to provide them with more surplus-value, they also expanded the whole scale of exploitation.

They did this by accumulation; that is, by using some of the surplus-value extracted from the working class to buy more means of production and labour-power, thus increasing their capital and consequently increasing the amount of surplus-value they could extract from the increased labour-force. So side by side with the extraction of absolute surplus-value went accumulation, the latter putting limits on the former. For besides the physical and physiological limits on the working day, accumulation lent strength to the working class in the struggle over its length. For, at this stage accumulation meant a proportionate increase in employment and a consequent diminution of the threat of unemployment needed to continue the extraction of absolute surplus-value. (I am not arguing that these factors operated the same way and to the same extent in all sectors of countries. For example, in many places the physiological limits to the working day were reached long before working-class resistance had any organised expression as can be demonstrated by the unbelievably low expectation of life of the urban working class in England in the first half of the nineteenth century.) The point is that the period of the extraction of absolute surplus-value and of accumulation using existing methods or production was limited. It was limited by the existing methods of production, in order to move on these had to be transformed and transformed in a specifically capitalist way. For this reason, Marx called this initial process that of the 'formal subsumption of labour to capital' because while the wage-labour relation had been established it had not yet started on the specifically capitalist development of the forces of production; that is, the real history of the capitalist mode of production had not yet begun.

This real history begins with a new method of increasing surplus-value, the extraction of relative surplus-value. If, instead of increasing the total amount of value each worker produces, the existing amount can be divided in proportions more favourable to the capitalist then there is an increase in total surplus-value extracted. This is what Marx called the extraction of relative surplus-value and it forms the basis for the 'real subsumption of labour to capital'. It does so because the only way to change the proportions in which the production of a given working day is divided between labour and capital, is either to pay the worker less subsistence or to enable him to produce that subsistence in less time. The former way by reducing the physical consumption of the worker, is limited by exactly those same forces that limited the extraction of absolute surplus-value, physiology and the class-struggle. The latter involves increasing the worker's productivity; that is, devel-

oping the forces of production. The way that this is done under
capitalism is by developing methods of production in which each
worker uses up more means of production in a given amount of time.
To do this involves replacing the individual worker's skill and muscle
as the basis of production, initially by the collectivisation of the labour
process. This leads eventually to a division of labour and a special-
isation of tasks within the production of a single commodity as well
as the previously existing one between those who produced different
commodities. The next stage is the substitution of non-human sources
of power for the muscle of the individual or collective worker. The
worker is now reduced to a machine-minder, individual skill is no longer
needed; the machine has taken over and determines the nature and
timing of the production process.

FORMS OF CLASS STRUGGLE, THE FAMILY AND THE STATE

Each stage of this process has associated with it forms of class-struggle.
Opposition to lengthening the working day, the formation of trade
unions and agitation for protective legislation against overlong hours
were forms taken by the working class in the earlier stages of
capitalism. Capital replied by resisting all these demands, though eventually, it had to give in on many of these, and by attempting to prevent
by legal and illegal methods, the formation of trade unions and
working-class parties. The extraction of relative surplus-value did not
make obsolete these forms of class-struggle, but did add new ones.
These were over methods of production as opposed to merely over the
length of the working day and wages. Without going into this in detail,
it is easy to think of examples; from the breaking of steam machinery,
through the struggle for legislation on factory safety to modern
attempts to resist productivity deals and the speeding up of assembly-
lines.

So we can see that Marxism does give us a method of analysing the
ways in which capitalist relations of production reproduce themselves
and in so doing change and develop the methods of production in
specifically capitalist ways. It also gives us, and this is crucial, a method
of analysing this process as a contradictory one and a continually
changing one, through the analysis of the forms of class-struggle. It is
here that the contrast with orthodox theory is at its most acute; in the

latter, class-struggle is obliterated let alone given any role in changing things.

I have not taken this schematic description of forms of class-struggle completely up to date, because that is done elsewhere in this book (see Chapter 7), but before concluding it is necessary to mention two aspects of contemporary capitalism which are essential to the understanding of reproduction and the class-struggle.

When we examined to what extent capitalist relations reproduced themselves we noted that they did not completely carry out the task with respect to the producers, the working class. Workers were paid a wage which could be spent on capitalistically produced commodities for their subsistence, but this did not take care of the production of the workers themselves. This, Marx claimed, could be safely left to the working class themselves. That may be the case, but that does not mean that our analysis should stop there. The forces involved in the production of people are also contradictory ones setting up relations of oppression and a struggle against oppression that is not to be understood by examining purely those relations under which commodities are produced for capital.

It is clear that people cannot be produced under capitalist relations. For if they were, they would have to be commodities themselves. But workers under capitalism are not bought and sold by capitalists, they are not slaves. Rather, they sell their own labour-power but for limited periods – they never sell themselves. So for capitalist relations to function, there has to be some other institution (set of relations) outside of those of capitalist production themselves in which people can be produced. That institution is the family, and the relations under which people are produced set up additional forms of struggle within the family to those discussed above, for example, over the control of women's fertility. While the family and many of the forms of struggle within it are not new, the entry of many married women into wage-labour has set up new forms for example, over unequal pay, sex discrimination and the provision of child-care. The consequent growth of the modern women's liberation movement has focused the attention of Marxists on this previously largely ignored area of struggle.[14]

The other aspect of capitalism that is crucial to our understanding of contemporary class-struggle is the state.[15] Indeed, class-struggle and the state are so intimately linked that we need an analysis of the former to understand the latter. To see this, we should go back to our discussion of reporoduction. We saw there that capitalist relations do, to some extent, reproduce themselves and the way that they do this is through the normal processes of capitalism, the buying and selling of commodities and of labour-power. This means that capital in its relations of production is restricted to the market in carrying on its own reproduction. Now this is quite a severe restriction. Capital in its relations of production is in the form of individual capitals; individual capitals do not have legitimate access to non-market forms of control; that is, they may not control by force. For this reason any control by force that capital needs should be located apart from individual capitals. This location is the state which therefore has a 'monopoly' of the legitimate use of force under capitalism. The legitimation of this monopoly, has this as its real basis; it also has many ideological expressions, for example in the idea that, though people have unequal shares in the economy, in the political system everyone has the same stake. Indeed, the very separation of a political role for the state acting on and above the class-struggle which is purely economic is a social construction; that is, it is part of the ideology of the capitalist mode of production which is but a distorted reflection of its reality.

Clearly no modern theory of the development of capitalism would be complete without an analysis of the state and the family as well as the direct relations of production. It is on these issues that the most fruitful debates in contemporary Marxism turn. Each different theory implies a different conception of class-struggle. While the uselessness of orthodox growth theory in considering such questions is apparent, the debates within Marxism on the forms and strategies of class-struggle will no doubt continue.

NOTES

1. The attempts of the new reappraisal of Keynes to re-establish all his macro-theories on a basis of postulates about individual behaviour in states of disequilibrium shows how important it is to orthodox theory to recaputre this wayward strain for mainstream methodology, by insisting that it conforms to the rules of individualism.

2. S. Himmelweit (1977) 'The Individual as a Basic Unit of Analysis', chap. 2 of F. Green and P. Nore (eds) (1977) *Economics: An Anti-Text* (London: Macmillan).

3. R. F. Harrod (1939) 'An Essay in Dynamic Theory', *Economic Journal*, **49**, and E. Domar, 'Capital Expansion, Rate of Growth and

Employment, *Econometrica,* **14.** Both of these papers are reprinted in A. K. Sen (1970) *Growth Economics* (Harmondsworth: Penguin Modern Economic Readings) the introduction to which is an excellent survey of orthodox growth theory.

4. Technical change can alter any one or more of the three ratios between capital, labour and output. Technical change that does *not* alter the capital/output ratio is called Harrod-neutral.

5. T. W. Swan (1964) 'Growth Models: Of Golden Ages and Pro-duction Functions', in K. E. Berrill (ed.), *Economic Development with special reference to East Asia* (London: Macmillan) pp. 4–5, reprinted in Sen, op. cit.

6. The terms 'natural rate of growth' and 'warranted rate of growth' come from Harrod, op. cit. The former, which equals n, the rate of growth of the labour-force, is supposed to be naturally given, while the latter equals s/v and denotes the rate of growth that the tech-nology and savings behaviour of the economy warrants.

7. This is rather an over-simplification of classical economics. In fact, they explained movements in all the relevant variables. Unique to classical theory, however, is endogenisation of population growth.

8. See R. M. Solow (1970) *Growth Theory* (London: Oxford University Press) pp. 2–3.

9. E. F. Denison (1970) *Why Growth Rates Differ* (Washington: Brookings Institution).

10. Solow, op. cit. chap. 1.

11. C. H. Feinstein (1964) *Domestic Capital Formation in the United Kingdom 1920 – 1938,* Cambridge: Cambridge University Press, and *National Income, Expenditure and Output of the United Kingdom, 1860–1960* (Cambridge: Cambridge University Press, 1972).

12. For an account of how *external* explanation has been used to mitigate the theoretical effects of capitalist crises see R. Sutcliffe, 'The Stabilisation of Capitalist Economies', in Green and Nore (eds) op. cit.

13. For an explanation of the concept of value and how capitalist exploitation occurs see S. Mohun, 'Consumer Sovereignty', in Green and Nore (eds), op. cit.

14. For a survey of one such area see S. Himmelweit and S. Mohun (1977) 'Domestic Labour and Capital', *Cambridge Journal of Econ-omics,* **1.**

15. A recent book of readings on the Marxist debate on the state is J. Holloway and S. Picciotto (1978) *State and Capital* (London: Edward Arnold).

CHAPTER 7

World Economic Crisis and Inflation

Ben Fine

WHAT BOURGEOIS ECONOMICS SAYS AND WHY IT IS WRONG[1]

Faced with the need to understand the world economic recession we are presented with an embarrassing wealth of objects for analysis. There are the indicators of the recession itself – massive unemployment, unprecedented general levels of inflation and monetary crises. These have to be set against the conditions which characterised the post-war boom. What are the effects and significance of the growth of multi-national corporation (MNCs), the increasing economic interventions of the state, the development of social democracy, the changing forms of imperialism, etc.? The problem is to extract from these phenomena those that are decisive and around which a general explanation can be organised. This is done in Section 1. In Section 2 the bourgeois theory of inflation will be reviewed, and it will be shown that the current coexistence of inflation and recession is explained according to the role played by expectations. In Section 3 the bourgeois theory will be criticised by offering an alternative framework for analysing inflation which draws upon the understanding of the recession presented in the first section.

1 CAPITALISM TODAY

A. CAPITAL, MONOPOLY AND THE STATE

Capitalism, like all modes of production, is composed of a set of social relations of production upon which is built a superstructure of political and ideological relations. For capitalism to continue in existence its reproduction must be guaranteed and this requires that class-struggle at all levels be contained within definite limits.[2] This is accomplished *as much* by the forms and objects that the inevitable class-struggle is encouraged and induced to take *as* by the relative strength of antagonistic classes. Even successful struggles by the working class can leave the fundamental relations of capitalist production untouched. Nevertheless, the development of capitalist production still requires changes in the relations of production, while the capital–labour relation remains. As a result the accompanying superstructure and the forms and objects of class-struggle will be transformed also. This process, however, should not be seen as an automatic and harmonious evolution.

So far, however, we have made no reference to the very motive of capitalist production – the thirst for profit. Historically, at its origins, capitalism satisfied this thirst by crude and oppressive methods, utilising the existing methods of production and exploiting them (or more exactly workers) to the full. As capitalism develops, machinery begins to replace the tasks undertaken by the labourer in production and more raw materials are worked up in a given time. Simultaneously, the growth of large-scale manufacture allows the productivity of co-operation, scale and division of labour to be utilised. With these developments, class-struggle focuses on unemployment (as workers are displaced and deskilled by the productivity of machinery) and working conditions (as machinery forces a new pace and division of labour). With increasing scale of production, workers are organised in larger and larger numbers at the point of production. While the capitalist purpose in this is the pursuit of profit, the workers' material interests are represented by the formation of trade unions, the organisational conditions for which are created by capitalist production itself.

The accumulation of capital brings with it capital's developed laws of motion. We have already implicitly argued that the pursuit of profit leads to an increase in the minimum level of capital necessary to achieve the levels of productivity that competition forces on the production process. Clearly, the more capital that can, metaphorically speaking, be collected into the control of a single hand the better. The means by which this monopolisation of capital can best take place is through the credit system (as illustrated by the development of the British financial system in the late nineteenth century). The funds of capitalists in general can be made available to a few capitalists in particular. This accomplishes what might be called a financial restructuring of capital, but it only creates the potential restructuring of capital in production. As we have already briefly seen this involves a development of the relations of production and this is tempered by class-struggle over the implications of restructuring capitalist production. There are the effects on individual work-places: unemployment at those small-scale factories that are closed down as inefficient, relative or even absolute falls in employment at those factories that are expanded, with speed-up of work and deskilling for those who remain employed. Besides these and governed by them are the effects in society as a whole. Whatever the pace of accumulation, it requires the centralisation or restructuring of capital in production. Consequently, there is a permanent pool of unemployed formed by those who are thrown out of work by closure or displacement by machinery. This pool is an important element in restructuring workers in production, for capital can draw on its reserves to fill the places that are created in expanding factories and form a new discipline on them and the existing work-force more readily.

Restructuring of capital is also essentially an uneven process. Sectors of production expand at different rates and with different rhythms. Production tends to become concentrated in specific areas, leading to overdevelopment in some instances and decay in others. Historically, this uneven development proved itself in the form of the separation between expanding cities and the depopulated country. Now it has application to the widening differentials between regions and countries.

These effects of restructuring are resisted by the workers, organised into trade unions. While the credit system proves a powerful level in financial restructuring, capital's offensive to reorganise the relations of production are limited to the market forces of economic compulsion and the ideological and political power that belongs to the ruling class. The mechanisms of reorganisation prove incapable of accommodating an accumulating capital that not only produces the effects of centralisation that we have already discussed, but also requires the continued production of profits. At times, the pressures to expand capital and satisfy the motive of profit-making prove incompatible, and the economy suffers a sharp financial crisis followed by recession.

Recessions are characterised by the coexistence of idle workers and machinery. Both in turn intensify capital's economic compulsion to reorganisation. Unemployed workers are essentially unorganised and can be more easily disciplined and reabsorbed into the process of production dictated by capital. But recessions also destroy capitals weeding out the weak and inefficient and allowing their resources to be centralised through bankruptcy, acquisition and merger. Consequently, recessions are an expression of capital's limited ability to be reorganised, but are also a powerful force behind renewed reorganisation. It is this that explains why capitalist accumulation does not proceed smoothly, but is punctuated by crises and recessions, giving rise to a cycle of production that is fundamentally a cycle of restructuring and destruction of capital.

However, it is not simply the relations of production that are reorganised; the means of reorganisation are themselves developed. This we have already discussed briefly in relation to the credit system. Here, the creation of a banking system allows financial restructuring to be accomplished more readily. Large-scale banks give rise to large-scale corporations and monopoly capital develops alongside and as a product of finance capital. It is the consolidation of the phenomena just discussed that gives rise to the period of *monopoly capitalism*. As we have seen, monopoly capitalism is to be associated with new objects of class-struggle – over unemployment, deskilling, speed-up of work – and new forms of struggle as the working class is organised into trade unions.

Capital accumulation is beset by crises that are intensified by the growing strength of working-class struggle. It becomes increasingly impossible to confine the effects of these crises to economic reproduction as the working class seeks the political rights and the exercise of political power to defend and advance their economic interests. Out of these conflicts within monopoly capitalism develops the stage of state monopoly capitalism (SMC), characteristic of the current post-Second World War period. Fundamental to this stage of capitalism is the increasing economic role played by the state. But this role must be seen relative to the cycle of restructuring that is fundamental to capital accumulation. The state does not intervene to control or abolish the cycle, but to promote it and moderate its effects on social reproduction. Consider this a little further.

In bourgeois economic theory, state economic intervention is usually divided according to the division of the theory itself into macro- and micro-economics. As a result, the role of the state in the discussion of growth and recession is usually restricted to considerations of Keynesian aggregate demand. Conversely, the role of the state in its policies towards nationalised industries, for example, is usually confined to considerations of micro-economic efficiency in the context of partial equilibrium and an otherwise fully employed economy. By contrast, our emphasis here is on the relationship between the state and the expansion, where possible, of capital accumulation. The state's role in capitalist society is primarily to guarantee *social* reproduction in general, to create cohesion and stability in political and ideological relations despite the antagonisms produced within these by the class nature of society and the disruptions accompanying capitalist accumulation in its economic reproduction. On the other hand, private capital as such is only concerned directly with its own individual economic reproduction (buying, producing and selling for profit) and this explains the necessity for the existence of the capitalist state. Once the state makes economic interventions, it can act as a force to moderate the conflicts associated with the accumulation of capital, as it widens its responsibility for guaranteeing social reproduction. Policies are developed oriented towards the level of employment, wages, etc.

The state's clearest intervention into the accumulation of capital is where it takes control of production itself – nationalisation. Here, together with its policies of aid, subsidy and supervision to private industry, its policies are generally directed towards a restructuring into large-scale profitable production. But the state also intervenes in exchange processes, becoming itself a dominant agent of credit, whether through its overall policies of 'demand management' or in its granting of loans to particular firms or industries. Intervention in distributional struggle between classes takes the form of incomes policy, and in addition taxation becomes a significant means by which profits are redistributed through the state as well as financing state expenditure, as Table 7.1 indicates.

However, state economic intervention must not be understood as the state simply acting as a surrogate for private capital. For, the state's economic interventions must have the effect of moderating the intensified crises associated with monopoly capitalism. On the other hand, the more intimate is the link between the state and economic reproduction, the greater are the potential political and ideological conflicts produced by conflicts over economic issues. The struggles for wages and employment increasingly become struggles within and potentially against the state.

As a result a political transformation is a prerequisite of state economic intervention. Typically, this takes the form of social democracy which has the effect of integrating the struggles of the labour movement into the state apparatus in correspondence to the state's economic interventions on behalf of capital. This is not simply an ideological

TABLE 7.1

Taxation as a percentage of GNP

	1929*	1974[†]
Canada	7.3	39.7
Denmark	7.9	53.4
France	10.3	41.1
Netherlands	11.4	50.6
Norway	8.4	52.9
Sweden	7.4	49.1
United Kingdom	17.5	38.7
United States	4.6	32.0 (1973)

Sources: *League of Nations Statistical Year Book 1930.*
[†] *TUC Economic Review 1977.*

necessity for capitalism (although this is important), allowing the state to represent its role in continuing capital accumulation as actions in the interests of society as a whole. More important, the struggles of the working class may be divorced from its point of strength and organisation – in the process of production – and be conducted through democratic channels where it will be weakened.

Now, the creation of social democracy is not essential for the state to be able to make the economic interventions – an alternative is a Fascist dictatorship. But if social democracy is established – and this will depend upon a successful working-class political struggle – working-class economic struggles will take new forms and have more immediate and direct political implications. This is because these struggles become articulated through the state. In the case of employment, workers struggle for state intervention to maintain jobs through struggles for nationalisation, import controls and aid to the industry concerned. As we have already seen, the satisfaction of these demands can be compatible with the continued promotion of capitalist accumulation. But it would be a mistake therefore to identify these struggles, limited to reformism though they may be, with the interests of capital as opposed to workers. For the working class will struggle to force the state to intervene in production in its interest as opposed to that of capital, which remains the production of profit through the reorganisation and accumulation of capital. This is clear in so far as the struggle develops for workers' control and the orientation of production for the maintenance of employment, the improvement of working conditions and the production of output according to the criterion of social use as opposed to profitable sale.

B.   THE WORLD ECONOMY

The significance of and stimulus to state economic intervention cannot be understood in isolation from developments in the world economy. State economic intervention and the internationalisation of capital together serve as a focus for understanding the post-war boom as well as the crisis that has followed it on a world scale. For if we contrast the post-war period with the inter-war period the importance of these developments stand out sharply. In the earlier period state economic intervention was severely limited (except in the case of the Fascist powers, where the political implications of state economic interventions could be suppressed). Of course, the internationalisation of capital has developed from the very beginnings of capitalism with the tendency to create a world market. But up to the Second World War, this was still restricted to competition between capitals on the basis of the imperialist division of the world into spheres of influence for the export of finance and commodities. After the Second World War, and associated with it the emergence of the dominance of American capitalism, new conditions for the international expansion of capitalism were created. Interpenetration of capitals between the advanced economies displaced the importance of the intensive exploitation of

TABLE 7.2

Value of world trade: percentage distribution

	1929	1973
Between developed areas	23.9	63.8
Between underdeveloped areas	12.0	4.3
Between developed and underdeveloped areas	62.6	32.0

empires. This is reflected in the changing patterns of trade and investment in the world economy (Tables 7.2 and 7.3).

However, more is involved than a simple quantitative shift in the orientation of trade and investment. In particular, a new form of internationalising capital has emerged, one that is only possible once the classic division of the world into economic empires has been broken down. It involves the internationalisation of the process of production itself. By this is meant the organisation of production within a single

TABLE 7.3

Percentage distribution of accumulated U.S. and
U.K. foreign investment*

		Developed areas	Underdeveloped areas
United States	1929	50.7	49.3
	1973	76.4	23.6
United Kingdom	1930	53.1	46.9
	1973	72.1	27.9

*Still in aggregate more than 70 per cent of world foreign investment
in 1973
Sources: *Review of International Trade and Development,*
United Nations, 1973.

TABLE 7.4

Number and distribution of affiliates of MNCs
(two affiliates in one country counts once) 1968/9

'Home' country	Affiliates	Percentage located	
		Developed	Underdeveloped
United States	9691	74.7	25.3
United Kingdom	7116	68.2	31.8
World	27300	73.6	26.4

firm across national boundaries so that, for example, parts may be manufactured in one or more countries but be assembled in another country and finally be sold on the world market. The 'factory' of the MNC increasingly straddles national boundaries (see Table 7.4). Nor is the internationalisation of production expanded at the expense of the internationalisation of other forms of capital. The figures on international liquidity (Table 7.5) illustrate the increasing state intervention into credit relations as reflected by the expansion of paper money.

TABLE 7.5

International liquidity

	1929*		1976[†]	
	$b	%	$b	%
Gold	10.2	69	42	18
Currency assets	4.5	31	166	70
IMF and Special Drawing Rights	–	–	28	12

Sources: *Bank of International Settlement.*
[†] *TUC Economic Review 1977.*

The data on world trade show how its growth has outstripped the growth of world production.

TABLE 7.6

Growth in world trade and production

Volume Index	1963	1972
Exports	100	213
Manufacturing production	100	123
Production of raw materials and agricultural goods	100	165

C. THE CURRENT ECONOMIC RECESSION

The foregoing analysis has argued that the two most important develop-ments of the post-war period are the growth of state economic inter-vention and the internationalisation of capital, particularly for the latter the internationalisation of productive capital as a point of depar-ture from earlier periods. Consequently any general understanding of the laws of development of capitalism, for example, as presented earlier, must have a specific application to capitalism's current development with these characteristics in mind. In these terms, the post-war world economy can be seen as developing an accumulation in the form of state economic intervention and internationalisation. More, these are the means by which accumulation was promoted. Consequently, it is not surprising that the post-war period should have witnessed a long period of expansion for the world economy, as the new forces under-lying that expansion permitted and fed a massive accumulation and reorganisation of capital on a world scale.

But why should such an expansion collapse into recession? The answer is to be found in general terms in the increasing incompati-bility of the internationalisation of capital with state economic inter-vention. Not that these tendencies are necessarily incompatible, for the state often adopts policies to promote the internationalisation of capital. Rather, it is the growing class resistance to these developments that eventually undermines the expansion. For because the *state* intervenes to internationalise capital, that internationalisation becomes restricted by the state's more fundamental role of guaranteeing social reproduction. But, because the state *internationalises* capital, social reproduction within the nation becomes restricted by the needs of international economic reproduction. As capital is accumulated and class-struggle intensifies, it is these conflicts between the needs of social and economic reproduction that come to the fore in the current period of capitalism.

To capture the characteristics of capital's international expansion, many theorists and particularly Marxists following Lenin have coined the term 'imperialism'. So far we have shown that the tendency towards SMC is an ambiguous development as far as imperialist expansion is concerned, at times obstructing and at times promoting the inter-nationalisation of capital by its economic interventions and moder-ation of wider social conflicts. As a result, it is hardly surprising that the extent of state economic intervention is unevenly distributed from country to country, according to the extent that each state is forced to moderate class conflict through economic interventions on the one hand and to the extent that MNCs can internationalise their operations unaided on the other.

More specifically, workers' struggles become directed through the state against the effects of international capitalist accumulation. They are oriented towards employment, welfare or incomes policy, they create an increasing tension between the fundamental need for economic reproduction in the form of capital accumulation and restructuring and the need for social reproduction and the moderation of economic as well as political and ideological struggle. These conflicts are more pronounced the more capital is internationalised since working-class struggle to defend its economic interests through the state increasingly obstruct the internationalisation of capital. Further, these struggles cannot be simply resolved by a transfer of capital abroad because they involve through the state the question of the stability of capitalist society as well as of the economy. In short, the development of SMC has not abolished the cycles of production associated with capital accumulation (as Keynesian theory focusing on the management of effective demand would argue), but has given them a new form of existence. The state through its economic policies may temper the rhythm and intensity of recessions and the social conflicts to which they give rise. But it does so at the expense of transforming economic struggles so that they have immediate political implications with the result that the free development of capital's international expansion founders on working-class economic and political resistance.

So far we have attempted to show two things. First, why is it that the development of capitalism should give rise to the increasing role of the state in economic intervention together with the internationalisation of capital in production. Second, why these developments should have given rise to the post-war boom but nevertheless lead to a recession. In the final part of this section it remains to examine the course that the recession takes in the light of this analysis.

The current recession, like all those that have preceded it, has the function for capital of laying the foundation for a renewed accumulation by restructuring existing capital. Now, however, this restructuring has the peculiar symptoms of being oriented towards the internationalisation of productive capital stimulated by state economic intervention. In addition, the state's interventions have the effect of moderating the social implications of the economic conflicts generated by the recession (often implemented through state economic policy), whether these concern struggles over employment, or the levels of real wages and welfare services as these are cut to redistribute profits to capital.

In some instances the growing strength of class-struggle and its expression politically has not only precipitated recession but has also led to profound changes in social organisation. Within Europe there have been crises in the dictatorships of Spain, Portugal and Greece. In the underdeveloped countries the complex interaction of the tendencies we have identified coexist through imperialist exploitation with backward capitalist and even pre-capitalist relations of production. As has been seen in Africa, Latin America and elsewhere, the process of capital accumulation, leading to reorganisation through recession, generates the necessity for sweeping social change.

2 ORTHODOX THEORIES OF INFLATION AND RECESSION

A. THE PRE-KEYNESIAN QUANTITY THEORY OF INFLATION

It is perhaps appropriate both logically and historically to begin a summary of bourgeois inflation theory with the quantity theory of money.[3] As proposed by Fisher, the equation $Mv = pT$ relates the supply of money M, the price level p, and the number of transactions undertaken T to the velocity of circulation v. As such, the velocity of circulation simply represents the efficiency of institutional arrangements for making transactions. On the other hand, in the almost identical Cambridge equation of the demand for money, $M_d = kpY$, the transactions demand for money, M_d, is related to the desired ratio of cash balances to money income. The condition for equilibrium in the money market, $M_s = M_d = kpY$, readily transforms into the determination of the price level, $p = M/(kY)$. From this it follows that the rate of increase of the price level (the rate of inflation) equals the rate of increase of the money supply since the two are proportional for given k and Y. Despite the fact, as we shall see, that economic theory has long since rejected this crude form of the quantity theory, it still remains a popular means of explaining inflation, summarised in the slogan 'too much money chasing too few goods'. The reason for this is in part due to the structure of the argument which has survived even if with modification. The focus on the equalisation of the demand for money to an exogenously determined supply almost inevitably leads to a theory of the expansion of the money supply as a cause of inflation.

For, whatever variables the demand for money is assumed to depend upon other than income and the price level, these are hardly liable to be considered to change sufficiently to absorb the increased money supply, if inflation does occur. Consequently, whenever there is inflation some form of the quantity theory or monetary explanation is bound to be proposed as in the modern monetarism associated with Friedman and his followers.

So far we have only discussed the rate of inflation in terms of comparative statics; that is, the association of a higher price level in equilibrium for a higher money supply. But inflation is a dynamic process and raises the question of the transition from one equilibrium price level to another, and also, if inflation is to be maintained, the mechanisms that lead from a continuously increasing money supply to a continuously increasing price level (for constant k and Y or at least for these rising at a slower combined rate than the money supply). The most obvious link between the formulation of static equilibrium and dynamic change in this context is through the excess demand for goods. Increase in the money supply leads to an increase in the demand for goods which cannot be met at the full-employment equilibrium so that prices rise. In addition, wages (and other incomes) must rise to restore the equilibrium conditions equating relative marginal products to relative factor prices, etc., otherwise there would be excess demands in these markets also.

It follows that, in the adjustment process, it is not simply the money market but potentially all markets that move out of equilibrium. This may appear to be of little significance given the eventual restoration of full-employment equilibrium. However, even if we accept the neo-classical version of the neutrality of money in the determination of equilibrium (except for the level of *absolute* prices) it follows that scope exists for economic policy to intervene to influence the path and speed of adjustment to equilibrium. Of course, it could be argued that the government should not have increased the money supply in the first place (if this, rather than a reduction in k or Y, is the source of inflation), and that *laissez-faire* is the best policy as far as the process of adjustment is concerned. But, clearly, the last proposition cannot be deduced from an inspection of the quantity equation alone, only from an understanding of the workings of the economy as a whole.

B.   THE KEYNESIAN THEORY OF INFLATION

The problem of adjustment, however, takes on even greater significance if we reject the neoclassical (and classical) notion of the neutrality of money in determining equilibrium, and recognise the possibility, as in Keynesian theory, of the existence of unemployment equilibrium brought about by the interaction of the money and real markets. For then it is not simply a question of increases in the money supply leading, according to the demand for money function, to the same real equilibrium at a different (inflated) price level, with only the path and speed of adjustment to worry about. It is possible that a new, even full-employment, equilibrium may be established without any increases in prices at all.

The reasoning underlying such a theory will almost certainly be familiar to the reader in terms of the *IS–LM* model. Restricting ourselves to the determination of equilibrium alone first and not arguing about movement between equilibria, it is well known that if prices (and/or wages) are sticky downwards then the desire to hold real cash balances *and* make sufficient real purchases may be thwarted by an inadequate money supply. Consequently, from the resulting unemployment equilibrium (in which the lack of money is partially reflected in lack of demand) a full-employment equilibrium can be achieved by expanding the money supply without leading to inflation. The demand for and supply of money are brought into equilibrium by an expansion of output.[4] In the *IS–LM* model, if the *LM* curve cannot be shifted to the right by a fall in prices to achieve full-employment equilibrium, then it can be shifted by an increase in the money supply. As a result the Keynesian model demonstrates that an expansion of the money supply does not lead to inflation as long as there is not full employment.

C.   THE KEYNESIAN 'INFLATIONARY GAP'

By the same token, however, the model does give rise to inflation for expansion of the money supply over and above the level necessary to achieve full employment. Consider, first, the Keynesian theory of the inflationary gap. If we construct the overall level of demand (expenditure) from the consumption function and autonomously given levels of investment and government expenditure, then in aggregate this may exceed full-employment output, the difference constituting the inflationary gap.[5] The outcome is supposedly an increase in the level of prices that reduces the real level of money expenditures to the level of full-employment output.

As it stands, this Keynesian explanation of inflation appears to be independent of the money market, no reference has been made to the supply of and demand for money. This is a result of the simplicity and incompleteness of the model. To begin with, investment is taken as exogenous and independent of the rate of interest. Second, if the inflationary gap is closed when prices rise, this presupposes a consumption function based on money rather than real income, otherwise as prices rise so would consumption expenditures in proportion. When the inflationary gap is closed, some proportion of the originally intended real consumption and investment must be decreased (leaving aside government expenditure) and this can only be done in a fuller model including a money market influenced by the rate of interest.[6] In fact, the simple inflationary gap model corresponds to the simple multiplier model. Just as this needs to be elaborated into the *IS–LM* model to incorporate an endogenous determination of investment, so the same applies to the Keynesian theory of inflation.

At this point it is necessary to consider then the Keynesian demand for money function. It is generally given in the form $M_d = pf(Y, r)$. The introduction of the interest rate r into the demand for money can be justified by a number of reasons. First, the rate of interest represents the interest forgone by holding money for whatever purpose (whether transactions or precautionary). Second, money may be held for speculative purposes. In particular, the lower (higher) is the rate of interest the higher (lower) it may be *expected* to be, giving rise to plans to purchase bonds later (now) at a lower price than otherwise.[7] For our purposes, the introduction of the rate of interest in the demand for money is not so important as the introduction of expectations. For it is these which can explain the market rigidities that give rise to unemployment and inflation, as we shall see. If neoclassical economics introduced the rate of interest into the demand for money without introducing a theory of expectations, then in the absence of market rigidities, its full employment propositions coupled with the neutrality of money would continue to hold as for the quantity theory.

However, when we elaborate the inflationary gap model into the *IS–LM* framework, the results are not substantially changed. Up to full employment, an increase in the money supply will expand output. Above full employment, the price level will increase in proportion to the increase in the money supply. There are, however, two exceptions. For the case of a vertical *IS* curve, in which investment is assumed to be independent of the interest rate, employment cannot be increased by shifts of the *LM* curve. An increase in the money supply is dissipated in a fall in the rate of interest with no effect on investment at (or below) full employment. As such, this corresponds to a rigidity in the workings of the investment market which can only be 'explained' by assuming investment is exogenous. On the other hand, in the case of the liquidity trap, in which the *LM* curve is horizontal, there is no similar rigidity in the money market. The increase in the money supply is simply held by individuals and not spent, in the expectation of increasing interest rates, so that the rate of interest is not reduced, stimulating aggregate demand and inflation at full employment (or output at below full employment). What we have shown within the Keynesian framework, with the introduction of a modified demand for money function in which expectations play a role, is that inflation can only occur for the expansion of aggregate demand (for example, but not necessarily, through an expansion of the money supply) above full-employment levels.[8] This is a necessary but not a sufficient condition for inflation, since expectations can give rise to a liquidity trap for which aggregate demand cannot expand. Nevertheless, inflation can only be sustained, in the absence of other exogenous increases in (government) expenditure, by increases in the money supply.

So far, within the Keynesian framework, we have only considered the different possible equilibria. We have not investigated the movement between equilibria. It has been presumed that an increase in the money supply results in an expansion of aggregate demand and this leads to an expansion of output below full employment, for example because the new equilibrium demands this. However, the actual movement of the economy from this original equilibrium may not follow this direction of movement, and, if it does, it may not do so fast enough. Consequently, an increase in the money supply may lead to inflation in the short run if prices respond to excess demand prior to the expansion of output. Consequently, while the equilibrium analysis may not be in dispute, different views can be generated about the relative merits of monetary as opposed to fiscal policy for achieving the desired full-employment equilibrium without too dilatory or dangerous a path of adjustment. These depend for their differences upon the relative speed and size of adjustment of prices and quantities and also the particular sequence of repercussions from one market to another. The more emphasis is given to the speed and size of adjustment of prices as opposed to quantities, the more likely is inflation in the short run. The same conclusion may be drawn, if it is presumed that goods and labour markets react more quickly than the markets tending to reduce the interest rate and increase investment.[9]

D.   THE PHILLIPS CURVE

The outstanding deficiency of the Keynesian theory so far elaborated is its inability to explain the coexistence of unemployment and inflation, and more seriously the simultaneous rise in the rates of inflation and unemployment characteristic of the current recession. In particular, the theoretical and practical crisis of Keynesianism can be expressed in the following terms. If unemployment is a symptom of deficient demand and if inflation is a symptom of excess demand leading to price increases, then there is the inconsistent coexistence of deficient and excess demand.

The most well-known response to this problem has been the Phillips curve. Originally it was observed that there existed an inverse relationship between the rate of wage increases and the level of unemployment. How could this be explained theoretically? First, it is presumed that there is a positive relationship between the rate of wage increase and excess demand for labour. Wages rise faster the greater is the demand for labour relative to the supply. Second, it is presumed that there is an equilibrium level of unemployment corresponding to the frictions in the labour market. There will always be workers streaming in and out of jobs, but at this equilibrium the number of unemployed will correspond exactly to the number of vacancies on offer. The excess demand for labour will be zero (and not negative despite the existence of unemployment, which significantly is 'voluntary'). Above the equilibrium level of unemployment, however, at a low level of demand for output, the level of unemployment will exceed the number of vacancies. Conversely, for low levels of unemployment, at times of excess demand for output, the number of vacancies will exceed the level of unemployment. All in all, it can be seen that there is an inverse relation between the level of excess demand for labour, measured by the number of vacancies relative to the number of unemployed, and the level of unemployment itself.

Now the level of unemployment is inversely related to the excess demand for labour, and the excess demand for labour is positively related to the rate of wage increases. It follows that the rate of wage increases is itself inversely related to the level of unemployment. Further, at the so-called natural rate of frictional unemployment at which the excess demand for labour is zero (vacancies equals unemployment) the rate of wage inflation is zero.[10] At higher levels of unemployment wages will fall, but they will rise at higher levels of unemployment. This yields a theoretical explanation of the Phillips curve. Further, it can be argued that the trade-off between the level of unemployment and the rate of increase in money wages is equivalent to a trade-off between unemployment and inflation (in the absence of money-illusion) as relative marginal productivities, etc., are equated to the appropriate relative prices.

As it stands, the Phillips-curve theory does purport to explain the coexistence of inflation and unemployment. But it does so in a way that is not so much consistent with as identical to the Keynesian inflationary gap approach. The major innovation is simply the argument that full employment is attained at a natural level of frictional unemployment. If aggregate demand is expanded above that level associated with the natural rate of unemployment, then employment will be increased only under the penalty of generating inflation. From the policy point of view the government has the choice, or is under pressure, to reduce the level of unemployment but must offset any gains from this against the resulting inflation.

Nevertheless, the Phillips curve as such is still unable to explain the simultaneous increase in unemployment and the rate of inflation unless by the suggestion that the natural rate of unemployment increases for institutional reasons. This would lead to a higher rate of inflation than previously for any given level of unemployment (for example, a positive rate of inflation at the earlier natural level of unemployment). However, as it is more or less impossible to argue that frictions in the labour market steadily increase over time, the existence of increasing inflation and unemployment would appear to invalidate empirically the statistical and theoretical justification for the Phillips curve.

Paradoxically, the theory of the Phillips curve was the result of a response to a statistical relationship, When the statistical relationship broke down, the corresponding theory was not rejected but modified to explain endogenously the shifts in the (no-longer-existing) Phillips curve corresponding to the necessary increase in the frictional level of unemployment. This was done by introducing expectations about the level of inflation.

Consider first an economy at the natural rate of unemployment. According to the Phillips curve the rate of inflation must be zero. But suppose that the rate of inflation is positive and constant and has been so for some time so that individuals expect it to continue to be so. How is this possible without the level of unemployment falling? First, it is necessary that the government be increasing the money supply at 3 per cent without excess demand being created.

Second, this occurs if 'contracts' (wage and price setting) are fixed at *expected real* levels in anticipation of inflation, as surely they will be. Putting the argument another way, if inflation exists and is anticipated at the equilibrium level of unemployment, the level of real demand and employment can only be maintained by the government by expanding the money supply to fund anticipated and contracted wage and price increases. In other words, the Phillips curve is shifted up by an amount equal to the (expected) rate of inflation.

So far, we have more or less restricted the analysis to the possibility of inflation at the natural rate of unemployment. Now suppose that the government attempts to maintain unemployment below the natural rate by expanding aggregate demand. Previously we would have argued from the Phillips curve that the result would have been a constant rate of inflation of say 3 per cent to close the inflationary gap. But if this 3 per cent inflation is anticipated aggregate real demand will be increased as (expected) depreciating money balances are run down. The result is a further increase in inflation, and a further upward revision of price expectations unless the government abandons its (over)-employment policy and no longer funds the self-fulfilling spiral of inflationary expectations. The cycle then repeats itself, leading to an accelerating inflation. Also, as we have seen earlier, to return the economy to the appropriate level of unemployment without maintaining inflation, for some period at least, unemployment will have to rise above the natural level. Within this framework, accelerating inflation and increasing unemployment can be explained in the short run if the government increases the money supply but at a rate slower than the expected rate of inflation, provided that sufficient expected real balances are held to reduce aggregate real demand. If the government does, however, attempt to maintain employment levels by expanding the money supply at the prevailing rate of inflation, then inflation will be accelerated.

E.   MONETARIST AND KEYNESIAN THEORIES OF INFLATION

It will probably not have escaped the reader that the modification of the Phillips curve presented above, to take account of expectations, leads to conclusions associated with Monetarist theory. On the other hand, it has been presented in such a way that it is has been linked directly with the Keynesian theory of the inflationary gap. Does this mean that Monetarist and Keynesian theories of inflation and macro-economics are more or less identical?

The answer is essentially in the affirmative. Earlier we argued that the dispute between monetary and fiscal policy was based on a shared theoretical framework, the differences lying in the structure and sequence of adjustment involved in the conflicting models. Hardly surprisingly, exactly the same applies when the Keynesian framework is supplemented with hypotheses concerning expectations. The Keynesian dispute with monetarism then does not concern the explanation of inflation *per se,* but only the structural, sequential and quantitative role played by the individual parts. More specifically, Keynesians in general anticipate that quantities are more responsive than prices to exogenous and endogenous changes. Consequently, less emphasis is laid upon the need for severe monetary policy to restore full employment without inflation, and more emphasis is laid upon deficiencies in output rather than excesses in demand as the source of accelerating unemployment and inflation. Thus, it is not a question of the influences at work, but simply of their relative strengths.

These, of course, are to be estimated statistically. It cannot be over-emphasised that such estimations hardly represent tests of or between the theories. On the one hand, inflation and unemployment can be distributed between the unobservable expectations and excess demand respectively according to the specification of the model. On the other hand, each model can be made sufficiently flexible to accommodate any empirical movement in macro-economic aggregates. However, there is a technical reason why Monetarist theory should gain an upper-hand (as well as its popular appeal and association with right-wing *laissez-faire* policy-making). Because increases in the price level and money supply have coexisted, it is quite clearly easier to build and estimate macro-econometric models in the monetarist tradition than any other. Monetarists, therefore, have a built-in bias, favouring their theory based on a stable demand for money function, which more or less automatically predicts a one-to-one correspondence between increases in the money supply and inflation.

F.   COST-PUSH AND DEMAND-PULL

While we have shown that the monetarist and Keynesian theories share the same Keynesian theoretical presuppositions, this has necessarily led to an approach to inflation centred on excess demand and consequently so-called demand-pull factors. But just as these factors, particularly in terms of the over-expansion of the money supply, give rise to popular conceptions of the cause of inflation, so do explanations based on so-called cost-push factors. The underlying idea involved here is that particular groups commanding receipt of economic resources attempt to push up their real share by pushing up their monetary revenue. Whether one group leads the others by attempting to increase its share while the others simply defend their own shares, or whether all groups simultaneously push to increase their shares in a redistributional conflict, the outcome is a spiral of inflation. The net outcome in real terms may in fact leave all shares unchanged, but the cake to be divided will be that much smaller because of the costs of inflation.

Now, not surprisingly, cost-push theories of inflation have also been dubbed conflict theories. Overall, we can identify three groups commonly seen as being involved in conflict: labour represented by trade unions, capital represented by monopolies, and the government represented by itself. Clearly trade unions wish to push up wages and monopolies wish to push up prices to increase their distributive shares. The government, however, simply wishes to remain in office, and is seen as doing so by acting in its interests (usually identified with labour), either by maintaining or expanding the level of employment or by maintaining or expanding the level of social services (particularly immediately prior to elections after which it is under less pressure to increase its popularity).

Having identified our conflicting groups, the various theories of cost-push inflation are open to us. We simply need to choose a starting group for the vicious circle of inflating claims and allow the other groups to respond accordingly. For example, trade unions push up wages, monopolies respond by a defensive mark-up of prices to maintain profits and the government expands the money supply to ratify these changes, otherwise allowing an unpopular increase in the rate of unemployment. Alternatively, the government prints money to expand popular social services, stimulating inflation and the defence of real wages and prices.

The glaring deficiency of cost-push theories of inflation is their failure to construct a theory of aggregate demand and/or output and employment. What is the size of the cake over which the various groups struggle, let alone the level of prices through which distribution actually takes place? Cost-push theories only look at the supply side, whereas demand-pull theories in their developed form consider both the level of aggregate demand and the supply of factors in markets for which inflation is anticipated (the supply of labour, for example).

As a result, recent developments in inflation theory tend to reject the dichotomy between cost-push and demand-pull, rather emphasising the interaction of supply and demand. The precise nature of this interaction forms the controversy between Monetarism and Keynesianism within the Keynesian framework to which we have already referred in the previous section.

Thus cost-push and demand-pull theories of inflation are not seen as alternatives but as complements.[11] The Phillips curve could as well be explained by the increasing distributional strength in struggle by labour as the level of employment rises, a struggle intensified in the case of anticipated inflation. But this would only investigate the supply curve for labour, and, unless it is to be argued that the economy is always on the supply curve, the interacting effects of inflation on demand must also be considered.

There is no doubt that cost-push theories of inflation are as one-sided as the quantity theory of money that began our investigation into inflation. Consequently, these theories must also be integrated into the Keynesian paradigm. This having been done, they have suffered against the benchmark of tests of and within that paradigm. This is hardly surprising. First, the growth of unemployment will act statistically against models that focus predominantly on cost-push. Logically this cannot render them 'invalid', provided an appropriate model is built that assigns inflation to the supply side and unemployment to the demand side. Second, however, cost-push models involve the construction of statistics appropriate to the measurement of 'push-fulness'. As these are notoriously vague (for example, how to measure union militancy) and difficult to construct, less effort has been made to justify cost-push than demand-pull oriented models of inflation.

The demise of the influence of cost-push factors in the study of inflation has had the wider implication of putting aside 'non-economic' and 'institutional' changes in the explanation of inflation. This has certainly lent support to Monetarist explanations of inflation, particularly those emphasising that the existence of trade unions (or other monopolies) can only redistribute employment or wages within the working class, but otherwise have little or no effect upon the overall equilibrium attained. Again, however, such extreme views do not have to be adopted and the existence of market power and the exercise of it can be theorised to have aggregate as well as redistributive effects on employment and output.[12]

G.   INTERNATIONAL ASPECTS OF INFLATION

It is not the intention of this chapter to survey international economics as well as the economics of inflation. But, if we are to relate theories of inflation to the current world economy then it is not possible to be silent on international aspects of inflation. Fortunately, the bourgeois theories of inflation in an international context are more or less identical to the propositions developed for the closed economy. The pretentious claim to deal with the world economy depends upon a sleight of hand that substitutes categories of international economics for those of the closed economy.[13]

Essentially this is done by replacing individuals and/or groups in the closed economy by nations. The overall framework of Keynesianism remains unimpaired, although the relative significance of cost-push/demand-pull and price/quantity adjustment remains a matter for controversy (and estimation). The interests of the nation are represented by as large an expansion of domestic output as possible, *ceteris paribus,* but the instruments for achieving this domestically (fiscal and monetary policy related to the money supply, interest rate, taxes and budget deficit) may lead to international imbalance (balance-of-payments disequilibrium or exchange-rate movement) or frustration as international monetary flows counteract domestic monetary policy.

All will be well as long as the overall level of demand in the world economy does not correspond to a level of employment above the natural rate. Otherwise, self-fulfilling expectations about inflations or movements in other variables (such as exchange rates) will be transmitted internationally and generate domestically the effects already analysed for the closed economy. Differences may exist over the appropriate international and domestic policies to be adopted to restore equilibrium according to the variety of Keynesianism utilised. Cost-push influences become transformed into conflicts between nations over distributive shares of output and employment and can be measured against indices of power and changes in power in the world economy.

H.   INFLATION AND THE CURRENT CRISIS

Our consideration of bourgeois inflation theory leads us to understand that the current world economy will be analysed and prescribed for on the basis of a number of fundamental propositions. First, there is an equilibrium (including a natural level of unemployment) which it is the object of policy to attain with minimum adjustment cost. Second, essential to this objective is the reduction of the rate of inflation so that the vicious spiral of self-fulfilling inflationary expectations is broken. Third, this can only be done by short-run policies that reduce the level of employment below the natural rate, so that inflation and expectations of it are reduced in the short run, and subsequently abolished in the long run, by deflationary policies. Fourth, this aggregate solution for the world economy must be distributed throughout the individual economies according to a combination of international political and economic settlements. Fifth, the individual national levels of deflation must be accepted within those nations. Sixth, in so far as these policies are not adopted and accepted at all of the international and national levels necessary, stagflation will persist and, if reflationary policies are renewed too early, return. Seventh, the movement of the world economy away from its initial path of equilibrium growth – the post-war boom – has to be explained by some disturbance stimulating inflationary expectations.

On the first six of these propositions we need make little more comment. They will be familiar to every reader in one form or another in the context of economic policy in their own country.[14] Different theorists and policy-makers give different emphases to different policies, but the outcome is always the same.[15] As suggested by the third proposition, real wage cuts, social service cuts and increases in unemployment, whether rationalised and implemented through incomes policy and or cuts in the budget deficit, growth in the money supply or government expenditure are all necessary to reduce the level of (expected) inflation in the short run and restore equilibrium in the long run. In addition, the economic theory that informs these policy suggestions is open to a presentation for popular ideology, that overexpansion of the money supply, state expenditure or wages causes inflation.

Explanations in response to the seventh proposition are open to more variability. Most popular is the reliance upon one or more 'exogenous' developments in or shocks to the economic system. For example, the rise in prices of primary commodities, especially oil, is seen as a stimulus to inflation in the developed economies (see also chap. 4). It can also be seen to lead to distributional conflict between the advanced and Third World countries, as well as posing the problem of financial recycling of the revenues involved. An alternative explanation relies upon the growth of trade union power, monopolisation and increasing state economic intervention in the attempt to maintain political power. Yet again it can be argued that American domination of the world economy has been challenged so that dollars are no longer accepted as a world money supply, releasing resources for American use in Vietnam or elsewhere. Characteristic of these explanations is that they concern forces that are accidental, temporary and, where economic conflicts and scapegoats are involved, open to satisfactory solution. Equilibrium can be restored given political agreement *and* temporary sacrifice.

3   INFLATION THEORY: A CRITIQUE AND AN ALTERNATIVE

A.   FORMS OF CREDIT[16]

It will perhaps have occurred to the reader that while both of the previous sections bear upon the causes of the current world recession, neither has any point of contact with the other. The bourgeois theory fails to deal with the accumulation and restructuring of international capital, the class antagonisms to which these give rise and the relationship between these and the role of the state in economic and social reproduction. The organising concept for the theory is the existence of an equilibrium and, associated with it, a level of frictional unemployment that is necessary for the smooth functioning of allocation through the market system. Clearly this equilibrium level of necessary, even 'desirable', unemployment is a pale reflection of the cyclical rhythm of unemployment associated with the accumulation of capital. Nevertheless, variations in the level of unemployment are explained in terms of the aggregate response of individuals to expected rates of inflation. The higher is the expected rate of inflation, the higher is the level of unemployment associated with a given level of actual inflation. Because of the post-war boom, it is presumed that the world economy has been more or less in non-inflationary equilibrium prior to an exogenous (or arbitrarily explained) disturbance that has led automatically to an inflationary and unemployment disequilibrium, or even stagflationary equilibrium, the cure for which is the short and sharp dose of deflationary policies.

On the other hand, the analysis offered in Section 1 does not confront the problem of explaining inflation, even if it does examine the forces promoting the post-war expansion and the limitations upon them. Nor, however, is an explanation of inflation precluded by the analysis, in the same way that the bourgeois theory's preoccupation with equilibrium precludes an understanding of the contradictory development of capital accumulation. Nevertheless, the concepts for analysing inflation cannot simply be borrowed from the bourgeois theory, for otherwise the explanation of inflation will be rooted within bourgeois theory. For example, radical theories of inflation often emphasise class-struggle as its cause in either one of two ways. Distributional struggle over wages forces up costs and consequently prices, further intensifying the conflict over the shares of available national income. Alternatively, it is often argued that class-struggle forces the state to borrow and expand the money supply, in order to finance social services or maintain the level of employment, consequently fuelling inflation. Theoretically, these two theories correspond to the orthodox explanations of cost-push and demand-pull inflation, even if the irreconcilable differences between classes are seen as the systematic source of disequilibrium rather than the intervention of expectations into the harmonious workings of the market.[17]

In order to construct an alternative theory of inflation, and one based on the accumulation of capital, we have to examine the concepts of credit and money critically. Orthodox theory, for example, rooted in Keynesianism, tends to see credit as an undifferentiated concept, the expansion of which, say in the form of an increased money supply, simply adds to aggregate demand and consequently brings on inflation in the face of the failure to expand output. Credit, however, can be extended for two rather different reasons. First, there is the motive associated with the ability to make exchanges. The time of sale and purchase is separated from the time of payment with either transactor making a temporary loan to the other according to whether payment is made in advance or in arrears of the exchange itself.

Second, however, credit is extended for the purpose of making a profit or, more accurately, to gain interest. It follows conversely that the borrower must have the intention of using the loan to contribute to making a profit, for otherwise the interest could not be paid (together presumably with something left over). Now in orthodox theory both of these forms of credit are synonymous, the first reflecting intertemporal preferences over consumption (interest being paid for a delay or advance of payment possibly in the form of a higher or lower price respectively – credit or cash terms) and the second reflecting intertemporal production possibilities.

However, from our analysis of Section 1, we have seen that credit of the second type, normally in money-form, is of considerable importance for the accumulation of capital. For the use of money as capital is the means by which financial restructuring takes place and is a means by which individual capitals seek to survive and compete during that restructuring by controlling and utilising as large a mass of capital as possible. It follows that the expansion of this form of the credit system is a necessary secular development for capitalism (although cyclical reductions in the credit system are also a feature of crises of recessions).

On the other hand, credit of the first type, even where it involves interest payments, does not belong to an analysis of the competition between capitals to expand productivity during the accumulation process. It merely involves a redistribution of the times (and also the sizes) of payments by consumers. Consider this in the context of the way in which wages are paid. Workers do receive and have received credit in many different forms. These range from the factory shops and pawnshops of nineteenth-century capitalism through to the hire-purchase and mortgage arrangements of the present day. Even where these forms of credit have not had the effect of simply reducing the value of real wages, they have always had the effect of adding coercion to the wage-labourer to work in order to maintain the levels of physical consumption, comforts and housing as the case may be. The same holds true for the instances where the worker makes savings and receives interest payments. For, in general, far from this reflecting the freedom of the worker to spread earnings over a lifetime of consumption, it reflects the means by which the worker is forced to work when able to do so in order to provide for the times when unable to do so (or to earn the deposits necessary for a house, car, etc.). The force of these remarks is to demonstrate that the role played by credit is to be located at two different levels of analysis, one to be associated with the competitive accumulation between capitalists, the other with the distributional struggle between capital and labour over the form in which wage goods are provided as well as the quantities provided.

In addition, the same sort of distinctions must be applied to state expenditure, the creation of a budget deficit and the state's interventions into the credit system (whether to expand the money supply or not). For these do not correspond to some amorphous set of undifferentiated payments or loans as in Keynesian analysis of aggregate demand. In contrast, the state's expenditure, for example, is in part made as capital – when funding investment in nationalised industries and aid to private capital – and presupposes an expansion of profitable production, and in part it functions purely as a means of allocating surplus already produced – when financing military expenditure or welfare services, for example – without presupposing a further expansion of output. Of course, it could be argued – and this is the basis for all bourgeois inflation theory – that if the credit had not been expanded and/or if the expenditure had not been made, and/or if output had expanded, there could be no inflation. But we can see that such arguments have no specific roots in an analysis of the capitalist economy, for which expenditures as capital specifically require an expansion of output whereas other expenditures do not, but draw upon existing resources.

Now reconsider the credit given in the processes of buying and selling. Again, this can be seen to have the effect of simply easing the process of exchange. But, where credit is granted, it does tend to affect the size of payment, in strict correspondence to the time of credit and rate of interest as the present value of the sum advanced depends upon these two variables. In addition, a class of merchant capitalists and banking capitalists can intercede between the buyers and sellers to improve the efficiency and make a profit on the business of arranging exchanges and loans. The result is that the first form of credit we have considered, that related to buying and selling, becomes subordinated to specific forms of capital specialising in these functions and making a profit from them. In other words, as capitalism develops, all credit tends to become linked to the existence of credit as capital, although it does not all become directed towards expansion of capital in the process of production, but can also be used for commercial and financial purposes.

This is confirmed if we reconsider the credit relationship between capital and labour. In the place of the credit between the worker and his employer's shop, which represents more or less directly a struggle over the level of wages, we find the credit between capital and labour mediated socially by the intervention of capital through bank loans, hire-purchase agreements and building societies. Similar conclusions hold if we consider state expansion of credit. Whether brought about through an expansion of the money supply or by borrowing, this usually involves a direct interaction with private financial institutions (or nationalised industries) geared to the making of profit on the basis of those credit operations. On the other hand, the state can appear at times to expand the money supply purely to make income 'transfers', for example, to increase old-age pensions. On accounting grounds, it is wrong to identify the expansion of the money supply with one object of expenditure rather than another (just as it is wrong to argue that a government deficit is caused by one set of expenditures rather than others). All we can say is that overall the level of the money supply has been increased. The problem is whether this constitutes an overall expansion of money as means of payment or more specifically as capital.

It could be argued that since pensioners, in general, are not capitalists no expansion of money as capital is involved. This would be wrong unless pensioners confined their expenditures between themselves and other non-capitalist agents. But this is scarcely the case. Rather, money-capital will have been expanded indirectly through the intermediary of the pensioners concerned. For the income 'transfer' immediately passes into the hands of capitalists (who sell the commodities to pensioners) and they can utilise as capital the money obtained. This of course differs from a straight expansion of the money supply to subsidise the capitalists concerned since it also involves, *ceteris paribus*, a distribution of surplus to pensioners. But these two effects are to be separated conceptually and that this is so is demonstrated by the fact that the state could have made that distribution through fiscal policy alone. It follows that the use to which the money expansion has been put corresponds both to a redistribution of surplus and a general expansion of money-capital. That the two effects have been accomplished simultaneously (and even this is not true) should not mislead us into believing that the expansion of the money supply has not been one of capital.

This has been a long and difficult section because it confronts the problem of the role of credit in such a way as to produce at times counter-intuitive arguments not only to those trained in Keynesian categories of analysis, but also to popular common sense. We have not dealt with every possible case of the nature of the credit relations between state, capital and labour, but the following general conclusions can be drawn. First, credit as a means simply of easing buying and selling must be distinguished from credit that is advanced as capital and which is necessarily linked to an expansion of output and payment of interest. Orthodox theory fails to make this distinction by aggregating together all factors contributing to effective demand (although it does determine the rate of interest by reference to the supply of and demand for money). Second, then, orthodox theory emphasises the role played by money as a means of payment in the formation of the level of effective demand. In contrast, it can be argued that it is the role played by money as capital that predominates even when money is expanded through the state purely for the purpose of making purchases possible in the first instance (for income transfers or military expenditure, for example). In addition, it can be observed that the development of the subordination of credit as means of payment to credit as capital stimulates the operations of financial and commercial as well as of industrial capital.

The paradoxical nature of these results cannot be overemphasised. At a time when the simple expansion of credit seems greater than ever before as loans are made to workers in various forms, as workers save and as the state expands the money supply to finance social services, it is being argued that credit is increasingly being expanded as capital! The paradox is resolved by not looking at these developments from the perspective of an individual, whether capitalist, labourer or Treasury official, but by examining the *capitalist* system *as a whole*. For then, these credit relations can be seen to be veils drawn over the form in which wages are paid and social services distributed[18] as opposed to the process of competition between capitalists to promote financial restructuring.

B.   CREDIT AS CAPITAL AND INFLATION

It is now our intention to draw the relationship between the role of credit as capital and the process of inflation. First, it should be observed that the fact that credit acts as capital neither implies logically that there should be price deflation, inflation nor stability. It depends upon the extent to which credit as capital is advanced successfully in terms of generating productivity increase and consequently extra surplus out of which interest can be paid. Consequently, in order to determine the rate of inflation we have to examine the forces behind a successful expansion of capital as well as those behind the expansion of credit as capital.

To a great extent we have already accomplished this task in Section 1. There we saw that accumulation necessarily assumed a cyclical pattern as the process of restructuring capital is punctuated by crises and recessions. The expansion of credit as capital tends to follow that same cyclical rhythm, as individual capitalists compete for credit to establish large-scale units of production with higher and higher levels of productivity. But as this process of competitive accumulation draws to a close credit as capital will have been over-expanded and lead to inflation. This follows from the fact that productivity increase and surplus production will not correspond to the levels presupposed by the advance of credit as capital. Nevertheless, it will appear as if there is too much credit relative to production and this gives rise to ortho-dox theory's preoccupation with aggregate demand as opposed to the role played by credit as capital in the accumulation process. Further, once begun, this inflationary process will tend to fuel speculation (for example, precisely in those commodity markets with increasing prices). Eventually, a crash in some branch of exchange or speculation will break, and the economy will be plunged into recession (the effects of which we discuss below as far as price movements are concerned).

Now, a natural question is why the expansion of credit as capital had to exceed the expansion of capital in production and why could it not have been restricted to non-inflationary levels even in the move-ment into recession. Even leaving aside the role played by speculation, such a question reveals a Keynesian understanding of the role played by credit, that the level of aggregate demand simply needs to corres-pond to the level of output. In contrast, we have argued that com-petitive accumulation requires the expansion of credit as capital to bring about the reorganisation and expansion of production, but it does not thereby determine the level of output (and surplus) produced, for that depends upon the strength and forms of class resistance to accumulation. If the credit expansion had been restricted, the effect would have been to precipitate the elimination of a number of capitals, and possibly a recession, as these would be unable to expand and so remain competitive. To suggest that credit expansion can at all times correspond to output expansion is to ignore the necessity of the cycle of production and the role played in it by competitive accumulation. It would be like suggesting that two teams after struggling to a five-all draw would have been better off to have settled for nil-nil at the outset!

So much for the tendency to inflation towards the end of the boom and its speculative sequel. In the following recession there is a tendency towards a depreciation in prices (and appreciation of money). The reason for this that, with the crash in the credit system and the move-ment into recession, there is an excess of capital in all its forms – in production, commodities and paper claims to dividends and interest. These all lose their exchange value relative to money, to one degree or another according to the process of competition between the capitalists concerned. Although there has been an over-expansion of money-capital as well as other forms of capital, the former tends to appreciate relative to the latter since it is the universally accepted means of payment and most advantageous means of hoarding idle capital. This means idle machinery and workers, a collapse in the values of paper assets and a *fall* in the level of prices. This would appear to leave inexplicable the coexistence of increasing unemployment and inflation, the development over which bourgeois theory only stumbles by appending a theory of expectations. But, as yet, we have not examined the role played by the state in the credit system and its relationship to inflation.

C.   THE STATE AND INFLATION

Earlier we have examined the increasing economic intervention played by the state and in particular its role in relation to the credit system. The role of the state in expanding credit must be distinguished from the private expansion of credit for two related reasons. First, it is not geared to individual private profit-making (although it does in general operate to promote the profitable expansion of production), and this allows the state to moderate the rhythm of the cycle of production and possibly to moderate its effects through its control of the level of credit in general. Second, the expansion of state credit may take the form of the expansion of the money supply.

Taken together, these two conditions mean that just as the state does not seek to make a profit out of its interventions into the credit system, so also it does not run the risk of its financial assets becoming bankrupted. Contrast the situation with the private credit system. There, for example, the collapse following a speculative boom leads to an uneven depreciation of the financial assets concerned as some become worthless and as others lose more or less value. For the state, the financial asset concerned predominantly in the formation of credit is money. The spread of losses over it must be even since it is a single and homogeneous asset. Consequently, the over-expansion of credit as capital through the state becomes an over-expansion of money and leads to a uniform depreciation of money, i.e. inflation, rather than an uneven depreciation of a mixed set of assets and credit relations. This is an effect furthered by another process associated with the development of state credit, the total displacement of a commodity money such as gold, by paper money. As a result, during a recession, the flight to money as such and away from other forms of capital is less pronounced (although it does lead to more pronounced movements between one form of international currency and another).

From these observations it follows that the rhythm of price increases does not follow the cycle of production as in the case of the private credit system. Rather inflation may accelerate during the recession even above the levels achieved during the previous speculative boom. Does this mean that inflation is simply explained by an over-expansion of state credit, particularly in the form of money? If so, the Keynesian (and in particular the modern Monetarist) theory would appear to have been restored with a vengeance and much needless rhetoric.

To demonstrate that this is not so the distinctive features of the theory of inflation constructed will be brought out. First, enough has been said about the differences in the concepts of credit (and money) involved that they do not bear repeating. Second, however, these different analyses of the credit system are not accidental, but naturally belong respectively to the Keynesian or Marxist analyses of the economy for which they are constructed and with which they are integrated. Thus, the Keynesian theory of credit can no more belong to a theory of the accumulation and centralisation of capital than the Marxist theory of credit (and its two forms) can have any relevance for Keynesian theory.

Third, then, this becomes specifically clear when it is observed that all bourgeois theory is organised around the concept of equilibrium. It is usually presumed that this equilibrium (and its associated levels of employment and natural unemployment) can eventually be maintained with price stability through an expansion of the money supply proportionate to the rate of increase of productivity. In contrast, we have argued that there is no such equilibrium and that these movements in the credit system cannot be taken to be exogenous nor be explained by an appended sociological theory of the motivation of governments to retain political power. Rather it is argued that there are systematic forces leading to an over-expansion of the credit system relative to the pace of competitive accumulation, and that this can give rise to stagflation, as opposed to deflation, the more the state intervenes in the credit system, as it must do, with the development of state monopoly capitalism.

NOTES

1. I have been helped in revising this chapter by the comments of the other authors on an earlier draft. I am particularly indebted to Simon Price for help in gathering the statistical tables together.

2. Consideration of economic and social reproduction is to be found in greater length in Chapter 6.

3. The quantity theory is considered at greater length in Chapter 5.

4. In addition, the rate of interest will have fallen, stimulating the investment that increases employment and output. We have not dealt here with the cases of the vertical *IS* curve and horizontal *LM* curve, for which employment cannot be raised, but neither of these necessarily lead to inflation.

5. This explanation is usually made by reference to the Keynesian 'cross'.

6. Alternatively, it could be argued that individuals suffer from money illusion.

7. The price of bonds yielding a steady income of one per annum can be shown to be worth $1/r$, that is to be inversely related to the rate of interest.

8. It is not necessary for there to be full employment in every sector of the economy, but it is necessary for full employment to be obtained in an essential (for example, skilled) sector of the labour force, giving rise to a 'bottleneck' to the expansion of output. Alternatively, there could be a bottleneck for some scarce resource, such as a primary commodity.

9. It can be observed here, however, that there are so many potential variations in the structure and specification of the Keynesian model that any empirical development of macro-economic aggregates can be accommodated by a whole series of conflicting models.

Each model has sufficient variation in the values of parameters, the variables to be included and the structure and lags in the model to 'explain' (if not predict) empirical economic developments. See Chapter 1 for a criticism of macro-econometric models. Also see Chapter 2, where it can be seen that the theory of the consumption function affects the size of adjustments. Indeed, Monetarists can argue that unless individuals suffer from 'tax illusion', an increase in government expenditure can at best be marginally inflationary at full employment if it is not financed by an increase in the money supply, since anticipated tax increases in the future will reduce desired present consumption.

10. It is necessary to observe that it is possible for real and money wages to increase at the same rate as productivity increases without price inflation.

11. However, it can be argued within the cost-push framework that the government acts in the interests of capital. See below, note 16.

12 The analysis of this properly belongs elsewhere, as it can be understood in macro-economics in isolation from the process of inflation.

13. There is a clear analogy here with bourgeois theory of international trade, which is treated more or less as a world economy of trading individuals (as nations).

14. It should be observed however that many governments present their economic problems as unique as an ideological justification for failure relative to other economies and for stringent economic policies to restore success.

15. For example, Monetarists emphasise deflationary policies through limitation in the growth of the money supply, trade unionists tend to support wage and price restraint in return for the *promise* of a commitment to policies stimulating growth and employment.

16. See also Chapter 6.

17. Radical theories also often see inflation as a state conspiracy to tax wages as do Monetarists!

18. It is not being suggested that these 'veils' have no effect as in bourgeois theories of the real economy and neutrality of money (e.g. the pre-Keynesian quantity theory). In particular, they concern both the forms taken by class-struggle over the level of wages and social services as well as intra-class conflict among the commercial, banking and industrial fractions of the bourgeoisie.

FURTHER READING

During the preparation of this chapter I benefited by consulting the surveys of Frisch (1977) and Laidler and Parkin (1975) to remind me of the orthodox approaches to inflation theory. The reader might prefer to consult a standard textbook such as Trevithick and Mulvey (1975). Those interested in radical theories of inflation might like to begin with Harvey (1977). A selection of writings by orthodox economists on the problems of and solutions to the current world recession is to be found in *Crisis '75 . . .?* (Institute of Economic Affairs, Occasional Paper 43, 1975).

Frisch, M. (1977), 'Inflation Theory 1963–1975: A "Second Generation" Survey', *Journal of Economic Literature*, 15 no. 4. (Dec 1977).

Harvey, J. (1977), 'Inflation Theory', *Marxism Today* (Jan 1977).

Laidler, D., and Parkin, M. (1975), 'Inflation: A Survey', *Economic Journal*, 85 (Dec 1975) 340.

Trevithick, J., and Mulvey, C. (1975), *The Economics of Inflation* (London: Martin Robertson).

CHAPTER 8

Neoclassical Theories of Discrimination: a critique

Stephen J. Lord

1 INTRODUCTION

This chapter is concerned with the existence and persistence of economic divisions within the working class of advanced capitalist countries, specifically those divisions associated with race and sex. It is a commonplace observation that some groups of workers – women and members of ethnic minorities, for example – are at a disadvantage in capitalist labour markets when compared to white males. Not only do they receive lower wages, but also they are often crowded into particular occupations and industries whose labour force consists of a high proportion of members of that group. Why is this so? Is this the result of the interplay of supply and demand in a competitive labour market, within which some individuals have a 'taste' or 'preference' for discrimination, or do these divisions arise from forces fundamentally related to the accumulation of capital, as Marxist economists have suggested?

This is the central issue that the following sections will examine. The main emphasis will be on a critique of neoclassical theories which attempt to account for discrimination in the labour market. The foundations of a Marxist approach will be briefly outlined in the final section, though the guide to further reading will hopefully enable those interested to pursue this more fully. The structure is as follows: Section 2 will describe some of the main employment characteristics of women and members of ethnic minorities; then the most important neoclassical model of discrimination developed by Gary Becker will be outlined, followed by a discussion of its major weaknesses and the modifications made to it by other neoclassical economists; finally, a more radical critique will be made of it, and the Marxist approach will be summarised.

2 WOMEN, MINORITIES AND THE LABOUR MARKET

Neoclassical theories of discrimination have been almost exclusively concerned with discrimination in the labour market, as indicated by differences in the wages paid to members of different groups, and their crowding into particular occupations, industries and jobs. In this brief summary we will concentrate on discriminatory practices that affect two main groups of workers – women, and members of ethnic or national minorities. The latter refers particulary to immigrant groups in Western Europe, in the case of Britain those from the New Commonwealth, i.e. India, Pakistan, Bangladesh, West Indies, some African countries and to blacks in the United States.

A cursory glance at some of the available figures would indicate that members of these groups are in a disadvantageous position in the labour market. In Britain, for example, the New Earning Survey showed that the average weekly earnings of full-time women in April 1977 was £50.0 exactly, while those of full-time men were £76.8; women thus earning 65.1 per cent of male wages. Owing to differences in the number of hours worked a week, a more reliable estimate of differences in wage rates is given by examining hourly earnings. The average hourly earnings of all full-time women, excluding those whose pay was affected by absence and excluding the effect of overtime hours, in April 1977 was 110.7 p. for manual workers, 143.7 p. for non-manual and 133.9 p. for all women workers. Comparable figures for males were 154.3 p., 227.9 p., and 181.5 p., so that the ratios of female/male earnings were 71.7 per cent, 63.1 per cent and 73.8 per cent respectively. There is some evidence that in recent years the difference between male and female wages has narrowed slightly, though there has been a noticeable stability of relative earnings between the two groups in the post-war period. Figures showing a similar earnings differential between men and women could be obtained for most countries. In the United States, for example, in 1975 white females earned about 61 per cent as much as white males.

There are also important differences between the wages paid to majority and minority groups. Though reliable figures are not easy to obtain for the United Kingdom, a study conducted by Politcal and

Economic Planning in 1974 suggested that the median gross weekly earnings of white men was £40.2, while for minority men it was £36.7, though there were substantial variations between the different minority groups and between different occupational categories. The differentials in earnings were much greater in non-manual occupations than for skilled manual and semi- and unskilled manual jobs, though this could partly be explained by the higher proportion of minority than of white men working shifts, which attract premium rates of pay. In the United States in 1975 black males earned 77 per cent of white male wages, though this proportion is found to vary cyclically, rising during economic expansion and falling during recessions.

Neoclassical economists argue that not all of this earnings differential can be attributed to discrimination. They assert that some of the differences in wages may be 'explained by referring to factors which affect the individual's productivity. This view derives from the human capital approach which indicates that differences in individual income arise from differences in the level of productive skills, talents and knowledge an individual has acquired through the educational system or through training and experience at work. Therefore, the wage differentials between members of different groups are 'standardised for differences in the amount of human capital they possess, and the residual is assumed to be a measure of the upper bound of 'pure wage discrimination'. Summarising these studies for male/female earnings Chiplin and Sloane (1976) conclude:

> both US and UK empirical findings in general suggest that a substantial though by no means overwhelming part of the gross differential between male and female earnings could be a consequence of discriminatory practices. Thus both macro standardisation exercises and micro studies at both industry and individual enterprise level by a number of investigators suggest that perhaps half or in many cases less of the gross differential is the result of discrimination. But much may depend on the number of variable investigators are able to include in their models. (p. 138)

A similar conclusion is reached when examining studies which examine black/white differentials in the United States. For example Arrow (1972) states: 'The studies tend to show that these factors will taken together, account for one-half or more of the observed incom differential, but there remains at least 40% unexplained.' (p. 85) However, this exercise in standardising for various factors which may affect the productivity of members of different groups, and assuming that the unexplained residual is an upper bound of discrimination, views discrimination in a very limited way and ignores the possibility of important 'feedback' mechanisms. Discrimination is a very pervasive force that affects all aspects of social and economic life. 'Pure wage discrimination' cannot be easily separated from the discriminatory treatment of particular groups in the provision of education and training, in housing, in the availability of health care, in the images presented by the media. Also, the statistical exercises ignore the impact that labour market discrimination may have on the achievement of particular productive characteristics. If, for example, women or blacks are likely to be shunted into low-paid, boring jobs which do not reward training or education, then it is not surprising that they will be less likely to undertake training, and will have higher rates of absenteeism and turnover, etc. These characteristics will be determined simultaneously with wages rather than prior to them.

Not only are there wage differentials between groups in the labour market, but there are also important differences in the attachment to occupations, industries and jobs. It is well known that female wage labour tends to be crowded into a relatively small number of jobs, in which the labour force is predominantly female. In Britian in 1977, for example, there were over 9 million women employed, of whom over two-thirds were in the service sector. Three service industries accounted for more than 50 per cent of total employment; distributive trades (17 per cent), professional and scientific services (e.g. typists, technicians, secretaries, teachers, nurses – 23 per cent), and miscellaneous services (laundries, catering, dry cleaners, hairdressers – 12 per cent). About one-quarter of female employment is in manufacturing industries, but of these over 50 per cent are in only four industries: food and drink, clothing and footwear, textiles and electrical engineering. The occupational segregation by sex would therefore tend to mirror the traditional relationship between men and women within the family unit. Part-time work is also much more widespread among women – over one-third of female wage labour is employed for 30 or less hours a week. If anything, these figures underestimate the crowding of females into 'women's work', as a more detailed breakdown of industrial attachment would indicate a greater segregation at the firm of establishment level. Very similar figures can be obtained for many countries. In the United States over a half of all working women are employed in jobs in which 70 per cent or more of workers are female.

There is also evidence to suggest that members of ethnic minorities in Britain are crowded into the less desirable jobs. For example a report by the Unit for Manpower Studies (1976) concludes:

> They are concentrated in conurbations where the pressure of demand for labour has usually been relatively high and in semi-skilled and unskilled jobs to which it is difficult to attract other workers because of such features as low earnings, a need to work unsocial hours and/or unpleasant working conditions. (They share these characteristics with earlier immigrants to Britain and with migrant workers in other Western European countries.) (p. 43)

In the United States blacks tend to be concentrated into the lowest-skilled and lowest-paid occupations, working in jobs which have great uncertainty of tenure, extremely low status in the eyes of both employer and employee, little or no chance of meaningful advancement, and unpleasant or exhausting duties.

This brief discussion of the wages earned and the work performed by women and by members of ethnic minorities certainly indicates that they are in a disadvantageous position in the labour market. Before we go on to look at the attempts by neoclassical economists to explain this disadvantage, we must raise the question of whether it is possible to treat female wage labour and minority group workers within the same explanatory framework. Although most neoclassical theorists have concentrated on racial discrimination it is usually assumed, implicitly or explicitly, that the basic models can be used to analyse sexual discrimination. For example, Becker (1957) believes his framework can be used for 'analysing discrimination in the market place because of race, religion, sex, color, social class, personality, and other non-pecuniary considerations.'

Additionally, Arrow (1973) argues: 'For the most part, the analysis (of racial discrimination) extends with no difficulty to sexual discrimination.' (p. 4)

This point will be discussed more fully in Section 5.

3 NEOCLASSICAL THEORY AND THE ECONOMICS OF DISCRIMINATION

We turn now to theories which seek to explain this discriminatory treatment. In this section we shall examine the model that has been formulated by Gary Becker, who attempts to analyse discrimination within a neoclassical framework.

The orthodox theory of the labour market can be traced back to the *Wealth of Nations* by Adam Smith. Wage differentials are seen as the outcome of the interplay of market forces. The theory assumes that in competitive equilibrium all 'factors of production' will get paid according to the value of their marginal product. Wage differentials can then be attributed to two sources. First, individuals differ in their endowments. Some individuals have more innate ability or productive skills, or receive more education or training, than do others. Second, individuals differ in their tastes. Some individuals have a greater relative preference for leisure over income, or value the non-pecuniary attributes of certain jobs, or have a greater aversion to risk, than do others. Firms are assumed to be profit maximisers, so that the forces of competition will ensure that equally productive workers will receive the same wages.

However, as we have seen, even after standardising for factors which could conceivably affect productivity, there still remains significant wage differences between members of different groups of workers. In view of the importance of this issue it is perhaps surprising how little attention it has received from economists until the last ten years or so. The first attempt to examine discrimination within a neoclassical framework was by Edgeworth in 1922. However, most of the recent discussion follow from the study *The Economics of Discrimination*, by Gary Becker, first published in 1957. Since then, many neoclassical economists have modified or elaborated Becker's original model, so that as Ray Marshall (1974) in a survey of neoclassical models points out: 'It should be emphasised, however, that the theorists who follow the neoclassical tradition differ among themselves; they agree only on the form of the theory, not on details or even on major conclusions.' (p. 849). This obviously creates difficulties for a brief summary of the neoclassical approach to discrimination. Becker's model, though, gives much of the flavour of the neoclassical analysis, so I will examine this first before looking at some of the subsequent modifications.

Becker sets himself the task of attempting to rectify the neglect of discrimination by economists. Though the analysis is presented in terms of racial discrimination, we have seen that he believes it is applicable to sexual, as well as other types of discrimination. Becker views the world in a conventional neoclassical manner capable of being analysed through the market-place interaction of autonomous individuals. He therefore makes the usual assumptions that individuals maximise utility, there is perfect competition and that all institutional arrangements are fixed and can be regarded as exogenous. As he is concerned to develop an explanation of pure wage discrimination, he further assumes that the relevant individuals or groups are equally productive – they differ only in colour, sex, etc., which has no bearing on the workers' productivity.

Becker starts his analysis by assuming that discrimination has its origins in individuals' tastes.

> Individuals are assumed to act as if they have 'tastes for discrimination', and these tastes are the most important immediate cause of actual discrimination. (p. 122)

Furthermore:

> If an individual has a 'taste for discrimination', he must act as if he were willing to pay something, either directly or in the form of a reduced income, to be associated with some persons instead of others. (p. 6)

Thus Becker sees discrimination as the result of individual tastes – in the same way that some individuals may have a taste or preference for apples rather than oranges. Tastes are usually treated by neoclassical economics as being exogenously determined, though in this case Becker does briefly discuss some of the factors which may affect this 'taste for discrimination'. It is taken to originate from the disutility of contact with certain individuals, although it is assumed that some direct contact must be necessary for the development of a desire to discriminate. In addition, this desire to avoid contact is sufficiently strong that individuals are prepared to pay for the privilege. As many writers have pointed out, this hardly conforms to reality; in many societies where discrimination is particularly virulent, blacks are employed as house servants; and it is especially difficult to maintain in the case of women.

Having introduced the notion of the 'taste for discrimination', Becker attempts to construct a monetary measure of it by using the concept of a discrimination coefficient. (In order to make the notation compatible with that of other writers I do not use Becker's notation.) If an employer can hire a black or female worker at a wage w, he is a discriminator if he acts as if the net wage were $w (1 + d_i)$, where d_i measures his discrimination coefficient. If the employer refuses to hire that worker at any wage he would have an infinitely large d_i. If the discrimination coefficient is negative it means that the employer has a preference for employing that individual – the case of nepotism or favouritism. Becker extends this concept of a discrimination coefficient to take into account discrimination by employees and by customers. An employee, offered the money wage rate w for working with members of the discriminated-against group, acts as if $w (1 - d_j)$ were the net wage rate, with d_j as his discrimination coefficient. A consumer, faced with a money price of p for the commodity produced (or sold) by black or women workers, acts as if the net price were $p (1 + d_k)$ with d_k as the relevant discrimination coefficient.

It follows from this concept of the discrimination coefficient that an employer will behave as if the net cost to him of favoured workers (W) is $W_w (1 + d_w)$, and the net cost of discriminated against workers (B) is $W_B (1 + d_B)$. If B workers are in fact discriminated against or W workers favoured, it follows that $d_B - d_w > 0$, so that equally productive B workers will only be employed if $W_w > W_B$. Thus, in equilibrium, discriminated-against workers will receive lower wages than other, equally productive, workers.

This analysis can easily be extended to take into account different categories of workers. Assume that there are two types of workers, skilled and unskilled. Then we can distinguish between intrafactor discrimination, the preferences, for example, of unskilled workers to work with unskilled members of their own groups, and interfactor discrimination, for example the preferences of skilled workers to work with unskilled members of their own group. If there is intrafactor discrimination, then, for example, unskilled workers will insist on higher wages if they are employed in a mixed labour force, than if they work only with members of their own group. This situation would lead to the segregation of the labour force rather than to wage differences. Clearly, interfactor discrimination is necessary (though not sufficient) for wage discrimination.

Becker uses an international trade model in an attempt to gain insight into the consequences of discrimination. He assumes that there are two 'societies' W and B, and that W owns relatively more capital and labour than does B.

Therefore,

$$\frac{C_w}{L_w} > \frac{C_B}{L_B},$$

where C_w = W capital, L_w = W labour, C_B = B capital, L_B = B labour. He further assumes identical linear homogeneous production functions, perfect competition and perfect substitutability of C and L between the two sectors. Before trade, $MPL_B < MPL_w$ and $MPC_w < MPC_B$, where MPL and MPC stand for the marginal products of labour and of capital in the two sectors. Therefore, W capitalists could get a higher return in B and B workers could get a higher return in W. Assuming the trade of factors rather than of commodities, each sector will find it advantageous to export its relatively abundant factor, until in equilibrium, $MPC_w = MPC_B$, and $MPL_w = MPL_B$.

If discrimination is now introduced into this model, so that W capitalists suffer a psychic cost whenever their capital is used by B, this will result in a reduction in the amount of W capital exported. In comparison with the competitive equilibrium without discrimination, MPL_B will decrease, MPL_w will increase, MPC_B will increase, and MPC_w will decrease. Because production is no longer efficient, Becker argues that discrimination will result in a reduction of the equilibrium incomes of W and B together. Also, B workers and W capitalists lose income, while W workers and B capitalists gain, though the gains to B capitalists are smaller than B workers' losses. Becker thus derives the rather surprising conclusion that by practising discrimination, W capitalists will suffer lower incomes.

4 NEOCLASSICAL THEORIES: SOME EXTENSIONS AND MODIFICATIONS

There are several important deficiencies in Becker's model of discrimination which other writers in the neoclassical tradition have attempted to remedy. These extensions or modifications have usually taken one of two forms. Some economists, most notably Arrow, have tried to develop models which stay within the competitive spirit of

Becker's approach. Others have modified Becker's assumptions either by emphasising the importance of non-competitive forces (trade unions, for example) or by removing the assumption that the relevant groups of workers are, in fact, equally productive.

This section will examine how neoclassical economists have attempted to cope with what are some of the more serious deficiencies with Becker's original model of discrimination. These are: the implications for the long-run persistence of discrimination, the use of international trade models for analysing who gains from discrimination, and the related problem of the derivation of individuals' 'tastes for discrimination'. Finally, I will briefly mention non-competitive and 'statistical' theories of discrimination.

A major problem with the Becker model concerns the long-run implications about the persistence of discrimination – the so-called dynamic instability problem. Becker shows that if employers have a taste for a discrimination, then the wages of the discriminated-against group will be lower than the wages of similarly productive workers who do not suffer from discrimination, i.e. $W_w > W_B$.

However, what is crucial for the long-run stability of this wage differential is not the average discrimination coefficients of employers but the marginal coefficient. If, for example, there are some employers who do not discriminate, they will only employ members of the discriminated-against groups, whom they can hire at the lower wage rate. Assuming competition, these employers will be able to undercut their discriminating rivals, employing greater numbers of the B group, until a long-run equilibrium is reached where $W_w = W_B$. Therefore, as long as there are variations in tastes, with at least one employer being a non-discriminator, wage equality will be the outcome, though there may be segregation of the labour force. It is also necessary for this international trade model to assume that there is only one traded commodity, or alternatively that all commodities are produced with identical production functions, otherwise the capital-intensive sector will specialise in production of the capital-intensive good and the labour-intensive sector will specialise in the labour-intensive commodity. As is well known from the theory of international trade, trade in commodities may be a perfect substitute for factor movement. Though factor–price equalisation is not guaranteed (we would have to further assume that the factor intensities of the two sectors are not too unequal, constant returns-to-scale production functions and no factor-intensity reversals) trade in commodities will work in the same direction as those employers who have no taste for discrimination in reducing wage inequalities.

Arrow has attempted to counter this criticism of the long-run instability of discriminatory wage differentials in neoclassical theory. He argues that if employers maximise a utility function that includes both profits and the ratio of W and B workers, i.e. $U = U (\pi, W/B)$, it is likely that this indifference surface is non-convex. If this is the case, Arrow proposes that the long-run adjustment processes do not work as perfectly as they are usually assumed to. Therefore:

> when there are significant non-convexities, the adjustment processes called for must be very rapid indeed; marginal adjustments are punished not rewarded. (Arrow, 1973, p. 20)

If the employer has invested in his work force either in hiring costs or in specific training costs, then he may not be induced to change his labour force in response to small changes in relative wages. Hence:

> If we start from a position where B workers enter an essentially all-W world, the discriminatory feelings by employers and by employees, both of the same and of complementary types, will lead to a difference in wages. The forces of competition and the tendency to profit-maximization operate to mitigate these differences. However, the basic fact of a personnel investment prevents these counteracting tendencies from working with full force. In the end, we remain with wage differences coupled with tendencies to segregation. (Arrow, 1973, p. 23)

However, this analysis implicitly assumes that no new factories, plants, shops, etc., are established. Otherwise these new establishments will hire only the discriminated-against group until wage equality is attained. In addition to this criticism, Chiplin (1976) has argued that Arrow's proof that utility functions which include the ratio of W to B workers are non-convex is invalid.

Freeman (1974) attempts to account for the long-run persistence of wage differentials by suggesting that discriminatory employers may remain in business because of limited supplies of non-discriminating employers. However, this would not appear to be a very convincing argument. Under competitive conditions the presence of only one non-discriminating capitalist would be sufficient to drive all the discriminating capitalists out of business. Also, we would not expect B capitalists to be discriminators, so they would additionally be able to undercut discriminating W capitalists. We must therefore conclude that the competitive model of Becker has at least one major drawback – it is unable to explain the persistence of discriminatory wage differentials over time, even if additional assumptions of non-convex indifference surfaces or limited supplies of non-discriminators are made.

A second objection to Becker's model of discrimination concerns his use of an international trade model. As we have seen, the competitive theory treats discrimination as if it is a restrictive practice that interrupts free trade between two independent 'societies'. Two problems arise with the use of this device. First, can discrimination be adequately represented by a model which examines restrictions between two independent sectors? Second, what does Becker's conclusion that discriminating employers necessarily lose income mean for their profitability?

The treatment of discrimination as an interruption to free trade between two independent societies is misleading. The discriminated-against groups (blacks, females) do not live in separate societies but in the same one as the discriminators. They may have few options and certainly not the option of refusing to trade with the dominant group. A satisfactory theory of discrimination surely requires an analysis of the methods by which members of the discriminated-against groups are integrated or incorporated into the economy and kept politically dormant, rather than the assumption that they belong to a separate, segregated society.

Becker also uses the international trade model to argue that discrimination by capitalists of the dominant group will in fact harm them in the sense that they must either pay or forfeit income in fulfilling their preferences. We can examine this contention in more detail by following Thurow's (1969) demonstration that the discrimination coefficient represents a downward shift in the W demand curve for B labour, i.e. D_1 to D_2 in Figure 8.1.

As Figure 8.1 indicates, the effect on W incomes will depend on the size of the discrimination coefficient, the supply elasticity of B labour and the demand elasticity by W for B labour. The effect on B incomes will be either through lower wages, or reduced employment opportunities, or some combination of the two. Assuming with Thurow, that the B group are likely to have a relatively inelastic supply function, it then follows that in most cases the W group will gain from discrimination.

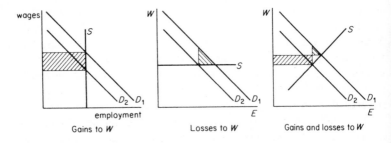

FIGURE 8.1
Capitalists' gains and losses from discrimination (shaded areas)

Optimal tariff theory can be used to calculate the discrimination coefficient that will maximise W income gains from discrimination.
Whether these income gains will accrue to W capitalists or W workers
will depend upon the exact nature of the utility function, as Arrow
(1973) has demonstrated. He argues that a plausible hypothesis is that
employers' utility depends only on the ratio of W to B workers, in
which case W capitalists neither gain nor lose income as compared with
the non-discriminatory position. It is therefore possible that capitalists
will increase money profits by practising discrimination, though for
Becker these pecuniary gains merely represent the payment for the non-
monetary costs of physical association.

The preceding discussion immediately leads on to a third weakness
of the competitive neoclassical analysis. Becker sees discrimination
as arising out of individual tastes, in which discrimination stems from
a desire not to physically associate with members of particular groups.
This would appear unrealistic, especially in the case of sex discrimination. Moreover, it is hard to see why capitalists would discriminate
against manual workers, with whom they have little or no physical
contact. This approach to discrimination also suffers from its specification of discrimination as being exogenous and therefore not explained. We are given no satisfactory explanation of the origin of discrimination. In order to tackle this problem, both Krueger (1963) and
Alexis (1973) depart from the conventional neoclassical assumption of
individual decision-making. Krueger assumes that capitalists will
attempt to maximise W incomes, while Alexis argues that envy–malice
considerations could result in W capitalists being concerned with the
relative share of wage income received by W workers. Neither explanation is particularly satisfactory. The reasons for this benevolence of W
capitalists are not given, and neoclassical theories are usually based

upon the assumption of individual preferences rather than on group interests.

The competitive model of discrimination would therefore appear to suffer from substantial limitations. There are also more radical criticisms of this sort of neoclassical model-building. Before going on to examine these and lay the basis for an alternative explanation, two additional approaches must be briefly mentioned.

Some writers have emphasised the importance of non-competitive forces – particularly trade unions – in perpetuating discrimination. Edgeworth (1922), for example, suggested that unions were responsible for the crowding of women workers into low-paid occupations in Britain. Similar allegations have been made about the exclusion of blacks by American trade unions. While there is no doubt that unions have played a role in perpetuating discrimination and in the exclusion of members of certain groups from particular jobs, it would be diffi- cult to maintain that unions were solely responsible for discrimin- ation. Explanations which rely on non-competitive forces have an *ad hoc* quality to them, and a more satisfactory analysis should in- corporate the actions of institutions like trade unions into it rather than assuming that their behaviour is exogenously determined.

An alternative approach, sometimes called the 'statistical' theory of discrimination, has been developed independently by Phelps (1972) and by Arrow (1973). The emphasis is placed not on employers' 'tastes for discrimination' but on their 'perceptions of reality'. There- fore:

> the employer who seeks to maximise expected profit will discrimin- ate against blacks or women if he believes them to be less qualified, reliable, long-term etc. on the average than whites and men, re- spectively, and if the cost of gaining information about the in- dividual applicant is excessive. Skin colour or sex is taken as a proxy for relevant data not samples. (Phelps, 1972, p. 659)

What is crucial for this analysis is where these beliefs come from. If they are, in fact erroneous we would not expect them to persist over time. If not, then the problem of discrimination is essentially defined away, since the different groups of workers are not equally productive. We are then left with no explanation of why there are systematic differences in productivity of the various groups of workers and we are no nearer a satisfactory analysis of the forces which generate discrimin- ation.

5   DISCRIMINATION AND MARXIST THEORY

The previous section has shown that there are significant weaknesses with the Becker model of discrimination: it does not explain the persistence over time of discriminatory wage differentials; it does not deal adequately with the question of who benefits from discrimination; and it does not satisfactorily account for the origins of individuals' taste for discrimination. In this section an alternative explanation of discrimination will be outlined which sees discrimination as being rooted in the working of the capitalist mode of production rather than as the result of exogenously determined tastes. First, however, some more fundamental criticisms will be made of neoclassical theory, which suggest that it is not just the details of Becker's model that are unsatisfactory, but that the whole approach is inadequate.

A major criticism of orthodox theory is that it attempts to construct models of the labour market using the individual as the basic unit of analysis. As we have seen, neoclassical models view discrimination as the outcome of the market-place interaction of individuals, some of whom have discriminatory preferences. We are given no satisfactory explanation of why these individuals happen to have such preferences; neoclassical theory conventionally treats preferences as being exogenously determined. This results in a circularity in the argument: discrimination is the result of individual preferences, and the only way we know that individuals have these preferences is because we know that discrimination takes place in the labour market. Without an analysis of why particular preferences are held, the theory becomes tautological, as Himmelweit (1977) argues, with the conclusions of the theory being derived mechanistically from the initial assumptions.

In addition, using the individual as the basic unit hardly captures the essence of discrimination, which is surely a phenomenon that involves and affects different groups in society. As mentioned before, even some orthodox theorists, for example Krueger (1963) and Alexis (1973), have rejected the individualistic approach and have tried to frame their analyses in terms of group interests. Not only are group interests ignored by the emphasis on individual behaviour, this method also makes it impossible to satisfactorily incorporate institutions into the analysis. The activities of institutions such as trade unions and the state obviously have a crucial impact on discriminatory practices, yet orthodox theory is forced to treat these institutions as exogenous, outside its analytical scope.

Perhaps the main weakness of orthodox theory is its inability to analyse social change. The concentration on relations of exchange in the market-place lead to these relations being treated as natural and eternal. There is no explanation given of how these relations come about, nor why there are differences in the position of some groups in the labour market – why, for example, blacks own less capital or why many individuals have only their labour-power to sell. By focusing on the individual, changes in the extent of discrimination can logically only be the result of changes in individual goals or constraints. This enables orthodox theory to play an ideological role as it suggest that the way to change discrimination or any other undesirable aspect of the economic system is not through political organisation, but by changes in individual behaviour. (For a further analysis of orthodox theory's inability to analyse social change, see Chap. 6.)

So far, it has been argued that orthodox theory is incapable of adequately analysing discrimination in modern societies. It will be suggested here that a Marxist analysis of the capitalist mode of production gives a more satisfactory framework for understanding the forces of racism and sexism. However, it must be pointed out that there does not exist a fully worked-out Marxist 'theory of discrimination', though in recent years a number of radical economists have attempted to incorporate an analysis of labour market divisions into Marx's theory of value, for example, Bowles and Gintis (1977).

In the first volume of *Capital* Marx shows how the processes of production in a capitalist society are incessantly transformed under the impetus of the principal driving force of that society, the accumulation of capital. For the working population this transformation manifests itself as a continuous change in the labour processes in each branch of industry, and as a redistribution of labour among sectors, occupations and industries. New skills are required, old skills become redundant. This process, Marx believed, would lead to an increasing homogenisation of the labour force, as social divisions were reduced, and as the labour processes associated with modern industry resulted in a constant deskilling of jobs. For example:

In the earlier epochs of history we find almost everywhere a complicated arrangement of society into various orders, a manifold gradation of social rank. . . . Our epoch, the epoch of the bourgeoisie, possesses, however, this distinctive feature: it has simplified class antagonisms. Society as a whole is more and more splitting up into two great hostile camps. . . . Bourgeoisie and Proletariat. (Marx and Engels, 1967, p. 80)

Also

Along with the tool, the skill of the workman in handling it passes over to the machine. The capabilities of the tool are emancipated from the restraints that are inseparable from human labour-power. Thereby the technical foundation on which is based the division of labour in Manufacture is swept away. Hence, in the place of the hierarchy of specialised workmen that characterises manufacture, there steps, in the automatic factory, a tendency to equalise and reduce to one and the same level every kind of work that has to be done by the minders of the machines: in the place of the artificially produced differentiations of the detail workmen, step the natural differences of age and sex. (Marx, 1967, p. 420)

Marx thus placed great emphasis on the impact of changes in the labour process of modern industry in leading to the increased homogenisation of the working class. However, since the 1960s a number of radical economists have suggested that there are important counteracting tendencies to the ones that Marx described, which have the effect of producing and reproducing divisions within the labour force. (See Rubery, 1978, and Bowles and Gintis, 1977.)

As mentioned above, Marx considered the accumulation of capital to be the main driving force of the capitalist mode of production. In order to accumulate capital the capitalist must obtain surplus value from his labour force, which is given by the difference between the value of output which labour power produces, and the value of labour-power itself. Thus the wage does not represent payment for the entire time worked, but rather just the amount of time that labour requires to produce its own consumption goods.

The value of labour power is determined, as in the case of every other commodity, by the labour-time necessary for the production, and consequently also the reproduction, of this special article. (Marx, 1967, p. 170)

This does not mean that the value of labour-power is merely a biologically determined subsistence level.

In contradistinction therefore to the case of other commodities there enters into the determination of the value of labour power a historical and moral element. (Marx, 1967, p. 171)

In order to increase the amount of surplus value produced, capital will attempt to increase the length of the working day or reduce the labour-time necessary for the production of wage goods – the extraction of absolute and relative surplus value. Marx also suggested that:

One consequence of the peculiar nature of labour-power as a commodity is that its use-value does not on conclusion of the contract between buyer and seller, immediately pass into the hands of the former. (ibid.).

As Bowles and Gintis (1977) argue, this means that the consumption of the use-value of labour by capital is problematic, as it depends not only on the technical abilities of the worker but also on the ability of the capitalist to induce the worker to perform.

The previous discussion immediately suggests the possibility that divisions in the labour force may be partly a result of the conflict between capital and labour over the extraction of surplus value. These divisions enable the capitalist to bargain separately with each group of workers, playing one group off against another, allowing him to impose lower wages or more unfavourable working conditions than would otherwise have been the case. Capital will use any divisive elements it can to fragment the labour force and to prevent any collective political or economic action. In addition, an important factor which may create a hierarchy in production is the resistance by the working class to the tendency of deskilling. Marx suggests:

By the excessive addition of women and children to the ranks of the workers, machinery at last breaks down the resistance which the male operatives in the manufacturing period continued to oppose to the despotism of capital (Marx, 1967, p. 402)

The struggle by white males against deskilling of production may therefore coincide with a struggle against the introduction of female or minority wage labour, which has as a consequence the incorporation of these groups at the bottom of the job hierarchy.

It may also be the case that some groups of workers may be paid a wage that is lower than the value of their labour power. Within the social deivision of labour in capitalism the task of maintaining and reproducing workers is largely given to women.

Then, as Beechley (1977) argues:

> In the case of married women, it is their dependence upon male wages within the family for part of the cost of production and re-production of labour power which accounts for the possibility of individual capitals paying wages which are below the value of labour power. The married woman does not, therefore, have to pay for the entire costs of reproducing her labour power, nor for that of her children who will become the next generation of wage labourers and domestic labourers. This argument, if correct, can explain why women's wages are significantly lower than men's. (p. 53)

Similar arguments may apply to the case of immigrant workers, if some of the costs of the production and reproduction of their labour-power are met in their country of origin. However, there may be less scope in Britain for this possibility, where, because of nationality laws, workers from the New Commonwealth have been entitled to settle with their families.

Finally, women and members of ethnic minorities may constitute an important segment of the industrial reserve army. This, Marx argues, is indispensable to the process of capital accumulation, as it acts as a reservoir of labour-power which can be brought into expanding branches of production and then disposed of when production con-tracts, and because it acts as a competitive force, helping discipline the rest of the labour force. Both women and immigrant groups constitute important components of this industrial reserve army, particularly as they may be partially dependent upon sources of income other than their own wages. Also, different probabilities of unemployment be-tween different groups reduce the likelihood of unity between the employed and unemployed, while concentrating the burden of un-employment on groups least able to impose political or economic costs on the capitalists.

This brief discussion has suggested an alternative basis for analysing the role of women workers and members of ethnic minorities in the labour market. Instead of discrimination being seen as a result of exogenously determined tastes, the differential treatment of different groups is considered as an integral part of the extraction of surplus value in the capitalist mode of production.

FURTHER READING

The standard neoclassical theory of discrimination is found in Becker (1957) and in Arrow (1972, 1973). A useful summary is in Marshall (1974)

For descriptions of the position of women and ethnic minorities in the U.K. labour market, see Mackie and Pattullo (1977) and Political and Economic Planning (1974).

Good summaries of the largely American literature on segmented labour markets are Bowles and Gintis (1977) and Rubery (1978).

For an introduction to Marxist theories of the labour process and the labour market, see Braverman (1974), Beechley (1977) Conference of Socialist Economists (1976) and Sivanandan (1976).

REFERENCES

Alexis, M. (1973) 'A Theory of Labor Market Discrimination with Interdependent Utilities', *American Economic Review*, 63 (May 1973).

Arrow, K. J. (1972) 'Models of Job Discrimination', in A. H. Pascal (ed.), *Racial Discrimination in Economic Life* (Lexington, Mass: Lexington Books).

Arrow, K. J. (1973) 'The Theory of Discrimination', in O. Ashenfelter and A. Rees, *Discrimination in Labor Markets* (Princeton, N.J.: Princeton University Press).

Becker, G. (1957) *The Economics of Discrimination* (Chicago: University of Chicago Press).

Beechley, V. (1977) 'Some Notes on Female Wage Labor in Capitalist Production', *Capital and Class* (Autumn 1977).

Bowles, S., and Gintis, H. (1977) 'The Marxian Theory of Value and Heterogeneous Labour: a Critique and Reformulation', *Cambridge Journal of Economics*, vol. 1, no. 2 (June 1977).

Braverman, H. (1974) *Labor and Monopoly Capital* (New York: Monthly Review Press).

Chiplin, B. (1976) 'Non-convexity of Indifference Surfaces in the Case of Labor Market Discrimination: Note', *American Economic Review*, vol. 66 (1976).

Chiplin, B., and Sloane, P. J. (1976) *Sex Discrimination in the Labour Market* (London: Macmillan).

Conference of Socialist Economists (1976) *On the Political Economy of Women*, C.S.E. Pamphlet No. 2.

Coulson, M., Magas, B., and Wainwright, H. (1975) 'The Housewife and her Labour under Capitalism: A Critique', *New Left Review,* **89** (Jan–Feb 1975).

Edgeworth, F. Y. (1922) 'Equal Pay to Men and Women for Equal Work', *Economic Journal,* **32** (1922).

Freeman, R. B. (1974) 'Alternative Theories of Labor-market Discrimination: Individual and Collective Behaviour', in G. M. von Furstenberg, B. Harrison and A. R. Horowitz, *Patterns of Racial Discrimination,* vol. 2 (Lexington, Mass: D. C. Heath).

Himmelweit, S. (1977) 'The Individual as Basic Unit of Analysis', in F. Green and P. Nore (eds), *Economics: An Anti-Text* (London: Macmillan).

Krueger, A. O. (1963) 'The Economics of Discrimination', *Journal of Political Economy,* **71** (Oct 1963).

Mackie, L., and Pattullo, P. (1977) *Women at Work* (London: Tavistock Publications).

Marshall, R. (1974) 'The Economics of Racial Discrimination: A Survey', *Journal of Economic Literature,* vol. 12 no. 3 (Sep 1974).

Marx, K. (1967) *Capital,* vol. 1 (London: Lawrence & Wishart).

Marx, K., and Engles, F. (1967) *The Communist Manifesto* (Harmondsworth: Penguin Books).

Phelps, E. S. (1972) 'The Statistical Theory of Racism and Sexism', *American Economic Review,* **62**, (Sep 1972).

Political and Economic Planning (1974) *Racial Disadvantage in Employment,* P.E.P. Report No. 544

Rowbotham, S. (1973) *Women's Consciousness, Man's World* (Harmondsworth: Penguin Books).

Rubery, J. (1978) 'Structured Labour Markets, Worker Organisation and Low Pay', *Cambridge Journal of Economics,* vol. 2 (1978).

Sivanandan, A. (1976) *Race, Class and the State: The Black Experience in Britain,* Race and Class Pamphlet No. 1 (London: Institute of Race Relations).

Thurow, L. (1969) *Poverty and Discrimination* (Washington, D.C.: Brookings Institution).

Unit for Manpower Studies (1976) *The Role of Immigrants in the Labour Market,* Dept of Employment, Project Report.

CHAPTER 9

Ideology, Knowledge and Neoclassical Economics: some elements of a Marxist account

Simon Mohun

INTRODUCTION

That modern economic theory is ideological, in the sense of justifying the *status quo,* or reconciling people to the workings of capitalism, is not an uncommon position. Yet modern economic theory has both a considerable and sophisticated technical apparatus, and a set of methodological procedures, which together give it pretensions not only to be a social science, but also to be scientific. Among those who criticise modern economics, there is little attempt to construct a theory of ideology, perhaps partly because there is little attempt by those who defend modern economics to construct a theory of knowledge into which to insert it. Accordingly, the first task of this chapter is to attempt within a Marxist framework to give some account of why neoclassical economics is ideological rather than scientific.[1]

The first section considers the exchange process and the circulation of commodities, and tries to suggest, first, why the appearances of capitalism take the particular forms that they do, and, second, that these appearances are systematically delusory in that they suggest that capitalism is something that can be analysed from an individualistic perspective. This theme is continued in Section 2, which tries to establish, first, the necessity of a class perspective in order to understand capitalism, and, second, and paradoxically, that adherence to an individualistic perspective is in itself to take a class position. Section 3 then applies this understanding to neoclassical economics and attempts to show on this basis its fundamental ideological character.

However, the analysis within Marxist discourse of a particular discipline as ideology is not in itself unproblematic. The first two sections are based closely on a particular reading of volume 1 of *Capital*, especially on parts I, II and VII; while the interpretation is a sufficiently common one to allow its restatement and its application to neoclassical economics in a straightforward manner, there is in fact no settled agreeement within Marxism on how to theorise and to apply the concepts of science, knowledge and ideology. Nor is it likely that there would be; first, in principle, since Marxism cannot be divorced from history, and, second, in practice, since the class-struggle in this century has continued to take unexpected directions (due to the longevity of reformism in capitalist societies and to Stalinism in post-capitalist societies, and to their interaction). Consequently, while all Marxists agree on the function of ideology as a justification of the *status quo*, there is considerable disagreement on just what ideology is and how it performs this function. Accordingly, the second half of this chapter shifts the focus to the Marxist controversies around these issues; but one consequence of the Marxist rejection of an harmonious and stable world of common interests must be the recognition that the resolution of these controversies can no more be prejudged than can the course of the class-struggle itself.

PART A: IDEOLOGY AND NEOCLASSICAL ECONOMICS

1 THE APPEARANCES OF CIRCULATION AND THE FETISHISM OF COMMODITIES

What characterises capitalist society as different from all other societies is the predominance of the process of exchange. It is not that prices, markets, demand and supply are peculiar to capitalism; rather, what is special is the generalisation of exchange to incorporate within its ambit the purchase and sale of labour-power for periods of time. Moreover, while the worker is free to sell his labour-power to whomsoever he chooses, he is not free not to sell his labour-power at all.[2] Consequently, an analysis of capitalism as an historically specific mode of production has to be structured around this fundamental perspective.

But this perspective is double-edged. On the one hand, the worker is separated from the means of production (i.e. freed from them) and thereby forced into the market to sell the commodities he possesses. Since he has no means of production with which to produce anything, he has to sell the only commodity which he does possess, which is his capacity to produce things, or his labour-power. On the other hand, however, in the market-place, he confronts the owner of the means of production as a free man, as his juridical equal. On the one hand he is forced into the market, and on the other hand he is a free agent. Both of these aspects are critical to an account of labour-power as a commodity, which is to say that both are critical to an account of capitalism *qua* capitalism.

Call these aspects Aspect I and Aspect II respectively. Then any theory which focuses exclusively on Aspect II will have as essential components the following ideas. First, private property: each agent in the market has a commodity to sell which is his own to dispose of as he wishes, and for as long as he does not so dispose of it he has unlimited and exclusive rights to it. Second, freedom: each agent is a free agent, free to leave and to enter the market at will, free to purchase and free to sell. Third, therefore, equality: commodity owners confront one another in the market as equals, exchanging equivalents via the agency of money. And fourth, optimality: it follows that only those exchanges take place which render at least one of the agents better off, and neither worse off. Of course, there are constraints on exchange (budget constraints, technology constraints), but these constraints are economic ones and in no way alter Marx's characterisation of the exchange process as 'in fact a very Eden of the innate rights of man'.[3]

Yet in all of this Aspect I has disappeared. It is hidden by the symmetry of the exchange-process; all commodity transactions are analysed in like manner by the equation of subjective preferences at the margin with price ratios. Thus formally there is nothing to distinguish the equation of the marginal rate of substitution of apples for pears with their price ratio from the equation of the marginal rate of substitution of income for leisure with the wage rate. Nor should there be, as long as theoretical attention is focused on the exchange process. As Marx writes, the labour of the individual asserts itself as a part of the labour of society, only by means of the relations which the act of exchange establishes directly between the products, and indirectly, through them, between the producers. To the latter, therefore, the relations connecting the labour of one individual with that of the next appear, not as direct social relations between individuals at work, but as what they really are, material relations between persons and social relations between things.[4]

This is really the heart of the problem. For under capitalism the social relations between the people who produce commodities actually appear as different from what they really are. Social relations are established by the production process, through the relationships of ownership/non-ownership of the means of production, but they are only given social justification by the process of exchange and the circulation of commodities. For it is exchange which establishes the social links between the different producers, which establishes, that is, a social division of labour, through its determination of which production processes are profitable and which are not. Yet profit is not produced by exchange; it is only realised in it. Hence the exchange-process does not define the content of social relations – it merely provides them with their context. To confuse context with content is to be blind to Aspect I, and to collapse Aspect II from a social process into a natural one.

Instead of being a social process which realises a particular set of social relations, exchange is transformed into an asocial process concerned with the relationship between commodities of determinate characteristics on the one hand, and individuals whose initial endowments are arbitrary and whose preferences are exogenous on the other hand. The question then of why a social process can be transformed into a natural one becomes a question of why it is that capitalist society necessarily appears to its agents (both capitalists and workers) as something different from what it really is. That is, why are its real forms of appearance delusory?[5] The answer comprises the Marxist theory of fetishism.

It is important to be clear at this point. It is not the case that the appearances of capitalism are an illusion which must be stripped away to reveal some inner essence which is 'really' what capitalism is. The appearances of capitalism are real enough, but they are delusory, deceiving the agents as to the import of their activities. So what are at issue here are the beliefs, the coherent or even not so coherent sets of ideas of the agents of capitalist society, and what it is that structures these beliefs in a particular way. This is precisely the terrain of the theory of ideology. For, more generally, what is at issue is the process whereby living subjects experience their environment. Its epistemological character is, therefore, one of exploring the necessary connections between, on the one hand, the social relations which define a determinate mode of production and, on the other hand, the ways in which these relations are experienced by the agents of that mode of production.[6]

However, Marxism reveals a radical disjuncture between social relations and the way in which they are experienced, a separation forced by capitalism itself. It follows that this disjuncture requires a theorisation of reality both to set against (real) appearances and to explain why those appearances take precisely the forms that they do. It is in this sense of arising from a deceptive reality that ideology is false consciousness. Hence an account of fetishism is crucial to an account of ideology. For it was suggested above that such false consciousness is generated by the collapse of social relations into natural ones, and that this actually does occur in capitalist society. It is clearly then incorrect to suggest that false consciousness means that agents simply deceive themselves, for the collapse really *does* take place. *What has to be explained is why reality is itself mystificatory.*

Consider a society comprising a community of individuals, all of whom have free and equal access to the means of production. Such communal ownership implies that the total labour-time of this soceity is allocated to various projects by agreement, in order to produce an aggregate social product. This latter is partly made up of produced means of production, which by assumption of communal ownership remain socially owned; and the aggregate social product is also made up of means of subsistence or consumer goods, which must be distributed by some method in order that consumption can actually occur. *For example,* let each individual's share of consumer goods be determined by the time he spends in production as a proportion of society's aggregate labour-time. Then labour-time serves as a measure both of the relative importance society attaches to different production activities, and of the share of each individual in aggregate social labour and hence of the individual consumption of that individual. In this sort of society the social relations which each individual experiences, with respect to the labour performed and the goods produced, are immediately transparent and quite unproblematic.

Now consider by contrast a commodity-producing society; that is, a society in which single or groups of individuals produce things independently of each other, and then bring those things to the market as commodities to sell in order to purchase other commodities. That each individual's labour has a social character is only revealed by the act of exchange, by the exchange-ratios established between the commodities, and thereby, and only indirectly, by the relations established between the producers. So to the producers themselves, that their labour is social labour, or has social validity, in fact appears as a property of the object produced by their labour.

For an individual's labour has in social terms a dual character. Obviously the labouring activity must be useful: it must produce something which satisfies a determinate social want, i.e. which is a use-value. But it is also the case that the individual himself has wants, whose satisfaction entails the generalisation of exchange such that the private useful labour of each producer is exchangeable (in the form of commodities) for the private useful labour of any other producer. Thus exchange equates the immense variety of private useful labouring activities which occur, and this equalisation is only meaningful in terms of abstraction from what it is that renders such activities different. This equalisation, therefore, can be considered as an equalisation of abstract human labour; that is, of value. The measure of this value can only be units of time, and by virtue of the social abstraction that is value, time only counts in so far as it is 'socially necessary'. Accordingly, that a private individual producer's labouring activity is socially useful takes the form in this society that the product of that activity be useful and, in particular be useful to others. Further, that his own particular activity is socially the equal of all other particular sorts of activities takes the form that the heterogeneous products of all the different activities possess the common quality of having value. Thus it is not labour which is socially apparent, but rather the value of the products of that labour; that more or less time is spent in labouring activity again is not socially apparent: instead the value of commodities is greater or less; and hence these value relations between commodities are the real appearances of the social relations whose collectivity defines the mode of production.

The difference then between the two sorts of society just contrasted is that, whereas in the first social relations are transparent and accessible to comprehension by virtue of participation in them, in the second the very process of the circulation of commodities, veils the social relations which exist. For the properties of commodities, as the products of labour, as social things, are ascribed to commodities as their natural qualities, as part of their material substance. This is precisely the process of fetishism. And the collapse of social facts into natural ones is by no means a simple error of perception – rather such perceptions are generated by the way in which capitalist society actually does appear, by the forms in which the social relations of capitalist society really present themselves. Thus the appearances of circulation are not illusions in the sense of being false representations of reality; they are real properties of an exchange process which, far from being an illusion, is the process which establishes the social relations between the independent producers via the exchange of their commodities. The argument, then, is that such a process generates fetishism and is thereby delusory.

2 THE CLASS RELATIONS OF PRODUCTION

If the fetishism of commodities arises through the collapse of a social world into a natural one, it is also the case that fetishism eliminates Aspect I and thereby confuses the context of social relations with their content. Since this content is defined with respect to the process of production, it follows that any journey from the context to the content of the social relations of capitalism must involve a shift of theoretical focus from the process of circulation to the process of production. And this requires further consideration of the consequences of the defining characteristics of capitalism.

The only commodity which the majority of people have in capitalist society is their ability to work; that is, they can alienate this ability from themselves as the commodity labour-power, selling it for a wage. On the other side of the transaction the purchaser of labour-power can then consume it in combination with his means of production (the production process), and use his juridical rights of ownership to appropriate the difference between the value of the commodities emerging from the production process, and the value of the commodities required to ensure that the living labourer can resell his labour-power each time period. Thus surplus-value is produced; it follows that for part of his working period the labourer produces a value equivalent to the value of his labour-power, and for the remainder of his working period he produces value with no equivalent, or surplus-value, for the capitalist. Yet each commodity owner can receive in the market the full value of the particular commodity he is selling, and still this process of surplus-extraction can continue.[7] The capitalist's money advanced to purchase means of production and labour-power is capital then in so far as it functions as an expansion of value: any one cycle of production concludes with the capitalist possessed of a greater sum of money than at its commencement. The initial sum of money advanced is money-capital; the commodities which it purchases are capital: the means of production are constant capital – constant, since value changes its location from the means of production as they are consumed (depreciate) to the product, but does not change in its amount; and labour-power is variable capital – variable, since this portion of capital advanced expands in value as workers produce more value than their labour-power possesses. Finally, the commodities produced are capital, and are sold for money, which as capital begins a fresh cycle of production. Accordingly, capital is a social relation between those who own the means of production and those who do not, a relation which is coercive since it both maintains and extends the scope of this binary opposition.

Now the conversion of money into capital actually occurs both within the sphere of exchange and outside it; within it, because the sale and purchase of labour-power as a commodity is necessary to the conversion; but outside it since what follows such a transaction is the consumption of labour-power entirely within the sphere of production thereby producing surplus-value. Such a linkage, or articulation, of circulation with production is obscured by the process of circulation itself. For the way in which the individual is paid makes it appear as though the wage measures the value which is placed on his labour, whereas, in fact, it is the value of his labour-power. What is thereby concealed is the division of the working day into a period during which the individual produces commodities whose value is equivalent to the value of his labour-power, and the remaining period, in which commodities are produced without equivalent and are appropriated by the capitalist.

What is important here, then, is that the equivalent exchange in the market between worker and capitalist is maintained wherein the former receives the full value of the commodity he sells; and yet surplus-value accrues to the latter through his organisation of the consumption of the use-value of that commodity in the labour-process and his sale of the products of that process. On an individual basis, the capitalist does not cheat his workers. But whereas, in fact, he pays for labour-power, it appears as though he pays for labour. Were the reality transparent, there would still be no cheating on an individual basis, but in the aggregate the totality of work performed would be seen to support a class which is wholly parasitical, and parasitical upon a property relation historically imposed by force. The appearance of payment for labour conceals this and thereby, as Marx writes, 'forms the basis of all the juridical notions of both labourer and capitalist, of all the mystifications of the capitalistic mode of production, of all its illusions as to liberty, of all the apologetic shifts of the vulgar economists.'[8] This suggests that, in order to penetrate further the veil of circulation, what is required is the consideration of classes rather than the consideration of individuals – for the cheating that does occur is an unconscious consequence of the division of classes with respect to the ownership of the means of production. This is substantiated further by the analysis of the accumulation process: the extraction of surplus-value and its reconversion into capital in a fresh cycle of production.

Consideration of capitalism as an accumulating system through time demonstrates that certain features possessed by the production process as an isolated single act, starting with inputs and finishing with outputs, in fact dissolve when the production process is conceived as a continuous and repetitive one. This is easiest to see if the assumption is temporarily made that the economy is in a stationary state wherein all surplus-value is consumed as revenue by capitalists, rather than ploughed back into production as capital. Three conclusions can then be drawn.

First the sale of the commodities produced by the labour of the preceding period provides the funds wherefrom the labour-power of the current period can be paid; and similarly for the labour of the current period and the labour-power of the next one. From the perspective of the *individual* (worker or capitalist) wages appear to be a value advanced from the capitalist's own funds. But from the perspective of the *working class*, wages are a value produced by the working class in the last period, and are advanced by the capitalist class to the working class in the current period in order that the latter may claim a portion of the commodities it has produced but which the former has appropriated. For it is only its class position with respect to such appropriation which ensures that the capitalist class has any funds at all with which to purchase labour-power and employ labour. But the forms in which this transaction appears – a contract between individual employee and individual employer – conceal the reality of the process:

the appearance is an individual relation of independence, but the reality is a class relation of dependence.

The second conclusion generalises the first: it must eventually be the case that the total value consumed by the capitalist summed across periods comes to equal the original capital he advanced. Consequently, once this has happened, his present capital, which by assumption of a stationary state is equal in value to his original capital, must solely consist of accumulated surplus-value, of unpaid labour which he has appropriated without equivalent.

The third conclusion is that the repetitive process of production reproduces the capitalist relation of separation between workers and the means of labour, or means of production, and hence perpetuates the worker as wage-labourer and the capitalist as capitalist. For the production process produces material use-values as capital, which is a means of creating more use-values, and thus capital. By contrast, the worker, the actual source of wealth, enters and leaves the process in the same state, for he has no means of making that wealth his own. Through his productive consumption of the means of production in the production process – which is also the consumption of his labour-power by the capitalist who bought it – he produces the products which, converted into commodities and thence into money, become the value which consumes his value-creating power, both next period, as means of production over which he has no command, and this period, as the means of consumption essential to his continued existence. And through his individual consumption of these latter, his labour-power is reproduced for further exploitation by capital. What is important here then is the capitalist's double benefit in converting part of his capital into labour-power; on the one hand, he increases the value of his whole capital through the labourer's productive consumption, and, on the other hand, he provides the means whereby the labourer is produced and reproduced as wage-labourer. For the worker's individual consumption is both the means for his maintenance and reproduction, and the means whereby, having consumed his means of existence, he is forced back into the market to sell his labour-power anew. Thus while it is purely contingent that individual worker and individual capitalist meet in the market-place as seller and buyer (of labour-power), at the level of classes, the capital-relation is continually reproduced.

These results, that the worker produces the capital advanced as wages, that all capital is capitalised unpaid labour, and that capitalist production continually reproduces the capital-relation, are easiest to demonstrate with a stationary state assumption. Relaxing this assumption and hence allowing accumulation only serves to reinforce these results. The analysis of the accumulation of value thereby shows how the exchange of equivalents in the market-place between buyers and sellers of commodities, an exchange characterised by private property relations sanctified by freedom, equality and optimality, is, in fact, only an apparently equal exchange. For, while the worker sells his labour-power at its value, what he receives in exchange is a portion of the product of previous surplus labour appropriated without equivalent in the past by the capitalist. And, in addition, the worker gives to the capitalist a greater quantity of living labour than is materialised in the wage-bundle of commodities he receives in return. What is crucial here then is the shift in focus wherein the equal exchange of the circulation process – in which everybody is paid the full value of the commodity he sells – is shown to conceal and to mystify the unequal exchange of the production process which is necessary for the maintenance of exploitation. This shift is not only a theoretical transition from consideration of circulation to consideration of production; it is also, and critically, a transition from consideration of relations between individuals to consideration of relations between classes. Marx summarises this as follows:

> The relation of exchange subsisting between capitalist and labourer becomes a mere semblance appertaining to the process of circulation, a mere form, foreign to the real nature of the transaction, and only mystifying it. . . . At first the rights of property seemed to us to be based on a man's own labour. At least, some such assumption was necessary since only commodity owners with equal rights confronted each other, and the sole means by which a man could become possessed of the commodities of others, was by alienating his own commodities; and these could be replaced by labour alone. Now, however, property turns out to be the right, on the part of the capitalist, to appropriate the unpaid labour of others, or its product, and to be the impossibility, on the part of the labourer, of appropriating his own product.[9]

It follows then that any analysis which has as its focus the circulation process and the exchange-relations established between individual commodity owners in the market will miss the structured relationship of inequality between classes in capitalist society, and will thereby ideologically support such a relationship through its analysis of the equilibrium and optimality properties of the exchange-process.

3 NEOCLASSICAL ECONOMICS AS IDEOLOGY

Modern economic theory has devoted considerable effort to the rigorous establishment of a set of propositions which are concerned with the relationships between the concepts of efficiency, competition, equilibrium and optimality. These propositions comprise both a theory of prices which govern resource-allocation decisions, and a theory of the relationship between the production technology and these prices; both have emerged from a careful investigation of the conditions under which Adam Smith's 'invisible hand' parable may be given substantive content. Indeed, the main achievement has been the rigorous specification of the conditions whereby an efficient allocation of resources can be attained by decentralising economic decisions through a price mechanism. Moreover since this analysis is established at a level of generality which focuses only on the allocation of physical quantities of resources and the associated valuations at that allocation, it is supposed to be institution-free. In other words, the analysis can be given an organisational interpretation which can incorporate any desired institutional framework; it is consequently immediately applicable both to present-day economies of completely different institutional persuasions, and to economies of the past whose institutional structures have long since disappeared.[10]

The association of equilibrium with optimality, and the assertion of the primacy of equilibrium, has the following consequence. Given the stringent conditions required for the results, all features of the world which do not conform to such stringency are relegated to the status of imperfections. For, because the building blocks of the model are atomistic individuals, each of whose preferences is to count, then the resultant outcome of the interaction of the decisions of these individuals is a correspondence between their subjective preferences and the allocation of resources - a harmonious conformity between subjective marginal rates of substitution and objective price-ratios. It follows that disturbances due to monopoly, or externalities, or information costs, are precisely that, disturbances to an otherwise harmonious picture which can be removed by *ad hoc* and piecemeal policy prescriptions.

In this respect, contemporary (neoclassical) economic theory is ideological. But not only in this respect; the theory is set up in such a way that it can only be ideological, and its purported, scientific status has reference not to present-day capitalist society (nor indeed to any other society) but rather to the study of programming techniques and of rational choice. It is important to understand why this is the case. Neoclassical economics is individualistic in that it assumes a given distribution of initial endowments among atomistic individuals (consumers and producers) who are supposed to maximise (a function based on an exogenous preference structure, and a profits function) subject to constraints (a budget constraint, and an exogenous technology constraint). Under suitable conditions the interaction of these decisions yields both a competitive equilibrium and a Pareto-optimal state (and, since the theory of resource allocation has an associated theory of competitive (shadow) prices, Adam Smith's intuition is vindicated). Beginning with quite asocial individuals a society is constructed purely by reference to a given initial situation, a given technology, and a given set of psychological characteristics. Since the individuals are asocial, so too is production, a process in which inputs are mysteriously transformed into outputs. And, since production is asocial, so indeed is society, in the sense that the *status quo* exists and always will exist: production is capitalistic (using 'capital', understood as means of production) rather than capitalist.

To clarify this, consider the following example from one of the best exponents of neoclassical economics:

Workers get paid for working; what do capitalists get paid for? For 'waiting' while roundabout processes of production percolate, or for 'abstaining' from some current consumption in favour of replacing or augmenting the stock of capital and maintaining or increasing future consumption. Since so much of the 'waiting' gets done in expensive automobiles and luxurious resorts, while the 'abstinence' excites little sympathy in an even slightly cynical observer, the whole apparatus begins to look like a transparent verbal trick. . . . But even so, there is no excuse for economists to lose the concept in their resentment at the language. One of the elegant showpieces of economics is its analysis of the resource-allocation implications of a system of prices or shadow prices. We have learned to free this analysis of ethical overtones. All that is necessary in capital theory is to draw a conceptual distinction between the imputed return to capital and the income of capitalists. Here, as elsewhere in economics, but with rather more irony here, the best way of understanding the economics of capitalism may be to think about a socialist economy.[11]

The supposed institution-free nature of the analysis is plain here, as is its predication upon asocial and ahistorical individuals.

But human beings are not abstract individuals in arbitrary initial situations, possessed of given and exogenous preferences, and having access to a given and exogenous technology. Rather, they are social phenomena, both the products of particular societies, and the spokesmen (whether conscious or unconscious) of these societies. Indeed, it follows from the discussion of the last section that the maintenance of an individualistic standpoint, since it cannot penetrate the reality of appearances to the reality of exploitation, is in itself a class standpoint: the standpoint of the bourgeoisie, or capitalist class.[12] For there is no way an individualistic perspective can achieve a comprehension of the class nature of society. In this sense individualism is a theoretical obstacle to the comprehension of the reality of classes, and of the appropriation by one class of the unpaid labour of the other.[13] Yet an individualistic perspective does arise out of the real appearances of capitalism. Exchange relations are the necessary starting-point both for and of the conceptions of their economic relations which individuals have; the experience of exchange-relations spontaneously generates these conceptions. The totality of such conceptions, or representations, is precisely constitutive of bourgeois ideology, for this totality comprises the way in which individuals experience their environment: an environment of relationships, contracted with other individuals, which generates a more or less coherent set of beliefs concerning this environment, a set of beliefs which are delusory. And theorisation based on these conceptions as axiomatic is bourgeois economics.

This is not a subjective phenomenon in the sense that some people try deliberately and consciously to deceive others: bourgeois ideologists are not 'bad' people. It is true that the emergence of neoclassical economics is roughly coincident historically with the emergence of a mass labour movement. And Marshall could write in 1897 about a strike of engineering workers: 'I want these people to be beaten at all costs: the complete destruction of unionism would be as heavy a price as it is possible to conceive, but I think it is not too high a price.'[14] Or Pareto could write in his *Manual of Political Economy*:

> the work of the liberals of the first half of the nineteenth century has paved the way for the demagogical oppression which is now dawning. Those who demanded equality of citizens before the law certainly did not foresee the privileges which the masses now

enjoy; the old special jurisdictions have been abolished, and a new one instituted, the arbitration boards favouring the workers. Those who demanded freedom to strike did not imagine that this freedom, for the strikers, would consist of beating workers who continued to work and setting fire to factories with impunity. Those who demanded equality of taxes to aid the poor did not imagine that there would be a progressive tax at the expense of the rich, and a system in which the taxes are voted by those who do not pay them. . . .[15]

And it is true that such opinions find a certain resonance today in various quarters of the economics profession (especially perhaps Chicago), although generally in more attenuated form. But it is also the case that Wicksell could go to gaol for his radical social beliefs,[16] and that Keynes believed that with sufficient accumulation there would be no need for its further encouragement through social mores, institutions, custom and practice – it would then be possible that 'the love of money as a possession . . . be recognised for what it is, a somewhat disgusting morbidity, one of those semi-criminal, semi-pathological propensities which one hands over with a shudder to specialists in mental disease.'[17] Ideology is false consciousness not in the sense of a conspiracy theory whose object is to deceive, but rather in the sense of a set of beliefs based on immediate appearances, appearances which are both real, as the way in which social relations appear, and delusory as to the content of those social relations.

It follows then that any theory which is based upon such immediate appearances will certainly capture that aspect of reality, but will be unable to explain why that reality is what it is, or takes the particular forms that it does. Accordingly, an individualistic standpoint, as the standpoint of the bourgeoisie, can only lead to a teleological justification of the *status quo*,[18] and to the extent that the *status quo* is deemed unsatisfactory this in turn can only arise from the superimposition of an ethical perspective. Not surprisingly, neoclassical economics conventionally divides into the familiar positive and normative economics.[19]

Such a teleology is seen mostly clearly in the emphasis on equilibrium analysis. The usual practice is to take maximising individuals with given preference orderings, given initial endowments and a given technology of production, and then, first, to ask whether an equilibrium exists (in the sense of no individual having any incentive to alter his actions), second, to ask whether such an equilibrium is unique, and, finally, to consider its stability.[20] Quite apart from the presumption of the elimination of conflict as the essential motor of change, and the presumption of harmony in this, the best of all possible worlds (under certain conditions of course on the shapes of sets, or the numbers of people involved), equilibrium analysis is apologetic in two senses.

First, the representation of the various equalities (or at more advanced levels, inequalities) which characterise the equilibrium conditions as a theorisation of real-world appearances is apologetic.[21] Consider just two examples, concerning the wage, and the rate of interest (profit). At equilibrium the wage measures both the marginal product of labour and the marginal rate of substitution of income for leisure, the former in the sense that, under competitive conditions, no entrepreneur will hire a worker who contributes less in revenue terms to output than he costs in terms of the going wage, and the latter in the sense that a worker will determine the quantity of his services he will offer for hire at the margin according to his subjective evaluation of the relative merits of income received in terms of the going wage as against the leisure he could have had were he not to work. But their individual representations of the wage transaction deceive both capitalist and worker as to its exploitative nature, for the commodity transaction is a fetishistic one, and the individualistic theory thereby generated is consequently falsely given credence as an explanation of what happens.[22] Similarly with the rate of interest: in a one-good world the rate of interest measures the value at equilibrium prices of the increase in the quantity of output produced by an increase of one unit of non-labour input employed, *ceteris paribus*. That is, in conventional terminology, it measures the marginal product of capital. And the rate of interest must also measure the subjective rate of time preference as between the consumption of output today and the consumption of augmented output tomorrow, or a measure of the subjective loss experienced if consumption is postponed one period. But again such an appearance is delusory, as the accumulation process mystifies living labour's property of transferring the value of the means of production to the product, making it seem as though such a property intrinsically belongs to the means of production (misleadingly termed 'capital'), and as though such means of production are productive when only human beings are. Marx summarises this twofold mystification as follows:

Since past labour always disguises itself as capital . . . bourgeois and political economists are full of praises of the services of dead and gone labour, which . . . ought to receive a special remuneration in the shape of interest, profit, etc. The powerful and ever-increasing assistance given by past labour to the living labour process under the form of means of production is, therefore, attributed to that form of past labour in which it is alienated, as unpaid labour, from the worker himself, i.e. to its capitalistic form.[23]

Clearly in its subordination to delusory appearances, bourgeois economics is apologetic. But it is also apologetic in a second sense, in terms of the language employed.[24] The labourer sacrifices leisure and receives income as a reward for his marginal contribution to production; the capitalist sacrifices (or forgoes) consumption of his capital, and his capital earns interest (profit) as a reward for its marginal contribution to production, this reward contingently accruing to the capitalist by virtue of the particular institutions of the society in question. The essential harmony of the system is thereby supposedly rendered transparent, which is wholly apologetic. But again, since language is primarily a matter of social tradition and only partly one of individual choice, this is not casuistry: it is the appearances of capitalism which produce this result. Marx summarises this as follows:

The habit of representing surplus-value and value of labour-power as fractions of the value created . . . conceals the very transaction that characterises capital, namely the exchange of variable capital for living labour-power, and the consequent exclusion of the labourer from the product. Instead of the real facts, we have the false semblance of an association, in which labourer and capitalist divide the product in proportion to the different elements which they respectively contribute towards its formation.[25]

It is easy then to see both the source and the function of national cake analogies.

But, while apologetics is structurally contained within bourgeois economics, it is not the whole of it. It is true that the most abstract categories of bourgeois economics, those which seem furthest removed from ideological content, comprise an abstract recognition of certain relations supposedly common to all societies rather than the cognition of the specificity of capitalism, and this in itself is apologetic in its elimination of capitalism from history and of history from 'capitalistic' societies. But, at the same time, at the level of visible appearances, everything does appear to happen as though the worker receives wages for the whole of his labour, and as though profit is produced by capital (in the conventional sense). The economic categories of demand and supply, price, wages, profit, interest and so on are visible relations of society, and do, therefore, have a limited 'pragmatic utility' with respect to the individual decisions that are taken.[26] They are not scientific, since they do not theorise the essential logic of capitalism. But for day-to-day decisions it is often not necessary to have a theory of the dynamics of the system as a whole; merely to have some idea of how particular variables move. Demand and supply will often do quite well for this. But what is thereby constructed is not a theory of capitalism, and consequently, periodically, these theorisations of appearances are sytematically rendered nugatory as the workings of the totality of capitalism produce crises. At the level of appearances these latter can only be attributed to exogenous shocks of one sort or another.[27]

Now this is hardly a satisfactory situation, and it produces two responses within bourgeois economics. The first is to try to confront the problems of social control and organisation which are thrown up by the capitalist world.[28] Since neoclassical economics cannot theorise this world, what is done is to take as a basis certain observed statistical regularities and to construct a practical discipline on this basis. Thus Keynesian demand management techniques have arisen since 1945, originally based upon the consumption function, and originally theorised on the basis of the formation and role of expectations in conditions of uncertainty. Neo-Keynesian economics attempts to continue this tradition, but the correspondence with the neoclassical world is evidently an imperfect one, and bourgeois economics is thereby seen to comprise the partially inconsistent elements of macro-economics and micro-economics.

The second response is to retreat from the problems of social control and organisation thrown up by the capitalist world, and to render theory innocent of such a world. This occurs in two ways. First, there is the attempt to replace the consumption function with a different observed statistical regularity (the demand for money function), and the attempt to theorise this on the basis of a choice – theoretic approach (monetarism). Such an approach is generally propounded within a perspective that the economy in the long run, with the absolute minimum of government interference (necessary to provide the legal framework to establish property rights, maintain law and order, regulate technical monopolies and establish the appropriate compensation for externalities, and to provide a monetary framework), is essentially a self-regulating system which will tend automatically to generate equilibrium at the natural rate of unemployment, at which all those able and willing to work can find jobs.[29] Market forces will, of course, ensure that the going wage rate is in the long run adjusted to whatever level is appropriate to generate the natural level of unemployment. But to characterise any particular amount of labour which is surplus to the requirements of accumulation, a *social* property of a particular mode of production, as a *natural* rate of unemployment (generated by the interplay of the essential harmonies of the system) is clearly fetishistic. Moreover, the problems of social control and organisation are within this framework deemed to be the result of government interference itself to an otherwise self-regulating system. The reactionary nature of such popular beliefs is a measure of what has been engendered by the collapse of the post-1945 long boom.[30]

The second way in which the retreat from the problems of social control and organisation occurs is through the elaboration, with increasing mathematical sophistication and formal elegance, of general equilibrium theory. Attempts are made, for example, to integrate macro-economics and general equilibrium theory within the neoclassical tradition on the basis of search and transactions costs and postulated different response coefficients of prices and quantities.[31] But the ideological frame of reference ensures critical silences. For example, what were the origins of capitalism? And how can the inequality in the ownership of capital be supported? The first question is elided by the elimination of history, and the second by the fetishism which separates the returns to factors from the incomes to people. To the extent that the questions are recognised at all, bourgeois economics gives the same answer to both, an answer which Marx outlined and dissected as follows:

> In times long gone by there were two sorts of people; one, the diligent, intelligent, and, above all, frugal elite; the other, lazy rascals, spending their substance, and more, in riotous living. The legend of theological original sin tells us certainly how man came to be condemned to eat his bread in the sweat of his brow, but the history of economic original sin reveals to us that there are people

to whom this is by no means essential. Never mind! Thus it came to pass that the former sort accumulated wealth, and the latter sort had at last nothing to sell except their own skins. And from this original sin dates the poverty of the great majority that, despite all its labour, has up to now nothing to sell but itself, and the wealth of the few that increases constantly although they have long ceased to work. Such insipid childishness is every day preached to us in the defence of property.[32]

PART B: MARXIST APPROACHES TO THE THEORIES OF KNOWLEDGE AND IDEOLOGY

1   EPISTEMOLOGY, BASE AND SUPERSTRUCTURE: SOME PRELIMINARIES

> Ideology is defined by the *Shorter Oxford English Dictionary* as 'A system of ideas concerning phenomena, especialy those of social life; the manner of thinking characteristic of a class or an individual.'

The Marxist theory of ideology is concerned with the problems of how such systems of ideas arise; why are they *systems* of ideas and what is their function? Further, since within Marxism ideology is counterposed to knowledge, or science, then to the extent that such a counter-position can be justified, a theory of ideology necessarily involves a theory of knowledge, and much of modern Marxism has been concerned with establishing the differences between knowledge and ideology, and the relations between the two.

Plato's allegory of the cave illustrates many of the issues involved. Consider a group of human beings imprisoned in a cave, with their backs to the mouth of the cave, bound in such a way that they cannot turn round and can only see in front of them. Behind the prisoners there is a fire, and between the prisoners and the fire there is a puppet show. What the prisoners see are the shadows cast by the fire on to the cave wall in front of them; the shadows are of the prisoners themselves and of the puppets behind them. By relating voices to the shadows, since they cannot see each other, the prisoners come to believe that the shadows are the sole reality. Eventually one prisoner manages to escape from the cave into the sunlight, and gradually comes to recognise the reality of the world and the derivative nature of the shadows which had previously deceived him. Clearly he must return to his fellow prisoners in the cave in order to tell them what is true and what is false, and to lead them out of the cave. But, having become accustomed to the sunlight, on his return to the cave he cannot himself make out the shadows properly. Consequently, his claims that the shadows, which he now sees less well than his fellow prisoners, are delusory, and that reality lies outside the cave, cause great resentment – so great indeed that, but for their chains, his fellow prisoners would kill this intruder from the outside world.

What is at issue in this allegory in the present context is a specification of the relationship between thought-constructs and the reality that those thought-constructs are supposed to explain, often treated as a problem of specifying the relation between the knower or subject, and the thing known or object. Such a specification requires in addition criteria whereby it is possible to assess a theory's claim to provide knowledge of reality, for otherwise there is no possibility of choice between competing theories.

These questions are extremely difficult to resolve satisfactorily. They comprise the classical problems of epistemology and are the source of many of the areas of debate within contemporary Marxism. The classical Marxist position begins from the premiss that

> In the social production of their life, men enter into definite re-
> lations that are indispensable and independent of their will,
> relations of production which correspond to a definite stage of
> development of their material productive forces. The sum total of
> these relations of production constitutes the economic structure of
> society, the real foundation, on which rises a legal and political
> superstructure and to which correspond definite forms of social
> consciousness. The mode of production of material life conditions
> the social, political and intellectual life process in general. It is
> not the consciousness of men that determines their being, but, on
> the contrary, their social being that determines their con-
> sciousness.[33]

In itself, this passage does not provide any solution to the epistemological problem of the relation between thought and reality, and contemporary Marxist approaches, by and large, are derived in reaction to the way in which Engels is conceived to have solved the problem. What Engels did was to assert that valid cognition of reality was guaranteed by the Marxist discovery that both cognition and reality are subject to the same laws (Hegel's dialectical laws of logic), and hence the discovery and application of these laws to both subjective thought and the objective world necessarily involves the correspondence of thought with reality. The tendential laws which Marx had discovered concerning human history were thereby extended to the world of nature, and the Marxism of *Capital* was thereby rendered both mechanistic and deterministic for the generation of Marxists whose organisations comprised the Second International.

This is most clearly seen by way of a contrast. Marx himself had continued the passage cited above as follows:

> At a certain stage of their development, the material productive forces of society come in conflict with the existing relations of production, or – what is but a legal expression for the same thing – with the property relations within which they have been at work hitherto. From forms of development of the productive forces these relations turn into their fetters. Then begins an epoch of social revolution. With the change of the economic foundation the entire immense superstructure is more or less rapidly transformed. In considering such transformations a distinction should always be made between the material transformation of the economic conditions of production, which can be determined with the precision of natural science, and the legal, political, religious, esthetic or philosophic – in short, ideological forms in which men become conscious of this conflict and fight it out. Just as our opinion of an individual is not based on what he thinks of himself, so can we not judge of such a period of transformation by its own consciousness; on the contrary, this consciousness must be explained rather from the contradictions of material life, from the existing conflict between the social productive forces and the relations of production.[34]

Now, although there are some ambiguities, Marx's conception of the capitalist mode of production was as a totality of particular relations of production which develop the productive forces in ways most adequate to the further (contradictory) development of these relations. That is, the relations of production are determinant. But the Marxism of the Second International overturned this hierarchy, substituting a conception of history whereby the technological development of the productive forces constituted its determining dynamic. The theoretical conditions for this substitution were given by Engels's elaboration of Hegelian laws of logic to both social and natural worlds, and the practical consequences were the assertion of the inevitability of socialist revolution, a revolution guaranteed by the determinism of the laws of development of the capitalist mode of production. Thus in 1892 Kautsky wrote that

> We consider the breakdown of existing society as inevitable, since we know that economic development creates with a natural necessity conditions which force the exploited to strive against private property; that it increases the number and power of the exploited while it reduces the number and power of the exploiters, whose interest it is to maintain the existing order; that it leads, finally, to unbearable conditions for the mass of the population, which leave it only a choice between passive degeneration and the active overthrow of the existing system of ownership. . . . Capitalist society has failed; its dissolution is only a question of time; irresistible economic development leads with natural necessity to the bankcruptcy of the capitalist mode of production. The erection of a new form of society in place of the existing one is no longer something merely *desirable;* it has become something *inevitable.*[35]

Since the working out of determinate scientific laws would lead to socialism, the justification for political action had to be imported from outside this frame of reference, as an ethical commitment to a 'better' society. This dualism between Marxism as the science of capitalist society on the one hand and socialist ethics as the doctrine of revolution on the other was simultaneously a theoretical rationalisation of and justification for the distinction between the Maximum and Minimum Programmes of Social Democracy, the former comprising the long-term inevitability of revolution, and the latter comprising the reformist day-to-day defensive struggles over living standards and so forth. As in the theory, where there was no necessary relation between science and ethics, so in the practice: long-run strategy and short-run tactics were increasingly divorced.[36] It only remained for the crisis of August 1914 to expose the reformist bankcruptcy of this position, when the major European Social-Democratic Parties chose to support their own national bourgeoisies in the forthcoming war. The ensuing carnage was symbolic of the ruins of the Marxism of the Second International.

Whereas Marx had talked of 'the economic structure' as being 'the real foundation' of society, upon which 'rises' a superstructure of law, politics, etc., he limited his discussion of the relation between superstructure and foundation, or base, to an assertion of 'correspondence'. In particular, he never theorised the nature of this correspondence. Was it, for example, an immediate correspondence? Or was it a correspondence which could only be established through several mediating linkages, rendering the correspondence relatively indirect – in which case, what sensible meaning could be attached to the word 'correspondence'? Engels approached these problems in a letter of 1890 in which he wrote

> According to the materialist conception of history, the *ultimately* determining element in history is the production and reproduction of real life. More than this neither Marx nor I have ever asserted. Hence if somebody twists this into saying that the economic element is the *only* determining one, he transforms that proposition into a meaningless, abstract, senseless phrase. The economic situation is the basis, but the various elements of the superstructure: political forms of the class struggle and its results, to wit: constitutions established by the victorious class after a successful battle, etc., juridical forms, and then even the reflexes of all these actual struggles in the brains of the participants, political, juristic, philosophical theories, religious views and their further development into systems of dogmas, also exercise their influence upon the course of the historical struggles and in many cases preponderate in determining their *form*. There is an interaction of all these elements in which, amid all the endless host of accidents (that is, of things and events, whose inner connection is so remote or so impossible of proof that we can regard it as non-existent, as negligible) the economic movement finally asserts itself as necessary. Otherwise the application of the theory to any period of history one chose would be easier than the solution of a simple equation of the first degree.[37]

Obviously Engels here is recognising a mutual interaction between base and superstructure with the former determinant in the last instance. In modern parlance there is a certain autonomy of superstructure from base, but ultimately this autonomy is only a relative one.

But the crucial questions of what determines the degree of relative autonomy that is possible in particular historical periods, and whether this is an appropriate way at all to approach the issues of dominance and determination in history, were not addressed by Engels.[38] Further, this silence in Marxism on the theory of the superstructure was not recognised by the Marxism of the Second International; since Marxism was the science of the deterministic laws of development of the economic structure, there was no need to consider problems of politics and ideology, for economic determinism collapsed all such considerations into reflections of developments of the economic base. However, the destruction of this position on the battlefields of Europe raised again the spectre of epistemology: what were the criteria for assessment of whether or not Marxism provides objective knowledge of the real world? This is a particular question of the correlative relation: ideology – superstructure: knowledge – base. Why is Marxism a science, and how can it distinguish knowledge from ideology? Hence at issue is the structure of Marxism as a theory: what is there internal to that structure which guarantees the validity of the knowledge Marxism claims to provide of capitalist reality?

Two broad answers have been proposed to this question. The first, in Hegelian Marxism, was formulated during the revolutionary upsurge of the post-1917 years under the impact of the Russian Revolution and in reaction to the mechanistic determinism of the Second International; associated in particular with Gramsci, Korsch and Lukacs, it is called 'historicism' by its opponents.[39] The second, a structuralist Marxism, was formulated, in partial reaction to 'historicism', primarily by Althusser and his school under the impact of the events of 1956 Khrushchev's revelations about Stalin in his 'secret speech', and the Soviet invasion of Hungary) and of 1959–60 (the Sino-Soviet split).[40] While both positions assert that the answer to the above question has to be sought in the dialectical method of Marxism, their answers yield rather different perspectives on the relation of base to superstructure, on the understanding of how bourgeois ideology maintains its hegemony over the working class and of how this hegemony can be displaced, and hence on the relation of theory to practice.

LUKACS AND HEGELIAN MARXISM

It is important to notice that two different questions are at issue here: first, the political question of the relation between theory and practice; and, second, the epistemological question of the relation between thought and reality. One of the characteristic features of the Hegelian Marxism of the immediate post-1917 years was the assertion of the identity of these two questions. A theory is scientific and hence provides objective knowledge of the real world if it is an expression of the class interests of the revolutionary class in a particular historical period Thus, for example, the classical economics of Smith and Ricardo was scientific because it was an expression of the interests of the revolutionary class of its day, the bourgeoisie. Since such economics, particularly Ricardian, provided justification for policy measures against the class of landlords (thus the struggle to repeal the Corn Laws), it was instrumental in providing the bourgeoisie with both a theorisation of reality adequate to the economic needs of the bourgeoisie, and an outlook which could be used to exert political and ideological hegemony over other classes (thus Bentham's utilitarianism, Mill's liberalism, Smiles's self-help, and the Manchester School's free trade) Thus a theory provides valid knowledge of reality to the extent that it serves the needs of the revolutionary class in its struggle for power Accordingly, Marxism is scientific to the extent that it serves the needs of the proletariat.

This conception is particularly clear in the case of the Marxism of Lukacs; Lukacs develops it alongside the closely associated conception that the proletariat is the one class in modern society with an interest in the acquisition of *total* knowledge: this marks the proletariat out as a revolutionary class whose interest is the abolition of classes as such and this distinguishes it from all previously revolutionary classes Thus he writes that

> It is not the primacy of economic motives in historical explanatio that constitutes the decisive difference between Marxism and bourgeois thought, but the point of view of totality. The category of totality, the all-pervasive supremacy of the whole over the parts is the essence of the method which Marx took over from Hegel and brilliantly transformed into the foundations of a wholly new science The capitalist separation of the producer from the total process of production, the division of the process of labour into parts at the cost of the individual humanity of the worker, the atomisation of society into individuals who simply go on producing without rhythm or reason, must all have a profound influence on the thought, the science and the philosophy of capitalism. Proletarian science revolutionary not just by virtue of its revolutionary ideas which

opposes to bourgeois society, but above all because of its method. *The primacy of the category of totality is the bearer of the principle of revolution in science.*[41]

Now the development of the productive forces of capitalism is a process of their increasing socialisation via the extension of the division of labour, increasing interdependence in productive activity, and the universalisation of production for the market. Capitalism socialises society in ways that the local particularism of previous modes of production could not. Thus in contrast to what was possible in previous modes of production, under capitalism social existence can be revealed as a social, not a natural, process, definitively the product of human activity. In this way the objects of knowledge (man in society) are identified with the process whereby that knowledge is acquired (also man in society). But it requires the proletariat for such a product to become a *conscious* one; for the proletariat to overthrow bourgeois class rule, to establish itself as the ruling class, and hence to abolish class society, it is necessary that it understands society, which is necessary and sufficient for understanding itself as a class. Thus Lukacs writes:

It was necessary for the proletariat to be born for social reality to become fully conscious. The reason for this is that the discovery of the class-outlook of the proletariat provided a vantage point from which to survey the whole of society. With the emergence of historical materialism there arose the theory of the 'conditions for the liberation of the proletariat' and the doctrine of reality understood as the total process of social evolution. This was only possible because for the proletariat the total knowledge of its class-situation was a vital necessity, a matter of life and death; because its class-situation becomes comprehensible only if the whole of society can be understood; and because this understanding is the inescapable precondition of its actions. Thus the unity of theory and practice is only the reverse side of the social and historical position of the proletariat. From its own point of view self-knowledge coincides with knowledge of the whole so that the proletariat is at one and the same time the subject and object of its own knowledge.[42]

It follows that only an investigation from the class standpoint of the proletariat can constitute a scientific investigation; all other investigations lead to a consciousness of reality that is false: ideology is therefore, false consciousness. Consider, for example, investigations on social phenomena which are based on the standpoint of the individual. Lukacs argues that it is impossible from this standpoint to achieve the perspective of totality; at best knowledge of aspects of particular areas can be obtained.

> The totality of an object can only be posited if the positing subject is itself a totality; and if the subject wishes to understand itself, it must conceive of the object as a totality. In modern society only the *classes* can represent this total point of view.[43]

The objects of knowledge are only constituted as knowledge to the extent that their functions in the totality to which they belong are understood. Only this conception allows the recognition that any theorisation based on the *appearances* of capitalist reality cannot produce *knowledge* of that reality, but rather can only comprise the *ideology* of the ruling class of that reality. Only the conception of totality allows a removal of this veil of appearances to uncover the essence of capitalist reality. Thus for Lukacs

> The knowledge of the real, objective nature of a phenomenon, the knowledge of its historical character and the knowledge of its actual function in the totality of society form, therefore, a single undivided act of cognition.[44]

The terrain of ideology was thus delineated as the crucial area of class-struggle, and class-consciousness the critical category. In the circumstances of the early 1920s, Lukacs's views proved the foundation of voluntarist and leftist political positions; the conception of the revolutionary party was reduced to an objectification of proletarian class-consciousness, and the actions of the party justified by what the class ought to think, even if it did not. However, the ebb of the revolutionary tide in Central Europe and the degeneration of the Bolshevik Revolution into Stalinism isolated such leftist currents, and the orthodoxy of Engels's Marxism was firmly reasserted by the Comintern. 'Historicist' Marxism was indicted for idealism; it stood accused of transforming the question of the *relation* of thought to reality into the very different question of how to *make* thought reality, and the means whereby this elision took place was the uncritical absorption of Hegelian dialectics into a frame of reference which was materialist rather than idealist. Despite their impeccable credentials as revolutionaries, theorists such as Lukacs, Korsch and Gramsci were accused of weakening the very frame of reference of Marxism itself by their incorporation into it of pre-Marxist methodologies.

But the orthodoxy of technological determinism was no substitute for the complex philosophical difficulties involved, and the collapse of the post-1945 capitalist boom in the West together with the accumulating revelations of Stalinist practice in Russia and Eastern Europe brought a renaissance in the study of the relation of base to superstructure, theory to practice, and thought to reality, a renaissance centred around the work of Althusser and his followers.

3 ALTHUSSER AND STRUCTURALIST MARXISM

Perhaps the most convenient peg on which to hang Althusser's discussions of ideology and of science is his rejection of empiricist epistemologies. At its simplest, empiricist epistemology asserts that all knowledge is based on the data of the senses, and that what it is possible to know can only be discovered through the organisation of sense-impressions. Now it is easy to reject extreme statements of empiricism, and Lukacs makes the point very clearly:

> The blinkered empiricist will of course deny that facts can only become facts within the framework of a system – which will vary with the knowledge desired. He believes that every piece of data from economic life, every statistic, every raw event already constitutes an important fact. In so doing he forgets that however simple an enumeration of 'facts' may be, however lacking in commentary, it already implies an 'interpretation'. Already at this stage the facts have been comprehended by a theory, a method; they have been wrenched from their living context and fitted into a theory.[45]

But it is not necessary to empiricism to presume that the mind is passive in the process of sense-perception, for the process of apprehension via the senses could be considered to contribute to the character of what is apprehended. But what is essential to empiricist epistemology is the idea that the senses must sense something, and that experience of this given something is the *only* source of knowledge. Thus knowledge is conceived in terms of statements which describe something given to the experience of human subjects.

Althusser generalises this, subsuming under the term 'empiricism' all epistemologies which are characterised by an *opposition* between a given subject and a given object, which, in the present context in particular includes those epistemologies whereby knowledge is obtained by the subject's abstracting the essence of the object. This means that, if the world is conceived as a world of appearances only, appearances which hide the essence and must be stripped from the essence to reveal the truth of the essence (rather like peeling layers off an onion), then such a conception is, according to Althusser, empiricist. Thus Althusser subsumes under the term 'empiricist' not only those epistemologies which are classically empiricist, but also those epistemologies which are metaphysical in the classical sense of the study of what lies behind or beyond appearances. This means that, for Althusser, both mechanistic Marxism and Hegelian Marxism are empiricist. Althusser's objection to empiricism is that to abstract the essence from a given real object must *imply* that knowledge (the essential essence) is contained in the real object as one of its parts. The object thus consists of two parts: the essential real, or invisible kernel, and the inessential real, or visible surface; the process of knowledge is a process of eliminating the latter to reveal the former. Accordingly, empiricism must concede that the object of knowledge and the real object cannot be identical. But then empiricism takes two objects, the object of knowledge (the essence of the real object), and the real object (which exists quite independently of the subject's knowledge of it, or his acquisition of knowledge of it), and, by reducing this distinction to one between parts of the same real object, renders knowledge of the object a part of the real object itself. As against this contradictory position, Althusser is insistent on the distinction between the real object and the object of knowledge: unlike in an empiricist epistemology, knowledge of the object is *not* part of the object itself.

This means that Althusser is asserting the necessity of a *rationalist* epistemology. Traditionally, rationalist epistemologies are those which argue that the intellect is in itself a source of knowledge, and can determine truths which are necessary ones. Hence they are superior to any truths derivable from sense-impressions, for the latter can only be contingent, since they are dependent on empirical accidents of one sort or another. Althusser's epistemology falls within this tradition: to the constituent parts of the real object (e.g. the world) and to the relations between these parts correspond certain concepts and relations etween these concepts; further, the correspondence is such that the concepts themselves yield knowledge of the real.

How they do this is through theoretical practice. Althusser argues that societies, or social formations, are composed of three major practices, by which he means processes of production or transformation. Economic practice concerns the transformation of nature into social products (the production process by human labour); political practice is concerned with the transformation of social relations ultimately by revolution); and ideological practice is concerned with the ways in which people's experiences of their social environment are transformed. Each practice involves a production process combining labour, raw materials and means of production, a production process which determines each practice. There is, in addition, a fourth practice. theoretical practice, which Althusser uses to distinguish science from ideology: theoretical practice transforms ideology into knowledge with theory. What must then be specified is the mechanism whereby the *production of the object of knowledge* produces cognition of the *real object* which exists outside thought in the real world.

It must be emphasised that this is *not,* for Althusser, a problem of guarantees. Indeed, all conceptions of knowledge which are dominated by the problem of criteria whereby that knowledge can be judged are called ideological. For Althusser, the problem of guarantees of truth itself an ideological one; Marxism by contrast is concerned with the mechanisms which generate or produce knowledge. In theoretical practice knowledge is generated by means of the construction of the objects of knowledge from referents (concepts, ideas, impressions and so on) yielded by all the different forms of practice (political, economic, ideological; even technical, scientific and so on). Since the object of knowledge is different from the real object, validation of that knowledge can only be a procedure which is internal to the theory itself. Thus Althusser writes that

the problem of the cognitive appropriation of the real object by the object of knowledge . . . is a special case of the appropriation of the real world by different practices. . . . Each of these modes of appropriation poses the problem of mechanism or production of *its specific 'effect'*. . . .[46]

r theoretical practice this effect is called the knowledge effect. And husser argues, somewhat opaquely, that

'The knowledge effect, produced at the level of the forms of ord
of the discourse of the proof, and then at the level of some isolate
concept, is therefore possible given the *systematicity of the syste*
which is the foundation of the concepts and their order of appea
ance in scientific discourse.'[47]

The argument is basically that scientific proof imposes upon the cat
gories of thought a certain order of appearance and disappearanc
given that the categories themselves only derive meaning from th
position in the system of which they are the elements. Thus, f
Althusser, the knowledge-effect is produced by an interplay betwe
the existence of the system ('the organisational structure of concep
in the thought-totality') and the existence of the forms of order of t
discourse ('the movement of succession of the concepts in the order
discourse of the proof'), an interplay in which existence of system
concepts predominates over their order of appearance.[48]

Now this position is not an easy one to maintain, and to see th
requires an outline of Althusser's position on ideology. What does
mean, for example, to say that the very specification of the proble
of the guarantees of knowledge is an ideological one?

Whereas empiricist epistemology talks of the subject and the obje
of knowledge, Althusser denies meaning to the term 'subject
knowledge'. For the objects of knowledge are constructed throu
theoretical practice operating upon areas identified by the soc
relations of the various practices. These social relations each have
certain structure within which individuals are only the 'support
personifications, or 'bearers' of the antagonistic poles of that structu
(Thus, for example, labourer and capitalist are constituted by th
different relations to the means of production, this structure, of n
ownership and ownership respectively, constituting the capitalist mo
of production.) Now it is the function of ideology to constitute
dividuals as subjects. It is ideology, according to Althusser, wh
transforms individuals from the bearers of structures into subje
who relate to their real conditions of existence as if they as subje
determine these conditions. Ideology is, therefore, the set of r
resentations of individuals' imaginery relations (a property of
process of knowledge which is not reducible to a property of
objects of knowledge). Two consequences immediately follow fr
this. First, any epistemology which identifies a subject of knowle
must by definition be ideological. And, second, ideology must e
in all societies.

Ideology is, therefore, an inversion, not in the Hegelian sense of taking the appearances of reality as the true essence of that reality, but in the sense of constituting the bearers of relations as subjects. Whereas Hegelian Marxism understands ideology as the action on a stage being a copy of reality, the play being a mirror held up to the audience, and truth as being the discovery of the author of the words and the director of the action (the hidden essence), for Althusser the theatre is one without an author, and the object of Marxism is not to see the play as a distorted or partial reflection of reality or as an *a priori* truth, but to investigate the mechanisms which produce what is happening on the stage. Whereas Hegelian Marxism attributes an unambiguous class connotation to ideology, seeing all contradictions as reducible (albeit in more or less complicated ways) to class-contradictions, structuralist Marxism denies such reductionism. Contradictions in one practice have no necessary forms of existence in other practices (although all contradictions are determined in the last instance by the economy).[49] Hence classes at the ideological level cannot be conceived in a reductive procedure (i.e. cannot be simply reduced to classes at the economic level), and the contents of ideology are, therefore, not the necessary forms of existence of classes at this level. Accordingly, the class character of an ideology is not determined by its content but by its form, that is, by the particular ways in which are combined or articulated the various ways in which individuals constitute themselves as subjects. The raw materials of ideology are non-class referents (racialism, patriotism and patriarchy, for example) which are then incorporated into class ideological practices, an incorporation determined both by the level of class-struggle, and by a representation of the world that is consistent with the existence of the relevant class in economic practice. The ideological hegemony of a class is, therefore, determined by the extent to which that class succeeds in incorporating into its own class ideological practice the various ways in which individuals constitute themselves as subjects. The ideological unity thereby created might well be coherent and logical (thus theology), or it might be riddled with logical inconsistency. In times of stability, logical inconsistencies do not matter very much, but in times of ideological crises, which given the nature of ideology necessarily involve individuals undergoing an 'identity crisis', contradictions are exacerbated, and the dominant ideological unity is dissolved and reconstituted on the basis of a different subjectivity or combination of subjectivities.

However, there are difficulties with Althusser's position on science, knowledge and ideology, and these difficulties centre on the concept 'theoretical practice'. The object of theoretical practice is the analysis of the mechanisms which produce the knowledge-effect, the mechanisms, that is, which produce theories which are scientific and thereby achieve genuine knowledge of the real. Thus the theory of theoretical practice gives a general criterion of scientificity through its analysis of the knowledge-effect. But, on the other hand, Althusser also asserts that there is no such general criterion of scientificity, for each science contains its own criteria of validity: if a set of statements makes sense within the particular theoretical framework under consideration, then it is scientific – otherwise it is ideological. Now the former position, that the analysis of the knowledge-effect provides a general criterion of scientificity, resurrects the spectre of guarantees. For the only way in which the construction of the object of knowledge, which takes place wholly in thought, also yields knowledge of the real, which exists outside thought, is through the assertion of a common structure to all practices. Only by such an assertion does it make sense to say that theoretical practice can achieve, through a general criterion, cognition of the other practices. But, if the relation between thought and reality is that they possess a common structure, then, while there is no need to ask for a guarantee of knowledge, a guarantee has been implicitly inserted, and the answer is uncomfortably close to the mechanistic determinism of Second International Marxism, since the latter asserted the correspondence of thought and reality through their conformity to the same laws.

Althusser attempts to resolve this problem by retreating from the position that the analysis of the knowledge-effect provides a general criterion of scientificity. He maintains the position that each science has its own criteria of validity, and now emphasises the role of class-struggle in theoretical practice. Indeed, whereas previously he had defined philosophy as the theory of theoretical practice yielding analysis of the knowledge-effect, he now defines philosophy as the representation of the proletarian class-struggle in theory. His contention is that class positions are represented in ideology by world outlooks which are antagonistic, and that world outlooks are represented in the domain of theory by philosophy. Further,

The ultimate stake of philosophical struggle is the struggle *for hegemony* between the two great tendencies in world outlooks (materialist and idealist). The *main* battlefield in this struggle is scientific knowledge: for it or against it. The number-one philosophical battle therefore takes place on the frontier between the scientific and the ideological. . . . The philosophical struggle is a sector of the class struggle between world outlooks.[50]

Again,

Philosophy represents politics in the domain of theory, or to be more precise: *with the sciences* – and, *vice versa,* philosophy represents scientificity in politics, with the classes engaged in class struggle.[51]

This reformulation rejects all epistemology, rejects all theories that involve the consideration of the validity of knowledge. Thus, for Althusser, there is dialectical materialism, or the class-struggle of the proletariat in theory, which has nothing to do with cognition; and there is historical materialism, or science of history, whose concern is the historical analysis of the development of the various sciences both as autonomous practices and in their relation to the social conditions of theoretical practice. Theoretical practice itself is reduced to a concern with the methodology and with the contents of sciences. Far from the autonomous position with respect to both base and superstructure in which theoretical practice had been located, alongside the sciences, Althusser now gives theoretical practice a superstructural position, materialised in what he calls the Ideological State Apparatuses, such as universities. And this means that theoretical ideologies are always present within the sciences, manifesting their presence as subordinations to specific class interests.

Sciences then are dynamic structures of concepts which are capable of continual *internal* development and transformation. Ideologies, by contrast, are static bodies of concepts incapable of such deepening or development, because their contents are generated not within the theory itself but by a social reality which is *external* to it. Althusser thus directs epistemology away from its classical concern with the relation between thought and reality towards its redefinition as historical materialism.[52] Since the sciences are assumed objectively to reflect the real in thought, materialist philosophy is restricted to a concern with the defence of already constituted sciences, each with its own internal criteria of validity, against the intrusion of ideology, as the representation of class interests.

However, if ideology is the representation of class interest within the sciences, it is also a system of representations, according to Althusser, which is indispensable to *any* society, since it is the transformation of bearers of structures into subjects constituted by the way in which those bearers experience and relate to their conditions of existence. There is clearly no restriction to class society entailed here. For if this latter sense of ideology is denied, and ideology were abolished along with the capitalist mode of production, then it follows that, in communist society, the essence of that society would be transparent in its appearances, and this reconstitutes the philosophical position on whose rejection Althusser had founded his own positions. On the other hand, if this sense of ideology is maintained, the thrust of Marxism as the theory of class-struggle is deflected into a sociology of the study of the ways in which social cohesion obtains in different sorts of societies. Thus the postulation of a class referent as the ultimate arbiter of the distinction between knowledge and ideology is vitiated by a failure to conceive ideology as anything other than an opposition to science.

4   PROLEGOMENA

It is clear from the preceding sections that both the state and the status of epistemology within Marxism are controversial. Second International Marxism mechanistically 'solved' the problem of the relation between thought and reality at the cost of the introduction of an arbitrary ethics to relate theory and practice. Conceived largely in response to the way the political consequences of this position made themselves felt in the conditions of the time, Hegelian Marxism saw the 'solution' to the relation between thought and reality as identical to that between theory and practice: they were but aspects of the same problem. But the failure to appreciate and to situate the emancipation of Marxism from its Hegelian origins ultimately doomed this project. For the valuable reassertion of the category of the totality and of the dialectical method was vitiated by a voluntarist political practice stemming from a tendency to collapse reality into thought. And when reality moved in a different direction, Hegelian Marxists were left exposed, easy targets to be picked off by Stalinist orthodoxy.

In sharp contrast both to the sterility of the latter and to the idealism of Hegelian Marxism, Structuralist Marxism proposes a quite different approach to the relation between thought and reality. This approach conceives as fundamental that the object of knowedge – the analysis of the capitalist mode of production – exists wholly in thought, and is therefore quite distinct from the real object: the reality of the appearances of actual capitalist societies. But while the thought object is thus sharply distinguished from the real object, the rationalism of structuralist Marxism ensures that the one corresponds to the other. Yet appeal to the concepts of practice and of class-struggle is necessary in order to banish the spectre of an epistemology of guarantees; the cost of this renders the distinction between knowledge and ideology rather difficult to grasp, if not completely opaque. And this arises from the dilemma that *either* some types of statements are privileged, in that they do provide criteria for the distinction between knowledge and ideology; but they must thereby also be the guarantees that this approach seeks to avoid. *Or* no types of statements are privileged, in which case Marxism appears to be reduced to a rationalism which is wholly relativistic and which one can take or leave according to choice. The obvious question thus arises: what then is the way forward?

It should first be said that at least two major lacunae exist in the above account. First of all, this essay has said very little about the theory of knowledge which can be constructed from Marx's own writings, writings within a philosophical tradition in which his immediate predecessors were Feuerbach, Hegel and Kant.[53] And, second, no reference has been made to the substantial literature on the philosophy of science and its relevance to social theory.[54] Neither study can be omitted in the project of constructing a science of society upon secure epistemological (and ontological) foundations.

That these foundations can only be materialist (or in modern philosophical parlance, realist) is straightforward enough: the observable characteristics of capitalist society must be explained in terms of unobservable structures and mechanisms in such a way that these latter explain both how and why the observable characteristics take the particular forms that they do.[55] The beliefs that people have concerning such forms can then be analysed in terms of their origins, their dissemination, and their eclipse by other beliefs. In other words, a materialist account of ideology requires as prerequisite an analysis of capitalism which can yield such an account. And this in turn requires the formulation of a concept of scientific knowledge which is appropriate to this task.

However, theory does not develop in this linear way, and the account in Part A of neoclassical economics as ideology is by no means vitiated as long as its provisional nature is respected. It shows the sorts of things it is possible to say without explicitly confronting the very fundamental issues, for these latter admit of no easy solution and much work remains to be done. If Part A stimulates the criticism of neo classical economics, it will have served its purpose. But its validation as a correct account depends on the task of constructing coherent and appropriate foundations. And the successful completion of such a task, and hence the vitality of Marxism itself, depends on the course of the class-struggle, a struggle in which *all* are participants, whether conscious of it or not.

NOTES AND REFERENCES

1. The economics to be considered is broadly that which resulted from the 'marginalist revolution' of the 1870s and which was rigorously reformulated in the 'mathematical revolution' of the 1940s and 1950. The phrases modern economics, neoclassical economics, and general equilibrium theory are used interchangeably. This is not to preclude the existence of other areas of economics, but the importance of neoclassical economics should be fairly obvious.

2. Not all workers are male, of course. But, since language itself is the product of a sexist society, it is difficult to cope with this in an elegant manner (elegance too being socially conditioned). Throughout the chapter, 'worker' can be considered as either male or female and the pronouns altered accordingly.

3. K. Marx (1938) *Capital*, vol. 1 (London: Allen & Unwin) p. 15

4. Ibid. p. 44.

5. It is important to emphasise that the forms of appearance are not illusory; they are undoubtedly very real.

6. This point, like many in Sections 1 and 2 of Part A, is made by N. Geras (1971) in 'Essence and Appearance: Aspects of Fetishism Marx's *Capital*', *New Left Review*, 65 (Jan–Feb 1971); reprinted R. Blackburn (ed.) (1972) *Ideology in Social Science* (London Fontana). This essay owes a great deal to Geras's article.

7. There is a conflation of value and price here which is perhaps permissible at the level of abstraction of the argument in the text but is strictly invalid without an understanding of money, or, at a lower level of abstraction, without taking account of competition.

8. Marx, op. cit. pp. 550–1.

9. Ibid. pp. 597-8.

10. The standard expository account is T. C. Koopmans (1957) *Three Essays on the State of Economic Science* (Maidenhead: McGraw-Hill) pp. 1–127.

11. R. M. Solow (1963) *Capital Theory and the Rate of Return* (Amsterdam: North-Holland) pp. 10–11.

12. This is why neoclassical economics is called bourgeois economics by Marxists.

13. For a further discussion of these points, see S. Himmelweit, 'The Individual as Basic Unit of Analysis', in F. Green and P. Nore (eds) (1977) *Economics: An Anti-Text* (London: Macmillan).

14. Cited in G. Therborn (1976) *Science, Class and Society* (London: New Left Books) p. 94.

15. Ibid. pp. 204–5.

16. Wicksell was imprisoned for blasphemy. He was very hostile to religion, and an outspoken advocate of birth-control, and of economic and political equality between classes, and between the sexes. See E. Lindahl, 'Introduction: Wicksell's Life and Work', in K. Wicksell (1958) *Selected Papers on Economic Theory* (London: Allen & Unwin).

17. Cited in D. E. Moggridge (1976) *Keynes* (London: Fontana) pp. 162–3.

18. This means basically that the *status quo* is a preconceived and predetermined end.

19. The division is bridged, of course, by the ethical postulate that individual preferences are to count.

20. See Chap. 6.

21. In many ways, all the chapters in this book and in Green and Nore, op. cit., are illustrations of this point.

22. Again it is worth emphasising that this is not just a mistake: the worker certainly would not be paid his wage if he only worked the hours necessary to produce commodities of value equivalent to the value of his labour-power.

23. Marx, op. cit. pp. 620–1.

24. This point is well made by B. Rowthorn (1974) 'Neo-Classicism, Neo-Ricardianism and Marxism', *New Left Review*, **86** (July–Aug), an essay first published in the *Bulletin of the Conference of Socialist Economists* (Autumn 1972 and Spring 1973). Rowthorn also makes other points similar to many of those in this section.

25. Marx, op. cit. p. 543.

26. The phrase is taken from M. Godelier (1972) *Rationality and Irrationality in Economics* (London: New Left Books) p. xxv. This book contains many interesting and stimulating ideas.

27. See B. Sutcliffe, 'Keynesianism and the Stabilization of Capitalist Economies', in Green and Nore (eds), op. cit.

28. Some interesting reflections on this are made by G. Lukacs, 'The Changing Function of Historical Materialism', in G. Lukacs (1971) *History and Class Consciousness* (London: Merlin).

29. This sort of analysis is exemplified, of course, by M. Friedman (1962) *Capitalism and Freedom* (Chicago: Chicago U.P.) chap. 1. For an effective demolition of the pretensions of this account, see C. B. Macpherson (1968) 'Elegant Tombstones: A Note on Friedman's Freedom', *Canadian Journal of Political Science,* and reprinted in C. B. Macpherson (1973) *Democratic Theory: Essays in Retrieval* (Oxford: Clarendon Press). This last book has much relevance to the critique of modern economics.

30. See, for example, E. H. Carr (1961) *What is History?* (London: Macmillan) pp. 135-7. It would be unusual today to find sentiments of the sort Carr was writing eighteen years ago, viz.

the transition from submission to objective economic laws which, though supposedly rational, were beyond man's control to belief in the capacity of man to control his economic destiny by conscious action seems to me to represent an advance in the application of reason to human affairs, an increased capacity in man to understand and master himself and his environment, which I should be prepared, if necessary, to call by the old-fashioned name of progress. (ibid. pp. 136-7).

31. A recent attempt is E. Malinvaud (1977) *The Theory of Unemployment Reconsidered* (Oxford: Blackwell).

32. Marx, op. cit. pp. 736-7.

33. K. Marx and F. Engels (1950) *Selected Works in Two Volumes* (London: Lawrence & Wishart) vol. 1, p. 329.

34. Ibid.

35. Cited in L. Colletti (1972) *From Rousseau to Lenin* (London: New Left Books) pp. 55-6.

36. Ibid. pp. 45-108, and for an illuminating historical account see C. E. Schorske (1970) *German Social Democracy 1905-17* (New York: Russell & Russell) (first published in 1955).

37. Marx and Engels, op. cit. vol. 2, p. 443 (see n. 33).

38. To anticipate the argument somewhat, Althusser graphically writes:

> in History, these instances, the superstructures, etc. – are never seen to step respectfully aside when their work is done or, when the Time comes, as his pure phenomena, to scatter before His Majesty the Economy as he strides along the royal road of the Dialectic. From the first moment to the last, the lonely hour of the 'last instance' never comes.

L. Althusser (1969) *For Marx* (London: Allen Lane) p. 113. Althusser comments in detail on Engels's letter in ibid. pp. 117–28.

39. The key texts are A. Gramsci (1971) *Selections from the Prison Notebooks* (London: Lawrence & Wishart); K. Korsch (1970) *Marxism and Philosophy* (London: New Left Books); and Lukacs, op. cit. (see n. 28).

40. The key texts are Althusser, op. cit. (see n. 38); L. Althusser and E. Balibar (1970) *Reading Capital* (London: New Left Books); L. Althusser (1971) *Lenin and Philosophy and Other Essays* (London: New Left Books) and L. Althusser (1976) *Essays in Self-Criticism* (London, New Left Books). An extremely helpful work is also A. Callinicos (1976) *Althusser's Marxism* (London: Pluto). Note also that the labels Hegelian Marxism and Structuralist Marxism are used purely as shorthand, and are not intended to be pejorative.

41. Lukacs, op. cit. p. 27. Emphasis in original.

42. Ibid. pp. 19–20.

43. Ibid. p. 28. Emphasis in original.

44. Ibid. p.14.

45. Ibid. p.5.

46. Althusser and Balibar, op. cit. p. 66 (see n. 40).

47. Ibid. p. 68. Emphasis in original.

48. Ibid. p. 68.

49. It is somewhat invidious to concentrate on epistemology in Althusser at the expense of the rest of his ideas. In particular the interested reader should explore the ideas of readings and problematics, over-determination, structure in dominance and structural causality in the works cited in n. 40.

50. Althusser, *Lenin and Philosophy* . . ., op. cit. p. 21 (see n. 40). Emphasis in original.

51. Ibid. p. 65. Emphasis in original.

52. Althusser, *Essays* . . ., op. cit. p. 124, n. 19 (see n. 40).

53. In addition to the interpretations to be found in Lukacs, op. cit. (see n. 28), and in Althusser and Balibar, op. cit. (n. 40), discussion of these issues can be found in Colletti, op. cit. (n. 35), L. Colletti (1973) *Marxism and Hegel* (London: New Left Books), and D. H. Ruben (1977) *Marxism and Materialism* (Hassocks, Brighton: Harvester Press).

54. An accessible and lucid survey in this area is R. Keat and J. Urry (1975) *Social Theory as Science* (London: Routledge & Kegan Paul).

55. This identification of materialism and realism is slightly cavalier, but it will suffice in the present context. Further, it should not need saying that the construction of secure epistemological and ontological foundations is hardly independent of an adequate specification of Marxist methodology. The recognition that neither is independent of the other is the source of most of the merits and most of the difficulties in the analyses of both Lukacs and Althusser.

Index